Michael Baumgardt

Adobe Photoshop 7 Web Design

with GoLive 6

Adobe Photoshop 7 Web Design
Michael Baumgardt

Copyright © 2003 by Michael Baumgardt

This Adobe Press book is published by Peachpit Press.
For information on Adobe Press books, contact:
Peachpit Press
1249 Eighth Street
Berkeley, CA 94710
510/524-2178 (tel) / 510/524-2221 (fax)

To report errors, please send a note to errata@peachpit.com
Peachpit Press is a division of Pearson Education
For the latest on Adobe Press books go to http://www.adobe.com/adobepress

Editor: Becky Morgan
Production Coordinator: David Van Ness
Copyeditor: Brenda Benner
Indexer: Karin Arrigoni
Interior Design: Mito Media, Inc., New York
Cover Design: Daniel Ziegler

ISBN 0-321-11561-9
9 8 7 6 5 4 3 2 1

Printed and bound in the United States of America

FOR AUDREY ROCHESTER

*It is when you give of yourself
that you truly give*

from "The Prophet", Kalil Gibran

I want to thank the following people
for their help and support:

● **Jill Merlin, Julieanne Kost** Adobe

● **JB Popplewell** Alien Skin Software

● **Christopher Stashuk** Aristotle **Little Rock, Arkansas**

● **Paul Ehrenreich** Blickpunkt Fotostudio **Munich**

● **Susan Ross** Logitech ● **Auto FX Software**

Thanks, Becky, for pushing through and even working on Memorial Day to get the job done. I am grateful to you and David Van Ness for the awesome work you did. A big thanks goes out to Gary-Paul Prince and all the others at Adobe/Peachpit Press who helped to market this book. Last, but not least, I want to thank Nancy Ruenzel for her continuous support.

A few years ago I made the transition from desktop publishing to Web design without anyone to show me the ropes. Originally, I wrote this book for Photoshop 5.0, and since then, Photoshop has come a long way toward being an indispensable tool. So has this book!

I don't say this without pride, but over the years, this book has helped thousands of designers make the leap into Web design; from the emails I receive, it seems that many readers like my approach to book writing. This book is broken down into three easy-to-follow parts that will teach you all you need to know and more.

Basics: The first section focuses on Web design—anyone making the leap from desktop publishing should read these chapters. They cover some of the fundamental concepts of Web design.

Photoshop and ImageReady: The second section features the Photoshop commands and techniques that are most important for Web designers to master. It should help Photoshop and ImageReady novices become pros. You'll also learn about compressing and optimizing image files—one of the most important tasks in Web design. Even pros will find plenty of new information here. I believe that no other book on Photoshop covers this subject in such depth.

HTML Authoring: The last section shows you how to bring Photoshop designs into GoLive to make a fully functioning Web site. These chapters offer tips on how to set up your site more efficiently, which will help even those with prior GoLive experience.

Those who have bought earlier versions of the book will notice that it has undergone a major overhaul. After three editions, it seemed time to create a new look. Hopefully, you'll agree that the current design tops the one in the previous editions. Although I put a lot of thought into the redesign, the layout is not the only thing that has changed. As well as featuring completely new content in many of the chapters, I've included more step-by-step procedures than ever before. Most importantly, I've reorganized the content to make it easier to find specific information.

I hope you find this book useful and enjoyable. If you have questions or feedback, contact me at:

Mbaumgardt@Mitomediabooks.com

Visit the book's companion Web site for
updates and to download tutorials:
www.mitomediabooks.com

Thanks to ...

Sabine & Christopher Bach; Friedericke Baumgardt; Heike Baumgardt; Hermann and Renate Baumgardt, my parents; Nina Bergengruen; Marion & Reimund Bienefeld-Zimanovsky; Karen Bihari; Tim & Jenn Bruhns; Hajo Carl; Angela Carpenter; Paul Ehrenreich; Ramsey Faragallah; Isabelle Girard and Allonzo; Alejandro and Christina Gjutierrez Viguera; Harry Greißinger; Silvia & Armin Günther; Tammi Haas; Juliet Hanlon; Peter Hoffmann; Nina Jakisch; Katja Lerch and Günther; Tom Nakat; Sabine & Joseph Plenk; Manfred Rürup; Marc Sheerin; Anja Schneider-Beck; Lisa Tran; Lars Wagner; Ilona & Vera Waldmann; Al Blanco, Jill Conway, Robert Duncan, Carla Elfeld, Jonathan Foragash, Nancy Fox, Graham Gardner, Catherine Ginter, Vernice Grant, Michelle Kinsey, Carmen Lentschig, Bill Manzulo, Tom Merrick, Vanessa Quiles, Nereida Quiles, Florence Quirici, Audrey Rochester, KC Rodriguez, Kristine Strachan Chiongban, Karen Yedvab, and last, not least, my friend Steve Zierer.

The first edition of this book was written (June to October 1998) in New York, Munich, Verona and Istanbul; the second edition (the first English edition) was translated and updated in New York and Port Chester (July to November 1999). The last edition was written in New York, Roveretto and Munich (September to December 2000) and the current edition from March to May 2002 in New York.

TABLE OF CONTENTS

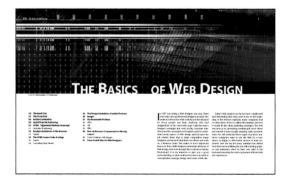

Web Basics

THE BASICS OF WEB DESIGN

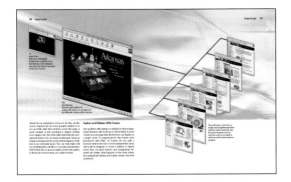

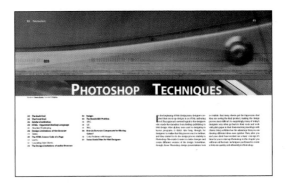

Techniques

WEB DESIGN TECHNIQUES

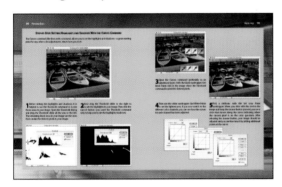

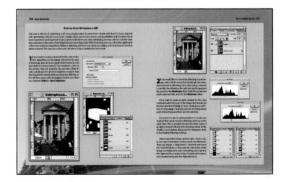

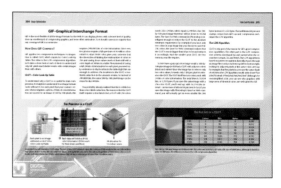

HTML Authoring

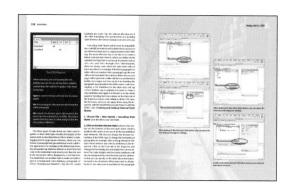

Files for the tutorials and the step-by-step procedures are available for download at www.mitomediabooks.com

Back   Forward   Stop   Refresh   Home

glo

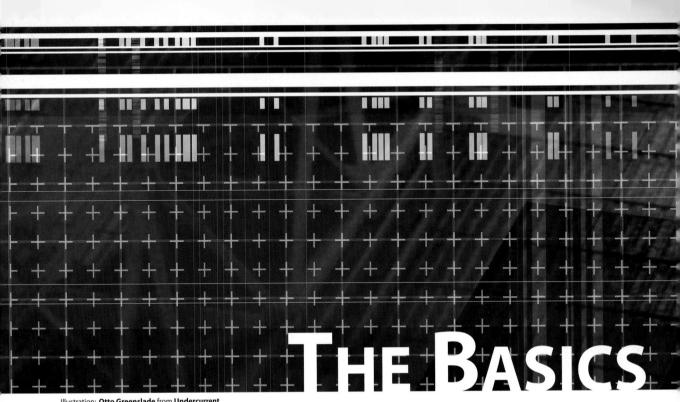

Illustration: **Otto Greenslade** from **Undercurrent**

THE BASICS

OF WEB DESIGN

In 1997, becoming a Web designer was easy. There were only a few professional designers around who understood how the Web worked, and the demand for those people was high. Anybody who had designed his or her own home page could become a designer overnight and work on big corporate sites. This is not the case anymore. Designers need to understand every aspect of Web design and, because the job market these days is quite competitive, many designers are forced to find their own clients and work on a freelance basis. This makes it more important than ever that a Web designer understand all facets of Web design. And even though this is a book on Adobe Photoshop®, it is my intention to give you a good understanding of what you'll need to know in order to conceptualize, manage, design and create a Web site.

Today's Web projects are far more complicated and demanding than they used to be. At the beginning of the Internet euphoria, many companies had no clear vision of how to utilize this medium and how it would fit into their marketing strategies. The Web was seen as an advertising medium, and most clients just wanted to have visually stunning online presentations. You will rarely find those types of projects anymore; companies want to use the Web for e-commerce, or simply to offer better services to their customers. Over the last five years, attention has shifted from the front end (filling the site with dazzling graphics and animation, often for their own sake) to the back end (ensuring the visitor a pleasant, efficient Web site experience).

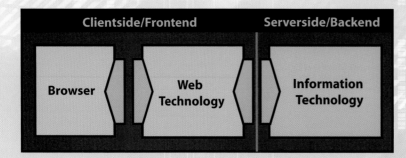

Clientside/Frontend		Serverside/Backend
Browser	Web Technology	Information Technology

The content of a Web site resides on a server, which transmits the pages when an URL is typed in a browser. Since the browser is installed on an user's computer, it is called a client. Anything that happens on the side of the client is therefore called client-side or front-end activity. Respectively, anything that happens on the server side is called server-side or back-end activity.

THE BACK END

Browser and server technology has seen major advances over the last years, and developing a Web site that serves dynamically created pages is easier than ever before. HTML authoring tools, such as Adobe GoLive®, offer the ability to utilize such application server technology as ASP (Active Server Pages), JSP (JavaServer Pages), PHP (Hypertext Preprocessor), and even shopping cart solutions. In the past, whenever a Web site utilized a form—an email subscription list, for example—the Web designer had to get a programmer, who would write a script that saved the data on the server. All this can now be done by a tech-savvy designer working directly in GoLive without having to edit the HTML code directly. I strongly recommend that you check out the form creation features in GoLive. The following sections present some other core server technologies that you should be familiar with.

PERL: If you sign up for an email newsletter, your information is sent to a server. Chances are that when you click the Submit button on the subscription Web page, a PERL script is triggered to save the data that you submit—that is, to store it in a database or text file. PERL (which stands for Practical Extraction and Report Language) and CGI (the Common Gateway Interface) are often discussed in one breath, but they are two different things. PERL is a programming language; CGI is a protocol that handles the data transfer between a browser and a server. Since PERL is free and works on every server, many Web developers use it to access the CGI to save and store the form data that a user has sent. Even though PERL is relatively easy to learn, it

comes with a challenge: Debugging and installing a PERL script can be tricky because there are many variables that can change from server to server. When you download one of the many available PERL scripts to use on your site, you have to know how your server is set up; but aside from that, it is worth learning the basics of PERL.

CGI: The Common Gateway Interface was created to handle the interactions between browsers and servers. If, for example, you click a Web link, a page request is sent from your browser to a server, and the server then transmits the HTML page. But CGI is also used when the information from a form is sent via either a POST or a GET method (these two methods tell CGI how the information was submitted and where to look for It).

While PERL and CGI work fine with smaller Web sites, they can be quite challenging to use with larger projects. (PERL is slow, for example, and can be very demanding on the server.) Developers looking for new, faster solutions have created application servers. An application server works by saving an HTML page along with some scripting code. When such a page is called, the server processes the scripts that are embedded in the HTML document and then displays it to the visitor (as a pure HTML page; the code gets stripped away). These scripts usually access a database where all the information is stored and then merge the information with the HTML document, in much the same way that a mail merging program merges the information from an address database with a text file.

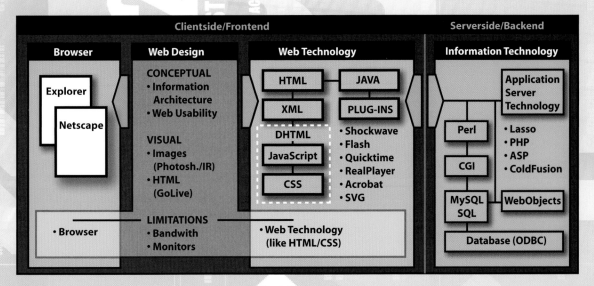

This graph shows how all the areas of Web design are linked. As a Web designer you have to bridge the gap that is caused by the limitations of the browsers and the Web technology.

ASP, ColdFusion, PHP and Lasso: These are all different application server technologies; Active Server Pages (ASP) is Microsoft's application server technology (www.microsoft.com). When a user requests an Active Server Page, the application server recognizes the document by the extension ".asp" and processes it before displaying it. Allaire, the company that originally created ColdFusion, was bought by Macromedia (www.macromedia.com). ColdFusion works like ASP and is easy to spot: Pages that use ColdFusion have the extension ".cfm". PHP is a great alternative to ASP and ColdFusion. Since it is open source, you find it installed on many Web servers, and Internet Service Providers charge far less for PHP servers than for ASP and ColdFusion servers. (You can read more about PHP at www.php.net.) Lasso was developed by Blueworld (www.blueworld.com) and is distinct from other application servers in that it can access FileMaker Pro databases. This makes Lasso very useful for anybody who wants to run a Macintosh as a Web server.

WebObjects: This technology was bought by Apple (www.apple.com) from NeXT. WebObjects allow a designer to put the functionality of a Web site into one program that resides on the server instead of having many little scripts. Everything resides in one large program, which can be created with an object-oriented language such as Java.

SQL and MySQL: Just as HTML is a standard for displaying Web pages, SQL is a standard for accessing the information in a database. SQL is relatively easy to understand and to learn. When used for creating dynamic Web pages, SQL commands are embedded in the HTML page and can then be processed by one of the application servers. MySQL is a particular database management system that supports SQL. It is very affordable (for some users it is free) and therefore widely used.

THE FRONT END

It could be said that the Web designer bridges the gap between Web technology and the browser. Design restrictions exist due to shortcomings of either the technology or the browsers, and it is the Web designer's job to resolve these shortcomings. Five years ago, the limitations imposed by browsers, computers in general, and the core Web technology were serious

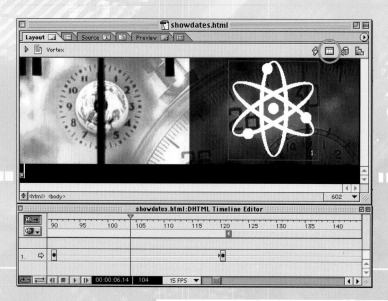

By clicking on the "Open DHTML Timeline Editor" button in GoLive, a timeline appears in which the HTML layers can be animated. To see an example of a DHTML Web site, go to www.vortex4u.com. This site uses DHTML to animate a couple of layers that move across the screen. In the "Show Dates" section, a graphic slides swings left to right in a loop, and on the "Press & Bio" page a butterfly moves randomly across the screen.

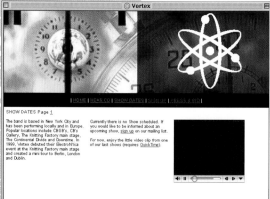

problems. These days, Web designers are lucky in the respect that the technology isn't the main challenge anymore. The following sections describe some of the technology that you will run into when working on a Web site:

JavaScript: JavaScript is a scripting language that can be inserted into HTML code and interpreted directly by the browser. Many interactive elements (such as rollover buttons) are created with JavaScript, so every Web designer should have some JavaScript knowledge. As in many other areas, Microsoft has managed to make the world more complicated by introducing its own version of JavaScript, called JScript. And yes, you guessed it: JScript is not totally compatible with JavaScript! However, if you stick to working with the ready-made JavaScripts that come as modules in GoLive, you won't need to worry; they work across all platforms.

Cascading Style Sheets: The idea behind HTML was to create a syntax for structural coding, and many formatting commands were left out intentionally. (HTML doesn't allow you to indent a paragraph, for example.) When the Web became so hugely popular, designers wanted to have more control over the formatting and design of Web text. Instead of incorporating extra commands in the HTML syntax, the World Wide Web Consortium decided to use an extension called Cascading Style Sheets (CSS). CSS offers a lot of control over formatting, but more importantly, it allows the designer to control the appearance of an entire site by changing a "master" CSS file. Another great feature of CSS is that it provides the designer with layers, and every Web designer should be familiar with these. (You can read more on CSS in the GoLive chapter.)

Dynamic HTML: This HTML syntax is no different from the one you use to create your Web sites. Dynamic HTML (or DHTML) is simply regular HTML used in conjunction with cascading style sheets and JavaScript. The goal of DHTML is to let designers create more animated Web pages. If you want to get your feet wet, you can try out GoLive's animation editor by clicking the film button in the upper-right corner of the document window ("Open DHTML Timeline Editor"). GoLive's animation editor resembles those found in 3D animation packages. To create an animation, place your elements in a layer and then record the move-ment across the screen. (Only layers allow absolute positioning through x and y values.)

XML: The idea behind Extensible Markup Language (XML) is to allow the designer to create markers that describe the content of a site. In order for a browser to translate these markers into HTML, the formatting of each marker is stored in an external document that is linked to the HTML page. A designer might, for example, create a marker for the price and the product name on an e-commerce Web site. This would allow the designer to change the formatting of all the prices and product names for the entire site by changing the XML master file. XML is essential for all dynamic Web sites, and every Web designer will eventually have to acquaint themselves with it, because it is also becoming increasingly important in the desktop publishing world.

Flash and Shockwave: Flash is a technology as well as the name of a software package by Macromedia. While Flash can also display images and other media, such as

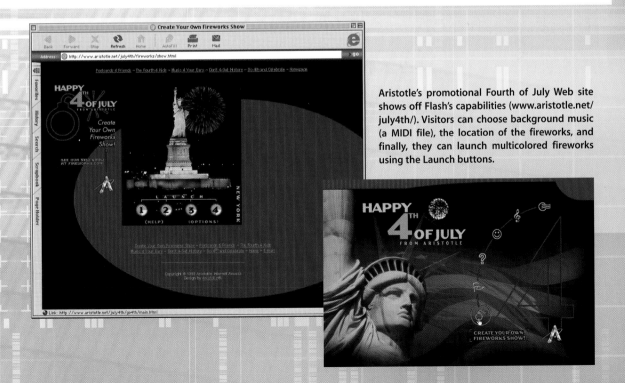

Aristotle's promotional Fourth of July Web site shows off Flash's capabilities (www.aristotle.net/july4th/). Visitors can choose background music (a MIDI file), the location of the fireworks, and finally, they can launch multicolored fireworks using the Launch buttons.

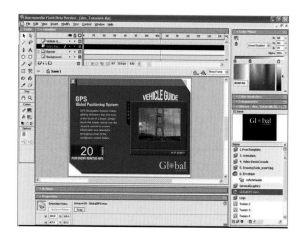

Macromedia Flash MX (as seen here) or Adobe LiveMotion allow you to create Flash animations.

QuickTime videos, its specialty is animating vector graphics. Over the years, Flash has become more powerful and scriptable. Many people are using Flash for developing applications. Shockwave, by contrast, is the name of a technology that allows you to embed applications that have been created with Macromedia Director. Director has been around for many years, and is popular for creating CD-ROM applications. It works mainly with bitmap images, and so it generates larger files than Flash does, but it also offers way more functionality. Shockwave and Flash are two separate plug-ins, and it could be said that the Flash plug-in is a slimmed-down version of the Shockwave plug-in. (Flash cannot play Shockwave applications, for example, but Shockwave can display Flash content.) But the difference between Flash and Shockwave also lies in the varying complexity and capabilities of the programming languages that they offer. The Director programming language, called Lingo, is more powerful than the Flash programming language, but it is also more difficult to learn.

PDF: Developed by Adobe before the Web became popular, PDF (Portable Document Format) was primarily intended for distributing documents in a cross-

The 4th of July Web site from Aristotle is a great example of Flash technology and a lot of fun: Click on one of the Launch buttons to trigger a rocket that explodes in one of four colors.

platform environment. Inspired by the success of the Web, Adobe developed a plug-in that enables browsers to display PDF files on Web pages. PDF documents can be quite advanced these days, incorporating hyperlinks, embedded videos, and even forms that can be linked to the server. To create PDF files, you need Adobe Acrobat®, which is able to convert any PostScript file to PDF format. With the free Acrobat Reader, which you can download from www.adobe.com, anyone can view, read, and print PDF files.

Java: Despite their similar names, Java, developed by Sun Microsystems, has little to do with JavaScript. Java is a high-class (and relatively advanced) programming language, similar to C++. Java allows you to create platform-independent applications that can be embedded on a Web page. With Java, virtually anything is possible, so if your Web project requires something that can't be done with Flash or Shockwave, you'll probably need to use Java.

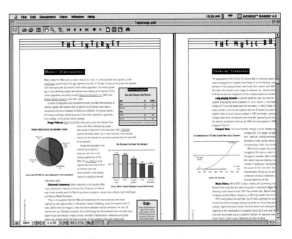

Adobe Acrobat allows you to store layouts with text and graphics in a platform-independent file format (PDF) that can be opened with the free Acrobat Reader. You can even embed those files in a Web page since Adobe offers a PDF plug-in for all the browsers.

ADOBE LIVEMOTION

Flash technology has become quite popular in the Web design community and has made the Web—for better or worse—a much more animated place. Until recently, Macromedia's Flash software was the only authoring tool available for creating Flash-based animations or interfaces. That has changed with the release of Adobe's LiveMotion.

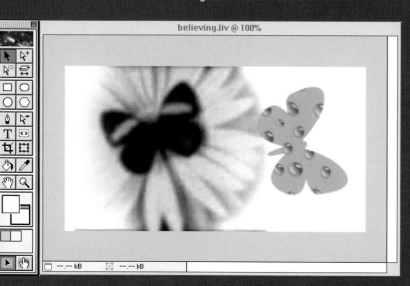

The main difference between the programs is that Flash offers a more versatile programming language. LiveMotion does provide behaviors like stopping or starting Flash movie playback (behaviors are similar to actions in Flash), but it's not comparable to Flash. But LiveMotion makes up for that shortcoming with versatility and ease of use: creating simple rollovers, GIF animations, and interactive Flash projects is much easier in LiveMotion than in Flash. Anyone who is familiar with Adobe products will soon feel comfortable with the LiveMotion interface, especially motion-graphics designers who have worked with After Effects.

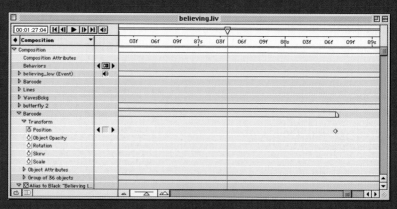

LiveMotion works with shapes that can be placed either directly using the rectangle, ellipse, or polygon tool, or by importing shapes from Adobe Illustrator. These shapes can be filled with images or patterns and can even have effects like emboss or drop shadows assigned to them. When you're done, LiveMotion will create an HTML page along with all the images and JavaScript functionality such as rollover effects.

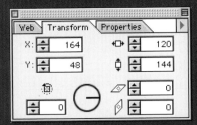

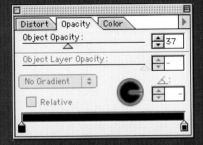

You can set the Transform and Opacity attributes conveniently from a palette.

To animate an element in the timeline, click on the triangle that is displayed before every track name. The triangle rotates 45 degrees and reveals three tracks: **Transform**, **Object Attributes,** and **Layer**. The **Transform** track controls the position, opacity, rotation, and skew and scale values for the object. Changing any of these is simple: clicking on the stopwatch button inserts a marker (or "keyframe") in the track underneath the object's timeline. Then the current position to the time can be moved to the end and another marker is set by clicking on the stopwatch button. In the **Transform** palette, these settings can be modified. To animate the object in relation to its anchor point, the Object Attributes like color or offset can be set in the **Layer** track. But LiveMotion's animation capabilities go even farther: you can nest animation loops in a timeline so that they play within one another (for example, you could loop a spinning globe and then animate it in the timeline). LiveMotion even shows the length of the loop so that while you are modifying the timeline, you can see how many loops will fit into it.

LiveMotion's strength is the ease with which it lets you create animations, but it also allows you to create some interactivity: mouse-over, mouse-down, and other rollover states can be assigned to buttons and saved as styles. A style, plus a behavior, can then be applied to navigational elements such as buttons to control the play head. Another great feature is that LiveMotion supports Photoshop filters. These can be applied nondestructively, so if you change your mind, just disable the effect in the Photoshop Filters palette.

Exporting and embedding a LiveMotion project in an HTML page as a SWF file is done automatically. LiveMotion even has a batch-replace feature that makes it easy to add LiveMotion-generated elements to existing HTML pages: the **Batch Replace HTML** command searches for HTML elements and then replaces them with LiveMotion-generated elements.

Overall LiveMotion is a great alternative to Flash and its ease of use makes it more suitable for designers whose focus is mostly on animation.

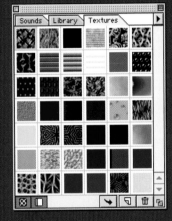

Applying textures is a great way to enrich an object while keeping the data demand low.

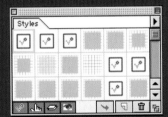

Creating rollover buttons is simple and convenient because the Styles palette can save rollover states.

QUICKTIME VR

With e-commerce being so important these days, chances are that sooner or later you'll have a client who is interested in new ways of presenting his products online. Companies offering special plug-ins for the virtual presentation are numerous and some of these technologies are very promising (check out www.viewpoint.com). One of the best technologies, however, has been around for some time and is available on over 50 million browsers: Apple's QuickTime. This means that there is a large audience already equipped to see a QuickTime VR movie—VR stands for virtual reality. These movies allow a 360-degree panoramic view of a location or the presentation of an object: dragging the mouse while clicking on the movie is enough to change the angle of view or zoom in/out and, if available, even link to different VR movies if the mouse is over a hot spot.

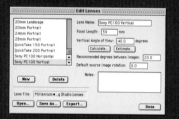

The most important step in creating a QuickTime panorama in QTVR Authoring Studio is telling the program what lens was used and the angles between every shot. QTVR Authoring Studio then aligns the images automatically.

To create QuickTime VR movies, you can use Apple's free QTVR Make Panorama 2, which you can download from www.apple.com/quicktime/developers/tools.html (only available for Mac). However, this tool has some limitations; for one, you can't stitch several images together. This means that you must either already have a panorama shot (some special cameras can produce these), or you must stitch several shots together in Photoshop. This process is tedious, because you have to adjust the transparency in the Layer palette to align the overlapping areas. A more professional solution is Apple's QuickTime VR Authoring Studio, which makes creating QuickTime VR movies a snap. If you need to make more than a couple QuickTime VR movies, it's worth buying this program. Creating a QuickTime VR panorama movie using Photoshop and QTVR Make Panorama 2 can take between two and four hours; with QuickTime VR Authoring Studio, it can be done in less than 20 minutes.

To create a QuickTime VR panorama movie, all you need is a digital camera and a tripod. When mounting the camera in an upright position on the tripod, make sure that the tripod is level with the horizon and that the nodal point of your camera is directly over the rotation point of the tripod. A common misunderstanding is that the nodal point is the same as the film plane, which is often marked underneath 35mm cameras, but the nodal point is the point inside your camera where the light rays converge and flip over. For most 35mm cameras and lenses, the nodal point is located somewhere near the center of the lens barrel. When shooting a QuickTime VR panorama, you must rotate around this point to eliminate the image mismatch caused by parallax error. You'll understand parallax error if you do a simple experiment. Close one eye and hold your index finger about six inches away from your open eye. Turn your head side to side and you will notice that your finger moves with respect to the background. This relative movement is due to the fact that you are not rotating your head around your eye's nodal point, which is somewhere in the center of your eyeball. Instead, you're rotating your spine, which is several inches farther back and to one side. It is this relative side-to-side motion that you'll want to eliminate when setting up a camera for VR panoramas.

Finding and adjusting to the nodal point of a camera is tricky, because each camera and lens combination has its own nodal point. With a standard tripod this is virtually impossible, because there is no way to adjust the camera correctly. For less than the price of Apple's QuickTime VR Authoring Studio, you can buy Kaidan's KiWi+, a tripod head that lets you mount the camera in an upright position and adjust the nodal point. It also has a twin axis bubble level for adjusting the tripod's horizontal position. The KiWi+ also ships with four detent (indexed) discs that provide click-stops for a variety of lens combinations. Check out www.kaidan.com to find the right product or even see some great examples of what you can do with QuickTime VR.

The KiWi+ from Kaidan is a great utility for shooting panoramic movies. It allows you to adjust the camera to the nodal point of the lens and it comes with detent (indexed) discs to rotate the unit in set degrees. For more information, check out www.kaidan.com.

If pictures are not taken in regular increments, the images have to be aligned manually in the Pair Alignment window. Even though this process goes quickly, it will take 10 minutes longer per panorama than if you use

After shooting a series of pictures, you need to combine them into one large panoramic image. If you are using QTVR Make Panorama 2, you have to use Photoshop to make your panorama from individual shots. With Quick-Time VR Authoring Studio, you can do everything within the program: the Authoring Studio even has an auto-modus that adjusts the images automatically. All you need to do is to enter the angle and the lens, and the

You can set the display settings for the final VR movie before it is saved.

The QuickTime VR panorama exported as an image.

stitch the individual pictures into one panorama in a matter of seconds. It does an amazingly good job, but you can also adjust images manually. All you have to do is export this image as a QTVR movie and QTVR Authoring Studio will automatically crop the panorama, sharpen it, and adjust the brightness. This software even blends the individual images at the edges to ensure a smooth panorama. If you set everything up correctly, the whole process will take only a few mouse clicks and the software will do the work for you while you have a cup of coffee.

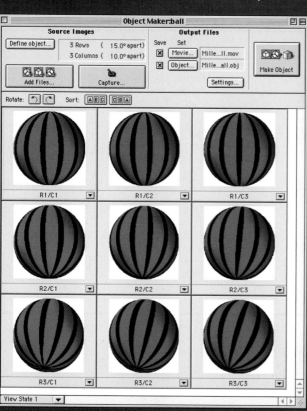

This object movie was created with a 3D animation program: you can clearly see how every picture shows the object at a slightly different angle.

Object movies

QuickTime VR also allows you to create object movies, which are great for showing an object from every angle, even with some animation. Creating an object movie is as straightforward as creating a panorama movie: after shooting several pictures, just import the images into the QTVR Authoring Studio's Object Maker. To enhance the experience, you can even allow a vertical rotation so that the object can be moved in all directions.

1. Planning the movie: We are so accustomed to movies as a linear sequence of frames that understanding how an object movie works can be a little challenging in the beginning. Think of a QTVR object movie as a grid: the pictures are arranged in sequence but instead of just being able to move forward and backward on the horizontal axis, you can also move an object movie vertically. Since this is a bit complex, it is a good idea to sketch it out so that you can visualize how to organize the project and shoot the frames (the sketch doesn't have to show all the frames, a 3x3 grid will suffice).

To create a VR object movie that can be moved along the vertical and horizontal axis, you have to create several rows and columns.

2. Choosing a capture device: The best way to capture images for an object movie is with a digital camera. Not only does this produce digital pictures, but it also makes it easier to align the images when they're stitched together. (Have you ever been able to mount a photo or film on a scanner without a slight angle?) In addition, digital camcorders and cameras let you preview results so that you can check the lighting, alignment, and positioning of the object. This is more important than you might realize: imagine that one picture in a series of 27 is not perfect. It is almost impossible to redo this single shot. Digital cameras are getting cheaper every day. For my shoots, I use a Sony PC-100 camcorder that can also take still images and save them on a memory stick. You can insert this memory stick with an adapter in the PC slot and mount it like a hard disk on the desktop. Transferring images could hardly be easier. Camcorders like the Sony PC-100 come with a remote control, which ensures that you never risk shifting the alignment between the camera and the object platform.

The final result in QTVR Studio: While holding the mouse button down, the user can spin the ball in any direction. Using a 3D program is a nice way to experiment with object videos. Most animation programs can export an animation as an image sequence.

3. Setting up the scene: The most difficult part of shooting an object movie is rotating the object around one axis. Doing this by hand is almost impossible. For budget-minded hobbyists, a lazy Susan spray-painted black should be enough. If you want a more professional device, I recommend the PiXi from Kaidan. This high-end object rig is specially designed for QuickTime VR shoots and can rotate even heavy objects in increments of 15 degrees.

4. Shooting the frames: Decide how many shots you want to take per row and column in your grid. Don't use too many grids, otherwise the movie will become huge. For example: rotating an object 360 degrees with 15-degree increments requires 24 pictures per row. If you plan on rotating the object along the vertical axis 90 degrees with 15-degree increments, you will end up with 144 pictures (6 rows with 24 pictures each). Since you are planning to use the object movie on a Web page, use 30-degree increments for the rows for a total of 12 pictures for the row. When using only three rows, the total number of pictures is 36, which will still be quite big for low bandwidth connections but is still acceptable.

The Kaidan PiXi is a professional object rig that is specially designed for QTVR object movies.

HTML - HYPERTEXT MARKUP LANGUAGE

If you choose Source from the View menu in Internet Explorer or Netscape Navigator, a window will open displaying the HTML code of that particular page. HTML uses only ASCII characters (ASCII stands for American Standard Code for Information Interchange), so it works on multiple platforms. This means that a Web page created on a PC can be read and interpreted by a browser running on another plat-

The HTML source code when opened in a browser.

form, such as a Macintosh. An HTML tag usually has a beginning and an end component, both of which are placed in angle brackets; the end tag sports a slash (/). Despite the long list of HTML tags, such as those for headers, paragraphs, justification, and so on, the language is relatively easy to learn, and you can create a Web page by writing HTML code in a text editor.

Structural Coding

HTML is primarily a structural language. While there are some formatting tags for font face and size, the main idea behind HTML involves defining structures. For example, in HTML, a header is marked as follows:

<H1>Headline</H1>

The browser is informed only that the text is a header, and not told which font to use or how large the characters should be. Each browser sets those

parameters independently, based on user preferences. Therefore, the same header may be displayed in 16-point Arial on one browser and 14-point Times on another. Obviously, this is a worst-case scenario for designers, and before Cascading Style Sheets were available, many designers sidestepped the problem altogether by avoiding the use of structural tags (such as <Hn>) in favor of the <FONT> tag with its Face and Size formatting attributes.

Absolute Positioning

HTML offers virtually no way of specifying absolute positioning. The original intention here was to display the same information successfully, regardless of operating platform or monitor size. In that context, it made sense that text should flow differently on a 14-inch monitor than on a 21-inch unit, and formatting the text was secondary. Web designers weren't happy with HTML's formatting limitations, however, so they started working around them by placing text and images in invisible tables (that is, tables with the Border attribute set to 0). Even though HTML and browsers now offer layers, using tables is still the safest way to lay out a Web page. Most HTML authoring tools offer a feature called Layout Grid. This grid is simply an invisible HTML table that is formatted in a specific way by the HTML authoring tool.

DESIGN LIMITATIONS OF THE BROWSER

During the browser wars between Netscape and Microsoft in the 1990s, every browser update was eagerly awaited by users and Web designers alike, because with each new version came a whole new realm of design possibilities. Back then, backward compatibility was a big issue: Designing a Web page for the latest version of a browser often meant that some visitors (those with older versions) were not able to see the page. This is not the case anymore; both Navigator and Explorer are quite up to par, and they have been available for quite some time. This doesn't mean that there aren't any more design limitations. It just means that Web designers don't have to worry too much about backward compatibility. If your Web site can be displayed successfully on a version 4.x browser, it will look good on other browsers as well. The following sections discuss some other design issues that you should be aware of.

Tables

Getting a table to appear and behave the exact same way on Internet Explorer as it does on Netscape Navigator can sometimes be quite a challenge. The reason for this is that certain table attributes are interpreted differently:

● In older versions of Netscape, tables with empty table cells would not display at the correct width, even if a width for the table had been set. This problem is not major, because it can be fixed.

● Navigator doesn't handle background images in tables very well. Older releases of Netscape (before version 6) display an image background in a nested table, even if the Background Image attribute hasn't been set. Explorer doesn't have this problem, but there are plenty of users out there who work with Netscape. If you are a Web designer who wants to use image backgrounds in tables, you need to check your Web site in all commonly used browsers to ensure that your pages appear as intended.

● Background images that incorporate transparency can't be used. Navigator will render transparent pixels to white if such an image is used as a table background.

● The more nested tables a layout has, the more unpredictable it is whether every browser will display the page correctly. Again, Netscape Navigator has a bad track record here. In order to create certain complicated layouts, a Web designer might have to nest tables in other tables. The rule of thumb is to nest a maximum of two tables (for a total of three tables). It is, of course, possible to nest more than two tables, but in doing so you run the risk that older Netscape browsers won't display them correctly.

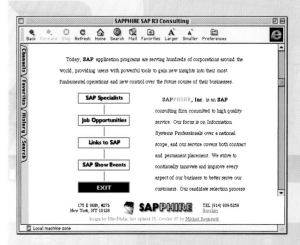

A Web site can look good in one browser but totally different in another. This could be due to incompatibilities of the HTML implementation in the browser or to the fact that the visitor's preferences override the settings of the Web site. In that case, the color and size of links or text is beyond your control.

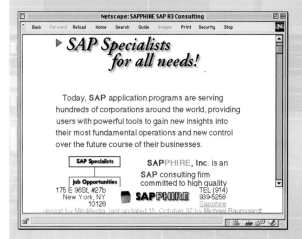

This is the same page in Navigator; if the user has changed the browser preferences to override, all the formatting of your fonts might be lost and the design can look very different.

THE HTML SOURCE CODE OF A PAGE

HTML documents are ASCII files; therefore, you can open and edit them in any word processor. HTML tags are identified by angled brackets. Every HTML document needs to contain at least the <HTML>, <HEAD>, and <BODY> tags. Most tags need to be paired; a tag that opens a block of text (<HEAD>, for instance) needs a companion tag to close that block of text (</HEAD>). Closing tags are identical to opening tags except for the "/" character.

<HTML>: This tag identifies the document as a Web page.

<TITLE>: The TITLE tag identifies the text that will be seen as a headline in the browser window.

<BODY BGCOLOR="#ffffff">: The BODY container holds all the text and graphics of the Web page between the start tag and the end tag. A tag often has several attributes. In this example, BGCOLOR defines the background color of the browser window.

<P><CENTER>: This is a paragraph tag. The embedded CENTER tag means that the paragraph is centered.

<MAP NAME="maintop">: MAPs are picture files, parts of which are defined as hot links. You can click a hot link to connect to another Web page.

<IMG SRC="images/maintop.gif" WIDTH="301" HEIGHT="27">: The IMG tag places a picture on the Web page. The attributes WIDTH and HEIGHT tell the browser the size of the picture. This way, text and layout can be displayed properly before the image elements finish downloading.

```
<HTML>
    <HEAD>
        <META NAME="GENERATOR" CONTENT="Adobe PageMill ">
        <TITLE>Eye2Eye Mainpage</TITLE>
    </HEAD>
<BODY BGCOLOR="#ffffff" LINK="#ff0000" ALINK="#0017ff">
<P><CENTER>
    <MAP NAME="maintop">
        <AREA SHAPE="rect" COORDS="211,2,300,26"
        HREF="press/indpress.html">
        <AREA SHAPE="rect" COORDS="148,0,205,25"
        HREF="bio/bioindex.html">
        <AREA SHAPE="rect" COORDS="69,1,144,25"
        HREF="tour/tourindx.html">
        <AREA SHAPE="rect" COORDS="2,1,61,27" HREF="cd/cds.html">
    </MAP>
    <IMG SRC="images/maintop.gif" WIDTH="301" HEIGHT="27"
    ALIGN="BOTTOM"
    NATURALSIZEFLAG="3" USEMAP="#maintop" ISMAP BORDER="0">
</CENTER></P>

<P><CENTER>
    <IMG SRC="images/e2e_main.gif" WIDTH="301" HEIGHT="211"
    ALIGN="BOTTOM" NATURALSIZEFLAG="3">
</CENTER></P>

<P><CENTER>
    <MAP NAME="mainbttm">
        <AREA SHAPE="rect" COORDS="94,3,167,26" HREF="exit.html">
        <AREA SHAPE="rect" COORDS="12,2,68,26" HREF="map.html">
    </MAP>
    <IMG SRC="images/mainbttm.gif" WIDTH="176" HEIGHT="27"
    ALIGN="BOTTOM" NATURALSIZEFLAG="3" USEMAP="#mainbttm"
    ISMAP BORDER="0">
</CENTER></P>
```

```
<PRE><CENTER>Click on CDs to listen to check out Eye2Eyes two available
records or ...To get on our mailing list, please send your address and
telephone number to
<A HREF="mailto:email@erols.com">email@erols.com</A>
</PRE>

<H6><CENTER>
    <A HREF="cd/cds.html">CDs</A> | <A
    HREF="tour/tourindx.html">TOUR</A> | <A
    HREF="bio/bioindex.html">BIO</A> | <A
    HREF="press/indpress.html">PRESS</A><BR>
    <A HREF="map.html" TARGET="_top">MAP</A> | <A
    HREF="exit.html">EXIT</A>
</CENTER></H6>

</BODY>
</HTML>
```

<A HREF="mailto: email@erols.com">: A link is a connection to another Web page. It is identified by an "A." Links are not restricted to the addresses of other pages or files; in this example, the link tells your e-mail program to create a message and sends it to the specified address.

<H6>: There are six different headline sizes and categories, numbered H1 through H6. H6 is the smallest headline size, and is often smaller than body text. The most common use of H6 headlines is for text links at the bottom of the page.

This is the page generated by this particular HTML code.

THE DESIGN LIMITATIONS OF EARLIER BROWSERS

	Background	Foreground	Tables	Frames
Navigator 2	Color + Image	Image	no Color	no Frames
Navigator 3	Color + Image	Image	Color	(only visible Borders)
Explorer 3	Color + Image	Image	Color + Background Img	invisible + Color
Navigator 4	Color + Image	Layers	Color + Background Img	invisible
Explorer 4	Color + Image	Layers	Color + Background Img	invisible + Color

A little history: while Internet Explorer and Netscape Navigator 4.x offered relatively similar features, the 3.x versions were quite different from one another. For example, Explorer could set a background color and image for a table or even make a frame invisible. When designing Web pages, you have to take older browser versions into consideration, however, you only need to be backward compatible with 4.x browsers.

Layers

At first glance, having the ability to stack elements on top of one another, as well as complete control over the placement of elements, seems great. However, the reality of layers is that they are just not the right tool for Web layout. Because text can flow differently on different computers, the length of a text layer can't be predicted, which makes it difficult to place items in proper relation to one another. Earlier versions of Netscape have an additional quirk: If the browser window is resized after the page has been loaded, then all the layers get screwed up. Layers can be used safely only for animation (with DHTML) where one layer with some text or an image moves across the screen. There are, of course, other uses too, but I recommend that you stay away from layers unless you are quite sure that you need them.

Cascading Style Sheets

At this point in time, no browser has a complete, fully functioning CSS implementation. There is always something missing, or some level of inconsistency across browser platforms. The very basic text formatting features can be used (and should be used), but many of the more advanced features will most likely not work consistently.

IMAGES

If you're making the leap from desktop publishing, you're probably accustomed to using image and graphics formats, such as TIFF and EPS, that give you the best possible image quality. On the Web, these formats are largely irrelevant, while JPEG, GIF, and PNG prevail. As you probably know, bandwidth is a big issue on the Web. Even with a 56 K modem you will most likely get only 45 K actual throughput, so large data transmissions are out of the question. Images usually make up 60 percent to 80 percent of the data on a Web page; consequently, file compression is a significant issue. JPEG and GIF are popular formats on the Web, because they employ effective compression algorithms that can compress graphics into relatively small files. This efficiency, however, comes at the expense of image quality.

JPEG, GIF, and PNG all have their advantages and drawbacks, which pertain mainly to their different compression algorithms. Generally, JPEG is used for photographs, GIF is used for graphics with solid-colored areas, and PNG straddles both worlds. Each of these image formats are explained in detail in their own chapters, but to help you get started designing right away, the following sections offer brief explanations.

THE BANDWITH PROBLEM

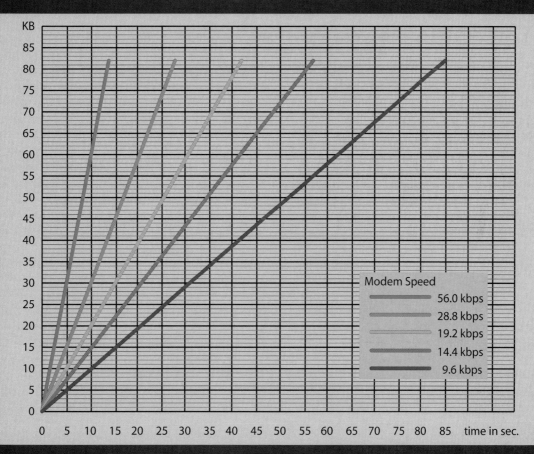

The transmission speed is never linear, as it is presented here. When designing your page, don't use the best-case scenario; even if the visitor has a 56k modem, it is more likely that he will end up with 46k transfer rate.

One of the restrictions of the Web medium is connection speed. There are still a lot of people accessing the Internet with 56 Kbps modems. (Just think of all the business people that only have modems on their laptops!) For designers, the bandwidth problem means that 40 K to 60 K should be the maximum amount of new transferred data per page. New transferred data refers to the fact that browsers store downloaded text and images in a local cache on the user's hard drive; stored data can be recalled from this cache much faster than new content can be downloaded fresh from the Web. If the browser detects that an image on a page has been downloaded before, it will load that image from the cache.

When you develop the design concept for your Web site, it's a good idea to use the same image elements as often as possible across your pages. For example, a company logo placed on multiple pages will be downloaded and stored in a visitor's cache after he or she visits the first page, which will speed up your viewers' browsing of other pages. Reusing graphics this way will let you add new graphics to other pages on the site while still minimizing user download time.

JPEG (Joint Photographic Experts Group)

JPEG can store up to 16 million colors, but it is not well suited for text or graphics, since its block-by-block compression algorithm introduces a blurring effect. Within each block, differences in brightness are retained, but subtle color changes are lost. Despite this loss of color information, it is amazing how good the image quality is, even at maximum compression. Compression factors range from 10:1 to 100:1, meaning that at the highest compression rate, a 1 MB image can be compressed into a 10 K JPEG file. This is ideal for the Web, but because JPEG compression is not lossless, you should always keep a copy of the original graphics file. Keep in mind also that JPEG lacks transparency—a feature offered by both GIF and PNG.

GIF (Graphical Interchange Format)

GIF uses a compression algorithm based on pattern recognition: If several adjacent pixels have the same color, GIF can compress them better, which explains why GIF is used for images that are more graphical in nature. GIF is not as successful as JPEG at compressing photographs, but it compresses large areas of flat color extremely well. GIF's compression factor with photographs is only around 4:1, but it has the advantage of compressing losslessly. Lossless means that after decompression, the picture looks exactly the same as it did before, and that repeated saves don't degrade the image like they do with JPEG. GIF images, however, are limited in the number of colors they can incorporate; the maximum is 256 colors.

GIF has two more handy features: It supports transparency and animation. In order to produce transparency, one color is defined as the chroma key color during storage. The browser then disables this color and replaces it with the background image. With GIF animation, you can set the duration of each image and define whether the animation should run once or in a continuous loop. (You'll learn more about this technique in the GIF Animation chapter.) GIF's transparency and animation features have greatly contributed to its popularity.

PNG (Portable Network Graphic Format)

PNG, a response to the restrictions of JPEG and GIF, was supposed to be the next step in image formatting for the Web. PNG combines the best of both worlds: lossless compression with up to 16 million colors, and 256 levels of transparency—which allow for semi-transparent color areas. Semi-transparency is particularly important when you want the edges of an image to blend smoothly with the browser background.

PNG also sports a great Gamma-correction function, which guarantees that images will be equally bright on all platforms. (Since Windows monitors are inherently darker than Macintosh monitors, Web pages created on a Mac look too dark when viewed on a Windows browser, and pages designed on a PC look too pale on a Mac. PNG's Gamma correction feature resolves this discrepancy, so PNG images display with the correct brightness on both platforms.)

Unfortunately, PNG is not well supported by all browsers. Some older browsers still require a plug-in to view PNG images, or won't take advantage of the 256 levels of transparency. PNG has two other major drawbacks: PNG files are much larger than comparable GIFs or JPEGs, and PNG does not support animation. As transmission speeds rise, however, PNG may well become more interesting to Web designers.

With PNG it is no problem to create objects with a drop shadow and have it integrate seamlessly with the design. As you can see in these images, the drop shadow blends with any background loaded into the browser.

HOW DO BROWSERS COMPENSATE FOR MISSING COLORS?

Dithering is a technique that mingles two main colors together to create the optical illusion of an intermediate color. This is basically the same procedure as printing with process colors; all the colors of the spectrum can be created by mixing different amounts (or dot sizes) of the four basic colors (cyan, magenta, yellow, black, or CMYK). The dots are printed at different angles to one another, and are so small they can hardly be discerned with the naked eye.

Browsers use a similar process—if a desired color is outside the range of the available color depth, the browser tries to create that color by mixing colors that are available. Two techniques are used—pattern or diffusion dithering. With pattern dithering, the intermediate color is created by using a regular pattern of pixels,

which can produce unpleasing, unaesthetic effects. The second technique, diffusion dithering, simulates the intermediate color by placing pixels in a random pattern. Of course this only appears to be random; it is actually based on a mathematical model that can differ from one application to another.

If an application doesn't simulate a color by dithering, it only quantizes the color, which means it is rounded to the next available color and the color shifts become even more apparent. So 99 percent red, for instance, becomes 100 percent, while 84 percent red becomes 80 percent.

The original image was saved as a 256-color GIF with an adaptive palette and also as a JPEG. Both images were then viewed in the browser with the monitor set to 256 colors. You can see the results in the images below.

Explorer (top) dithers the GIF using diffusion dither, Navigator only quantizes the color value (bottom image). *Pictures are scaled to 120 percent.*

The same image saved as a JPEG (best quality) is displayed in both browsers with diffusion dithering. Explorer (top), in my opinion, yields the better result.

Color Problems with Images

Using color in desktop publishing is a snap compared to the challenge it represents in Web design. The five-percent dot gain that DTP designers have to deal with seems like nothing compared to the color variables on the Web: monitors that display 256 colors to 1 million colors, varying Gamma values across platforms, and an assortment of browsers that display images differently. But since these factors are all out of your control, you have to learn to learn to live with them: When saving a JPEG image, for instance, adjusting the brightness to compensate for Gamma differences is about all that you can do. GIF images behave a little more predictably, especially when colors are limited to the Web-safe palette, which is displayed consistently on all browsers and platforms.

Optimizing an image for both computer platforms requires finding a middle ground. Otherwise, images optimized for the Macintosh will appear too dark in Windows, as you can see in this example. The top image is the Macintosh version, at the bottom, the same image as it appears in Windows.

On the top, a typical GIF with an adaptive 16-color CLUT. The image below shows how this GIF will appear in a browser on monitors with 256 colors. You can clearly see the additional dithering that happened due to the fact that the colors in the adaptive color palette weren't Web-safe.

Using the Web-safe palette, however, amounts to settling for the lowest common denominator: Visitors with high-quality color displays will see the same "low-quality" pictures as those with older equipment. This is why few Web designers use the Web-safe color palette; most save GIF images with an adaptive or selective color palette and then test the results in multiple browsers, on multiple platforms, at 256 colors. If colors are acceptable under these varying circumstances, the designer can rest assured that the image will look even better on monitors that display thousands or millions of colors (more on this in the GIF chapter).

SOME USEFUL SITES FOR WEB DESIGNERS

Do you want to know what's happening in Silicon Alley, the heart of the New York Internet scene, or do you just want to find out more about HTML or JavaScript? You may find the following online sources helpful:

www.wwwac.org
The site of the World Wide Web Artists' Consortium (WWWAC) is the best place to locate Web designers, programmers, and Internet fans in New York City. The WWWAC holds monthly meetings and offers special interest groups that focus on a variety of topics, such as interface design and database integration.

www.nynma.org
The New York New Media Association, which also hosts regular meetings and special interest groups, provides job postings on its Web site. If you are looking for a Web design job in New York City, this is a great place to find one.

www.searchenginewatch.com
This site provides excellent information that will help you to optimize your site to ensure good results with search engines.

www.webposition.com
WebPositionGold can optimize your site for better search engine ratings. It generates HTML pages designed to rank your pages near the top of an engine's search results, and it automatically submits your pages to the major search engines.

www.virtual-stampede.com
One of the first programs available to do batch registrations for Web sites, Spider Software has now been rewritten and released as NetSubmitter Professional. This is a great (and affordable) tool for registering your site with the search engines. I highly recommend it.

http://dreamcatchersweb.com/scripts/
This site has some useful PERL scripts that are not too difficult to install. (If you are interested in more free PERL scripts, you can easily find them by doing a Web search.)

www.w3.org
The World Wide Web Consortium is the organization that develops and approves new versions of HTML. Check it out whenever there is an abbreviation that you don't recognize; it will most likely turn out to be a term that the W3C is currently working on.

developer.netscape.com
Not quite sure which HTML tag is supported in which Netscape browser? This site will tell you. If you want to learn more about HTML, this is a particularly great source.

msdn.microsoft.com/workshop/entry.asp
The Microsoft Developer Network and the Web Workshop have merged. This is an online source that you can use to find out about the HTML implementation in Explorer. It also has a very good introduction to HTML.

www.coolhomepages.com
This site lists some of the best-designed Web sites on the Internet. The featured sites are organized in categories, which makes this site a great source for inspiration—or a great place to promote your own Web site.

REVIEW.**NOTICE**

Developing

Illustration: **Bradley Grosh/Antony Kyriazis** from **Fuse**

A DESIGN CONCEPT

Learning to design Web pages in Photoshop is not difficult. Even if you are not an experienced Photoshop user, you can probably learn most of the important techniques in two days. However, if you have a small design studio, you don't have the luxury of a large team of specialists; you'll need a pretty good understanding of some aspects of Web design that have as much importance for the success of a Web site as a great design, including information architecture and Web usability.

Larger Web design agencies go through several phases of working with the client to come up with the best solution. Usually the first person who works on a Web project (aside from the account manager or the contact person) is the information architect. This is the person who tries to get a clear picture of what it is that the client wants to accomplish. For an e-commerce Web site, this person would look at what kind of products the client wants to sell. For a content Web site, the information architect would look at what types of information there are. He or she then comes up with a concept of how this information, or content, can be grouped, which has a direct influence on what the navigation will look like. So, ultimately, the information architect is the one who gives the designer an outline of what the design needs to accomplish. The information architect may also work with a Web usability specialist in these early stages, although often the person responsible for information architecture also handles the Web usability.

After the designer gets the outline for the information architecture, he or she creates a couple of sketches of the main page and any subsequent pages. When I say sketches, I literally mean sketches drawn with pen or pencil. Many Web designers say the trend to use traditional media is not to save time or money, but to avoid having the client relate to preliminary drafts as the final product. A pen or pencil sketch is very clearly a work in progress.

After there is some agreement with the client, the final design concept is created in Photoshop and presented. If there is some budget for Web usability, the next step is to create a mock-up Web site and get some testers from the targeted audience. Only at this stage is there is some certainty that the Web site fulfills its purpose. At this point, the design usually gets into a second round in which the information architect and the designer work out the problems.

So if you are a one-man show and are just getting into Web design, this chapter will give you some information on Information Architecture, Web Usability and Design Concepts.

INFORMATION ARCHITECTURE

"Information architecture" was a major buzz phrase among Web designers in the early days. Clement Mok, founder of Studio Archetype, a well-known San Francisco-based design firm, actually went so far as to give his company's name the subtitle "Identity & Information Architects." Before the Internet bubble burst, information architects were in high demand, as many Web design companies went looking for new hires with experience in this field—simply because it can make the difference between a good and bad

Web site. Information architecture is no less important today, but a lot of companies are more hesitant these days to include it in their budgets. The same is true for Web usability. But for small Web agencies, this can actually work to your advantage if you are willing to put in the time to learn all about it.

So what does "information architecture" actually mean? The best way to describe it in one sentence is to say that it refers to structuring information and content based on a logical and consistent navigational concept. This may seem simple at first blush, but in reality it's the biggest challenge when designing for the Web.

Designers who come from the print world may have a particularly hard time here, because designing for print uses an established set of rules and concepts that we're all so accustomed to that we don't think about them any more. For instance, every book has a table of contents, an index, and chapters that divide the content into units. Book designers and readers are so familiar with this navigational concept that nobody has to think about how to structure or use a book. But on the Web, information is not organized or accessed in such a linear way. There are many more options for structuring content and navigational elements.

You can draw a parallel to the development of the user interface on computers. In the beginning, computers and their applications did not provide standard functions—not even simple, familiar commands like Cut, Copy, and Paste. Today it seems the most natural thing to copy something to the clipboard and paste it into another application, but if you've ever observed someone learning to use the computer, you remember how hard it was at first to wrap your mind around these concepts.

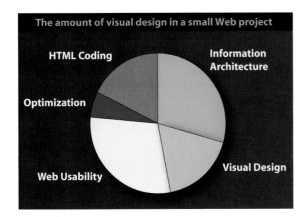

Approximate division of site development time.

Keep this in mind when you start developing Web sites, because not everything that seems logical to you will seem logical to your visitors. Increasingly, large Web design companies use test groups to study how users respond to sites, giving them specific tasks, such as looking for a particular document or service, to gain some feedback.

Only a few years ago, when the Web first became popular, many sites were laid out like printed brochures in terms of both their navigation and their content, simply because those sites were built by desktop publishing designers who used concepts from the print media with which they were familiar. Fortunately, Web design has matured, and through survival of the fittest, standards have been established that you now find on many successful sites. Looking at these sites is a good way for print designers to make the transition to the Web. But still, Mark Crumpacker, former Creative Director at Studio Archetype, believes that multimedia designers have a much easier time transitioning to Web design because multimedia is interactive and therefore similar to the Web.

Many of today's information architects have an editorial background, and they spend a great deal of time analyzing current trends and looking at how comparable sites are structured. Let me introduce the basic concepts and outline the questions you should ask yourself before beginning a Web design project.

Web Site Structure

Many Web sites are so confusing that visitors get lost, can't find what they're looking for, or—in a worst-case scenario—can't even comprehend what the site is about. Even Web sites that have a clear and consistent navigational structure can have the fundamental flaw of unclearly structured content. A common mistake sometimes found on large corporate Web sites is that they inundate visitors with hundreds of products or throw unrelated content at visitors all at once. To avoid this, you should always take a step back and think though the process and goals of the site, instead of building a site that reflects some other existing structure. For instance, Motorola structured its first site to reflect the company's internal divisions. As Crumpacker (who used to be the information architect for Studio Archetype) points out, that might make sense to the people in the company, but not to site visitors. To Crumpacker, information architecture fails if it doesn't focus on the needs of the target audience. This is crucial for the success of a Web site.

The UPS Web site is a great example of Studio Archetype's work, and of how a thoughtful analysis of the audience and its needs can make a huge difference. When UPS approached Studio Archetype with the task of redesigning its site, the firm was faced with the challenge of dealing with a lot of existing content and ensuring that site visitors wouldn't get lost. It was apparent that the problem lay in the site's structure and specifically in the way it broke the content up into categories.

To get a better idea of how to approach the problem, they studied the user. The typical customer was most interested in tracking the current location of a package, calculating shipping costs, and learning where to drop off packages or how to schedule pickups. Studio Archetype simply reorganized the information and the content around those four central tasks. After the new version went live, phone calls to UPS dropped by 20 percent, according to Crumpacker, which shows how much positive impact a well-structured Web site can have on customer support.

Christopher Stashuk of Aristotle used JavaScript to create rollovers, which are not only trendy but they also allow designers to use navigational elements that integrate well into the design, as in this example. Instead of using buttons, the links are all blurred text, but as the mouse rolls over them, they are replaced with a clearer version of the text.

Consolidating the Content

Reducing the amount of information on a Web site and consolidating similar topics into a single topic set are essential tasks for producing a good site. Rikus Hillman from Pixelpark in Berlin, who has worked on the online magazine Wildpark, is familiar with this problem. Wildpark started as a complex site, but the creators soon decided that they should reduce the number of categories from ten to four. With this simple change, the magazine's structure suddenly became much clearer, and it became easier for the editors to point out new content to the viewers. But reducing the number of categories was just a start; the information itself also needed to be reworked. Most articles and stories in online magazines are too long, says Hillman, a problem that arose early on because many editors came from traditional print magazines. The Internet requires a different approach to text.

When Studio Archetype was given the job of reworking the Adobe corporate site, the firm's information architects set themselves the goal of reducing fourteen sections to six. With Adobe's help, they regrouped the information to make navigation simpler for visitors. For example, the original site drew a distinction between graphic and prepress products, but for the user, those two categories overlap, so separating them created confusion. "We didn't quite achieve the goal of reducing everything to six sections," says Crumpacker, "but we came close. We ended up having eight categories on the Web site."

Navigation

Some Web designers create a fancy interface and expect that visitors will be able to navigate in it. Very often this is not the case, and the visitor may have serious difficulties finding the desired information. You can avoid this pitfall by using clear and consistent global, parallel, and local navigation.

● Global navigation allows the visitor to move between the main sections of the site. It should be present on every page.

● Parallel navigation applies to subcategories or subsections within each section that require a consistent navigational structure. It should be present on every page within a section.

● Local navigation works like a table of contents. You use it to find information within a page. It may look like a table of contents at the beginning of the page, or it might be a list of links in a sidebar.

For most Web sites this navigational system (with global, parallel, and local navigation) is the best way to go.

In the future, as Web design becomes more like multimedia design and as the Internet community embraces new technologies, information architecture will have to solve ever more complex problems. With extensions to HTML, information is becoming more

The DAT's Digital main page with the QuickTime VR navigational element that Christopher Stashuk developed can be seen here on the right.

dynamic, and the conventional page metaphor, where visitors click from one page to another, will be only one solution among many. Perhaps, as in Clement Mok's vision, future Web interfaces might allow visitors to walk through a virtual world in which they hear ambient sounds and information is presented in a three-dimensional world. I am intrigued by the idea of using ambient sounds for navigational purposes, but that is light-years from now. But wait! Aren't Internet years like dog years? We will probably see this sooner than we expect.

WEB USABILITY

After information architecture, the next popular buzzword was Web usability. The reason this term came about was simply competition. More and more Web sites offered similar, if not identical, services. A good

Christopher Stashuk used QuickTime VR to help users navigate DAT's Web site. Because QTVR allows a 360-degree view of a scene, Christopher used it to put text links on the imaginary "wall." QTVR can also embed hyperlinks, which makes for an innovative navigational element. Not everyone will get the concept right away, though, so Christopher also included traditional text links.

COMMON INFORMATION ARCHITECTURE MISTAKES

How do you approach the concept of a Web site and achieve effective information architecture? The easiest way to show you is to point out the most common mistakes:

Too Many Categories

Reduction is the key to success. Combine information and avoid too many categories. The rule of thumb is that there should be no more than seven categories; scientific studies have established that this is all that most visitors can remember.

Getting Trapped in Established Structures

Does the structure of the Web site make sense, or is it simply based on the company's departmental structure or some other preexisting concept? Always ask yourself if the categories are logical from the visitors' point of view.

Inconsistent Navigational Organization

Is your navigational concept simple and straightforward? If not, start over. Your concept should include clear global, parallel, and local navigational structures.

Burying Information in too Many Levels

Many Web sites branch out like a tree, but if your tree includes more than four hierarchical levels, it is probably too complex. Creating a visual representation or chart of your design will help you control the site's hierarchy.

---

example are the search engines that were a dime a dozen. With so many around, users preferred those that were easier to use. Web designers and information architects had to look into how to improve the usability of a Web site to create a better product for the end user. So today it is not enough to just offer stunning design. Clients, especially those offering a service or content, expect a Web design agency to make their Web site more user friendly than the competition.

While this all makes sense, the question remains, what is Web usability? I wish I could give you an answer in a nutshell, but the truth is that this field is relatively new and therefore there isn't much literature available. Of the few books you can get, the most popular ones are *Information Architecture*, by Louis Rosenfeld and Peter Morville, and *Designing Web Usability*, by Jakob Nielsen. Nielsen managed to get himself known as an expert in the field and thus his book was quite popular for some time. However, his book is mostly for Web designers who have little experience, though it's ideal for helping corporate people to get a feel for the subject. The best information on Web usability is available online at Nielsen's Web site (www.useit.com/).

The problem with Web usability is that, even though most designers and clients are aware of its importance, nobody is willing to spend much time and resources on it. As a result, there are only a few people who deal with this subject professionally. This is unfortunate, but I believe it can also work to your advantage if you are willing to read up on it. Here some basics about Web usability that will help you improve your own projects:

Content authoring: Years ago I did an interview for the magazine *PAGE* with Jason Pearson, one of the founders (and the designer) of the CD-ROM magazine Blender. That was even before the Web had such a boom, so the term Web usability wasn't even around yet. However, when I asked Jason what he had learned from creating a CD-ROM magazine, he said that the biggest challenge was to write content for

CONTENT SURFACING

Content surfacing is a popular technique of information architecture, since it allows a visitor to locate new content on your site immediately rather than having to look for it. In the same way that a newspaper grabs readers with a headline and breaking news, you can pull the reader into your site with something new on your first page.

This might be just a photo and a headline, or it could provide a little summary or the story's lead-in sentences. Either way, it is a great way to grab visitors' attention and tie them to the site. Studio Archetype's site was a good example (unfortunately, since they merged with Sapient, it is no longer live). The main page was built using a modular structure, meaning that the images in the middle of the interface could be exchanged easily. A click on the image brought the visitor right to the story within the site. You should use this technique on Web sites with frequent updates, since it is one of the most important ways of motivating visitors to return on a daily basis.

The old Studio Archetype Web site was one of the better known promotional sites. Designed by Mark Crumpacker to embody Studio Archetype's philosophy of information architecture, it was a great example of a clean and consistent navigational concept. This shot also shows the concept of content surfacing, in which images are updated regularly and linked to new content within the site.

the screen, because of the limited screen space and the attention span of the readers. Writing for the Web has the exact same problem. When you create content for a Web site, you can't use the same linear style as for the print medium.

Put some thought into how you can streamline the content by linking to less important information with hyperlinks. Hyperlinks allow the user to scan through the text, so be sure to use only the most important words as links. Avoid the pitfall of making an entire sentence a hyperlink—use a maximum of five words. Also don't use the phrase "click here" as a link—it doesn't provide any information. You'll also waste an opportunity to get a higher keyword rating from the search engines because many rate keywords that are hyperlinks higher than other content on your page.

Another great tip to improve usability is to use "link titles." This is a feature of Internet Explorer and Netscape Navigator (4.0 and higher). Users who mouse over a link see some text that displays additional information at the mouse position. To use this feature, use the attribute "Title" in the HTML code for hyperlinks. This could look, for example, like this:

```
<A HREF="...""Title="what is this link about?">hyper-link</A>.
```

Screen real estate: The rule of thumb (according to Jakob Nielsen) is that content should account for at least half the page. The optimum would be a ratio of 80 percent content to 20 percent screen real estate for other elements like navigation or banner ads. To analyze a site's use of screen real estate, take a screen shot of a page and measure the ratio of content to other elements. Do this by blocking out the main regions on a Web page and then counting the pixels for each region using the Measurement tool in Photoshop, which will give you the width and height in pixels of any marked area. Also check out how much screen real estate is wasted on white space (look at it as space that is not used for anything). You might wonder why this is so important since extra space on a Web page doesn't cost anything, but the more users have to scroll to find the content, the less likely they are going to have a great user experience.

Information architecture: Yes, information architecture can be seen as part of Web usability. Since I already touched on information architecture, I just want to remind you again that consistent navigation is key to good Web usability. If you are serious about Web usability, test the navigation on a small test group. Are the icons or text links unambiguous?

Response time: Web usability studies show that the top priority for users is the download time of a page. Response times of less than a second would be ideal, but that is rarely possible, even with cable modems and DSL. If visitors have to wait longer than 10 seconds, they get impatient and may leave the site. Adobe GoLive has a feature that calculates the estimated download time of a page at different connection speeds. Use that feature to ensure that the page download doesn't take more than 10 seconds on a 56 Kbps modem.

Usability tests: Designing a Web site without some usability testing is really a big risk. Jared Spool and his colleagues found in a study of 15 large U.S. commercial sites that users successfully completed a task or found information only 42 percent of the time. This means that 58 percent of users failed to complete a task or find any information. This is unacceptable and it should make clear how important it is to conduct usability tests of a Web site before its launch. The interesting thing about usability tests is that even a small group of five testers can typically uncover 80 percent of the site-level usability problems and about 50 percent of the page-level usability problems.

● Site-level usability looks at the home page, the information architecture, navigation and search, the linking strategy, overall writing style, page templates and layout, site-wide design standards, as well as the graphical language and commonly used icons.

● Page-level usability looks at specific issues related to the individual pages, including the understandability of headlines, links and explanations; the intuitiveness of forms and error messages; as well as individual graphics and icons.

If you create your own usability test, create one or more user models, which is basically nothing more than envisioning some of your anticipated "typical" users and their needs. Then create a set of tasks that those users would most likely perform and have your test team execute the tasks. To evaluate the usability, you may want to look into the heuristic evaluation proposed by Jakob Nielsen (read more about how to perform such a test on his Web site: www.useit.com/papers/heuristic/heuristic_evaluation.html). A heuristic evaluation is a quick and inexpensive evaluation of a user interface. To conduct a heuristic evaluation you have to get a small group of evaluators to examine the interface and check its compliance with usability principles.

DESIGN CONCEPTS

As I said at the beginning of this chapter, Web design is really a combination of conceptual design (information architecture and Web usability) and visual design. After our excursion into conceptual design, it's about time we talk about some of the specific design concepts and conventions. In the first chapter I already introduced you to some of the design issues and limitations of HTML and Web browsers. All those limitations have an impact on your design, and over the years, designers have come up with some workarounds. Today the Web has some established standards that are widely accepted and used.

Sidebars

One of the most popular Web design concepts is using a sidebar that contains all the navigational elements. This can be done with frames, but as I will explain later, frames have some disadvantages, and most sidebar designs are based on an image that is used as a background tile. Sidebars can also be created by using an HTML table that stretches over the entire length of a page (see also the explanations in the next section).

In this screenshot the navigational parts are marked with red, the white space with blue and the content with green. You want to be aware of your "screen estate" and how you use it.

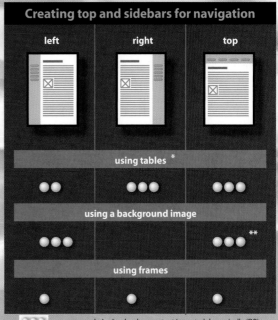

When creating your design concept, you have to choose between top or sidebar navigation. In this overview you can see which navigational concept works best with frames, tables or using a background image.

THE TUNNEL CONCEPT

Printed brochures often use a great-looking cover to grab the reader's attention. The tunnel concept does the same thing by using a splash screen—an attention-capturing image that appears briefly before giving way to another image. Visitors have to click through one or more splash screens before they get to the main screen with the content and the navigational interface. A Web site using a tunnel concept might also use a flashy exit page, which can leave a big impression, but you don't see this very often.

In the beginning of the Web era, many companies were concerned primarily with having a nice-looking site, mostly as a way to show off and convey that the company was at the forefront of technology. These days, most companies are more interested in e-commerce, or they want to use their sites to improve customer service. Forcing visitors to click through a series of pages before arriving at the main page is—especially in a time marked by a decreasing attention span—just not appropriate anymore. So I strongly recommend against using the tunnel concept or even a splash screen, which was quite popular in the beginning of the Web when connection speeds were slow. Back then a splash screen would often be used to present the visitor with a fast-loading page and then have the next page download in the background while the visitor was occupied reading the introduction on the splash screen. But since most people have at least 56 Kbps modems, visitors want to get to the content without interruption. There are some rare occasions when the tunnel concept or a splash screen might be appropriate, but in general I advise you against using it.

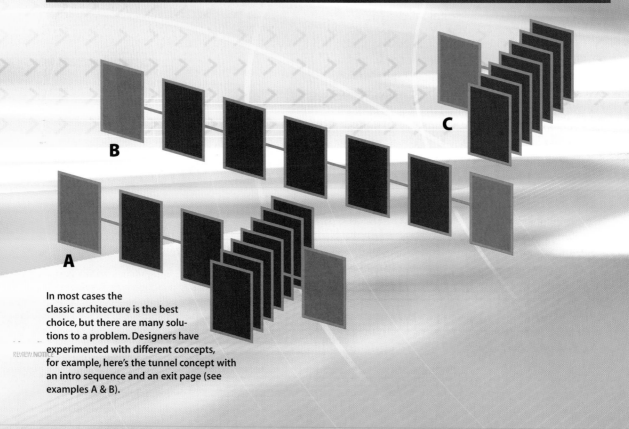

In most cases the classic architecture is the best choice, but there are many solutions to a problem. Designers have experimented with different concepts, for example, here's the tunnel concept with an intro sequence and an exit page (see examples A & B).

However, Web designers still mostly use a background image because there are some issues with tables and image backgrounds. Rather than taking up several pages explaining the issues and giving examples, I'll just say that it has a lot to do with backward compatibility. One more thing: You may have noticed that the sidebar is almost always on the left side, even though from the standpoint of ergonomics and user interface it would make much more sense to have the navigation bar on the right side; after all, the scroll bar is also on the right side of the window. But one issue with having the navigation bar on the right is ensuring that the navigation bar is always visible, even on small monitors. There is actually a way to do this, so let me just give you some guidelines on navigation bars:

If you want to have your navigation bar on the left, use an image that you load as background in the browser. How such a background image is created is discussed in a later chapter.

If you want to have a navigation bar on the right, use tables instead. The advantage of tables is that you could give the cell that contains the navigation a fixed width and set the table cell for the content to be flexible. When visitors adjust their browser windows, the navigation bar will always stay visible, but the table cell with the content will get smaller. This requires that you have content that can easily reflow, like, for example, text with some embedded images. Content that requires a certain width might cause the navigation bar to disappear.

Topbars

Having the navigation in the sidebar is becoming less popular—you see designers increasingly using a topbar for the navigational elements. The decline of sidebars is possibly related to the fact that they use up so much screen space. Or perhaps designers just got bored with sidebars. Nowadays you see many Web sites with navigation at the top of the page. Like a sidebar, a topbar can be created with a tiling background image, but the problem is that the background image eventually repeats on the vertical axis and therefore limits the maximum length of a page.

Apple's Web site has influenced quite a few Web sites, not so much by using top navigation, because that has, of course, been done before, but through the special 3D type of its tabs.

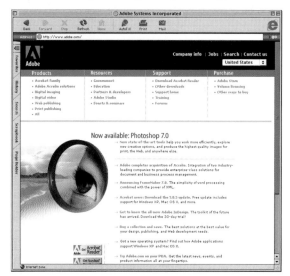

Adobe's Web site also uses a topbar that is made out of an HTML table that stretches across the window. The site also uses navigation in a sidebar.

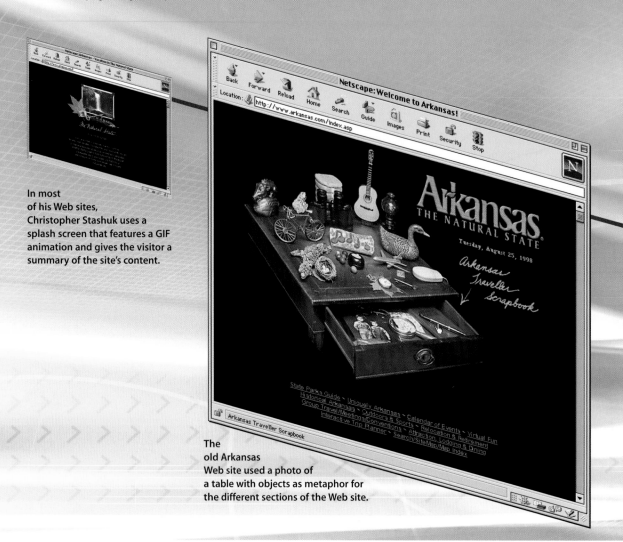

In most
of his Web sites,
Christopher Stashuk uses a
splash screen that features a GIF
animation and gives the visitor a
summary of the site's content.

The
old Arkansas
Web site used a photo of
a table with objects as metaphor for
the different sections of the Web site.

It's possible to load a background image into the browser without tiling by using Cascading Style Sheets (for an explanation on how to do this, see the GoLive chapter), but the more popular solution is to use an HTML table that stretches across the page. A good example of this technique is Apple's website (www.apple.com). The HTML table that holds the navigational buttons has an image background. Using an image as background for a horizontal navigation works best in an horizontal layout. This can work really well for something like a timeline or a product presentation (IDEO's Web site is a great example; see the Web gallery in this book. However, they use a table for that).

Topbars and Sidebars with Frames

One problem with topbars or sidebars is that navigational elements will scroll out of view if there is more content on your page than the browser can display on a single screen. To compensate for this, frames were introduced with HTML 2.0. Frames let you split a browser window into two or more independent areas, which allows designers to create a sidebar or topbar where they can place buttons and navigational elements. No matter what happens to the main frame, the navigational sidebar and topbar remain onscreen at all times.

The architecture of the site is simple and straightforward. But whether visitors find their way through it depends on how clearly the sections are labeled and how well the information is grouped.

INTERVIEW WITH TOM NICHOLSON

Tom Nicholson is an unassuming man. When he occasionally hangs out with his coworkers and employees after work, he's just one of the crowd. But when he gets into talking about information architecture, both customers and employees are under his spell. No question, he is a man with a lot of experience who can provide highly valuable input.

His company, Nicholson NY, started with interactive media way back in 1987. At that time the Web boom was far in the future, and Nicholson was working on multimedia. Today, the company (now www.iconlab.com) has over 100 employees and occupies several floors in the Puck Building on Lafayette Street in New York's SoHo.

You worked with interactive media back in 1987, at a time when computers were still relatively new technology. What was that like?

We have been in the business for twelve years now, from 1987 to 1999, and we started with interactive media, which was quite different back then from what it is today. Using computers to create interactive media was not as common at the time, and I had to spend a lot time on core issues like how do you balance "user drive" versus what we call "editorial drive" in order to get something communicated in this new medium.

Do you remember any particular project from back then? It would interest me to see what you were thinking about interactive media ten years ago as opposed to what you think of it today.

The first project that I did and that really launched my career in that area was a pretty large scale project involving six million visitors to the World's Fair in Knoxville, many of whom had come to the US to learn about energy. I developed six or seven interactive programs using touch screens and computer graphics, and merged them into interactive experiences, such as an energy glossary that listed 500

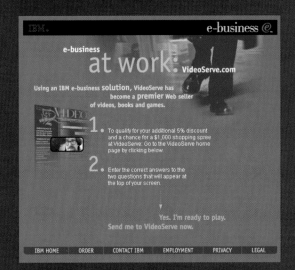

IBM, one of Nicholson's clients, wanted a special Web page for their e-commerce campaign.

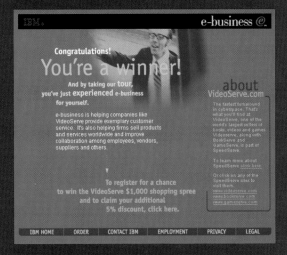

The IBM site also reflects the visual style of Andreas Lindström (see interview at the end of the chapter), who acted as art director of the site.

The splash screen of the Sony Web site.

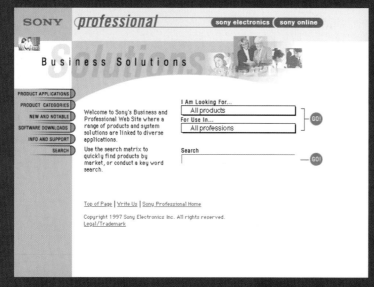

For a corporate Web site, the Sony site is amazingly hip and cool—another Andreas Lindström creation. Tom Nicholson and his team tried to group as many categories as possible to make it easy to locate products and information.

words—all dynamically animated on screen. They included videos and a lot of technical terms. We also did projects for IBM and Citibank.

When did you get into Web design?

It was many years after that...around 1991 when Newscorp came in and wanted to create an AOL-killer; it was supposed to knock AOL out of the box. It was our first online experience, and it led to the first Internet Web site developments. That was when the company started to grow from fifteen people to 100.

You really watched Silicon Alley rise, so to speak?

We were the first interactive agency in Silicon Alley. When we started, there was basically nothing here.

When you look around on the map there is CKS Modem, who were founded in 1987, the same year we were, but that was it.

What would you say is the strength of the agency? I suppose it is the strong background in interactive media?

Yes, I think so. We were leveraging what's possible with interactive media at a time when nobody else was doing it. But we have certainly grown beyond being just a design firm. What is happening in the Internet industry is that it's becoming more and more important to incorporate all aspects of Web design and Internet and offer a full solution for the client. Besides working with interactive content and information design or information architecture, we have been building e-businesses for our clients—doing everything from Internet business strategy through creative execution and technology development.

That brings me to my next question. Information architecture is one of the buzzwords of the Internet. What does it mean to you?

Information architecture is nothing more than formatting information in a way that communicates. It's kind of a mental model, where you try to share your mental model with another person by using words, pictures, and so on. The user interface

plays a big part in this. For instance, in the print world the information architecture is very much established and fixed; with a book you have three ways of accessing information: from the front with the table of contents, from the back with the index, or by just browsing through the content. But in a flexible environment like Web design there are an almost infinite number of ways of representing the information.

Can you give an example?

Let me tell you about a project that we did in the past. It was a kiosk system for a museum, but it could just as easily become a Web site once bandwidth is not a problem any more. An archeologist discovered

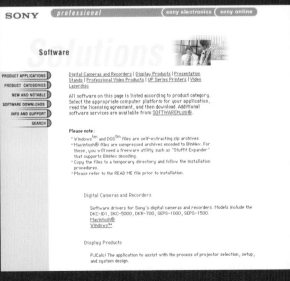

Although the Web site uses a conventional sidebar, the use of different colors gives each section its own identity.

something new on this Indian reservation: he found these stains in the ground that he concluded were from a seventeenth-century fort. He started digging, and sure enough he learned that it was a fort, and he found all these components of life in a village.

Instead of content surfacing, the site uses a dedicated news section.

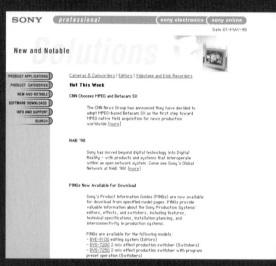

So if somebody came to you saying, "I want to convey this to the public," well, one way to start might be to get an editorial person to figure out what the content is. It might look like "Tell us everything about the fort: Who lived there? Where? Why were they there?" and then you could present it interactively on the Internet. Somebody else might

break it down to the fortification itself: arms and defense mechanisms, daily life, food, social interactions, and so on. This version of the Web site would probably have buttons labeled "Life in the Village," "Food," "Arms," and so on. That's a lot like what you see on the Web today.

Yet another way of approaching this would be to ask yourself, "What is the closest mental model to the subject?" It happens that in this case it is the fort itself, because that's the artifact that offers all the information. So why not just give the fort to people and let them move through it, and interact with it; eventually you would learn all about life on the eastern seaboard. The key to designing an interactive environment is that you can have many different interfaces, which offers great possibilities for adapting to people's different learning styles. The more you can adapt to those differences, the better.

That example really illustrates the possibilities of interactive media. Instead of simply communicating linear information you can model it around the real world. Do you have any more examples? Or can you make a general assessment about what you think constitutes good and bad information architecture?

There are many basic principles that apply. You have to start by thinking about basics like the graphic user interface, what makes for good graphic design, and how well the information has been put in an hierarchical structure.

Then there is the rule of seven: people can only remember seven independent things. They can hold in their short term memory seven independent entities that have no relationship to each other. Some people can do eight, or maybe nine, but most people are limited to seven. That's why telephone numbers have seven digits; that's not an accident. So when it comes to designing a Web site you should stick to seven groups, and then work out a hierarchy with a consistent interface for those seven.

But what happens far too often is that a company has several different sections and departments, and each of them has its own Web site. Sometimes they put an umbrella site on top, but then you don't have any consistency, and the deeper the people get into the site the more confusing it gets.

There are many sites that have that kind of "bad" information architecture. It's a common occurence, because the Web is changing so fast. Our Sony project is a good example. Under the professional products group they had a number of different marketing groups, all of which were independent and all of which used their own printed material. That didn't matter, because those

customers didn't cross paths with each other. Now, all of a sudden, Sony needs to come together on one Web site—as a Web design agency we were faced with the challenge of reorganizing all this content without getting trapped by the structure of the company.

Sony had several departments, which was an efficient way for them to run their business, but the customers had no perception of that. All the user cared about was that he

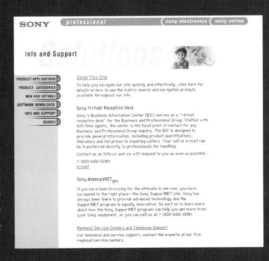

An e-commerce site must have a dedicated page for customer contact.

wanted to buy a monitor, for example, and he didn't care which products group the monitor department belonged to. So the first thing we had to do was to go in and work across the groups to create consistency, which was essential for the success of the Web site.

On the old Baldor Web site (www.baldor.com), the navigational elements are placed inside a frame that is always visible. A pop-up menu like the one Christopher Stashuk used here is another great navigational element.

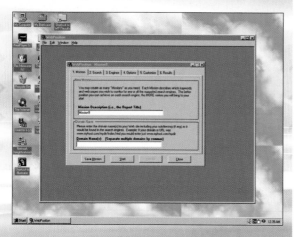

WebPosition is a powerful tool for checking the ratings and position of a Web site with the major search engines. You can find more information at www.webposition.com. If the search engine rating is very important to you, avoid using frames—they have a negative effect on search results.

Frames require an additional document called a frameset, which contains such information as the frames' dimensions and which HTML page should be displayed in which frame. Each frame can be addressed using a target attribute, which is essential in creating navigational bars. Frames were a great improvement over no frames at all, but in the first version of HTML, you couldn't make the borders invisible. The attributes that I have just mentioned didn't exist when frames were first introduced. Only later did Explorer and Navigator offer these essential attributes, but by then frames had lost popularity among Web designers.

Web designers soon realized that frames have some serious drawbacks. The most important of these is that Web sites with frames often fail to get good results from search engines. This has to do with the way search engines work: they index the text in an HTML document and count how often a certain keyword appears on a page. Unfortunately, if you use frames, the search engine never gets to see or index the real content of your Web site. The search engine "sees" only the frameset document, which contains only a few lines of HTML code. To make matters worse, the pages with content replace each other in the frame, which makes it virtually impossible for the search engine to list a specific page.

I don't want to go into too much detail on this; all you need to know is that using frames can be counterproductive if you want to create a content Web site. There are ways to use frames and still have your site appear high in the ranking of a search engine, but optimizing sites for search engines is extremely complex. If you want to find out more about how to do so, go to a search Web site and search for the keywords "search engine." You will find a number of sites that offer advice or even the service of optimizing your Web site for you. Use careful judgment if you decide to use one of these services, because truly effective optimization for search engine promotion requires someone to monitor the changes that happen constantly among the search engines—they change the way they index more frequently than you might think,

CREATING DYNAMIC WEB PAGES

The days of static HTML pages are over. Most Web sites these days are created dynamically by merging the information in a database with the page templates on a server. Lorin Unger from Citysoft (New York/Boston), a Web services company specializing in database-driven Web solutions using ASP and ColdFusion, talks about the challenges of creating dynamic Web sites.

One of Citysoft's past projects was an application for a school management organization that manages multiple schools in Florida, Arizona and Pennsylvania. The organization was looking for a tool to handle their pre-enrollment administrative processes up to the point at which the student matriculated into the school system. Even though all the schools were managed by one organization, they all had individual requirements that needed to be accommodated in the solution.

"The challenge in particular with this project was that there were a large number of stakeholders in the project. At the corporate level they were primarily concerned with the efficiency of putting the information in and having a secure system. Their focus was also on creating reports from their data. Then there was a call center that operated across the schools, which was mostly concerned with quick access of the information. Their focus was on the efficiency. At the last level were the actual representatives of the schools, who needed various functions on inputting and outputting information, but only to their particular school," recalls Lorin. According to him, the challenge was more in terms of gathering the requirements than in the actual development process.

"We had to make sure that all of the stakeholders had been heard from. It is important to not get any contradictory pieces and then try to second-guess their business process. It was important that everybody who needed to know about certain functionalities did in fact know. For one, of course, for the robustness of the application, but also because at the end of the day, no matter where the miscommunication happens, the reflections will be on us," says Lorin.

He approaches such a task by creating a site map, which is basically just a series of boxes that are connected to indicate how different pages are related. "No details, no interface references, nothing like that. Once that is agreed upon I create actual wire-frame diagrams of the screens. Again without any design attributes like colors or fonts, just what kind of functionality [e. g., input forms and result screens] exists where on the page." Once the client agrees on the design and feels that it fulfills their needs, the interface designer comes in and creates the artwork. Only after all the other steps are done and finalized does the HTML programmer recreate the design in HTML.

because they are constantly trying to improve the accuracy of their results. A good place to get more information about what's happening is search-enginewatch.com.

Most Web designers, knowing the importance of a good search engine ranking, have gone back to frameless designs. However, if your Web site is database-driven, using frames doesn't make a difference (a search engine can't index content in a database, so you might as well use frames).

There are also design issues with frames: for instance, if there is more content in a frame than it can display, it shows a scroll bar. (You can prevent this by setting the Scrolling attribute to "No," but then some

BROWSER OFFSET

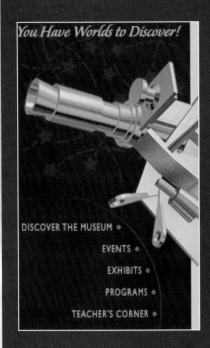

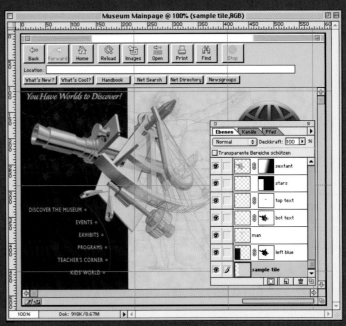

Placing elements over the edge of the sidebar, as shown here in an earlier version of the Arkansas Museum of Discovery Web site (www.amod.org), could cause problems because of browser offset. Browser offset is the amount (measured in pixels) that the content of a page is shifted away from the top-left corner. Browsers used to do this automatically to ensure that text would have a little offset. However, this offset was different for each browser, and designers had a hard time doing simple things like placing a larger image over the edge of a sidebar, as you can see in this example. As you can see in the smaller picture, the sextant and the navigational

links were saved as transparent GIFs (gray area) with enough room between the navigational links and the edge of the sidebar. This would compensate for an offset of several pixels in either direction, but this was, of course, not the best solution. Luckily when the 4.x browsers were released, they offered the capability to set the browser offset to any value the designer wanted. Most users now have 6.x browsers so you don't need to be too concerned about browser offset anymore. Before you start a project in GoLive, though, you should always set the offset in the HTML authoring tool.

navigation might get cut off when the frame is too small to display all the content). While a scroll bar in a frame with content is not an issue, it is a problem if it appears in a navigation bar. Keep this in mind if you decide to use frames when you design your page.

HYPERLINKS

The Web uses hyperlinks as a way of connecting different information and pages. Since hyperlinks are so essential to the medium, you, as the designer, will spend quite some time designing them. The most common kind of navigational controls use text or image links to connect pages and information. If you've ever seen a Web site with several buttons, then you saw a set of images that were defined as hyperlinks.

Designers often take the easy route and use three-dimensional buttons as navigational links because it's a simple way to display a clickable area, and such buttons are unambiguous. However, there are only a few Web sites where such buttons are actually well integrated and look good. One of them was the Studio Archetype Web site. These buttons used icons as well as text to communicate where they led, and the icons glowed when visitors moved the mouse pointer over them. This interactivity, where a navigational element changes when the mouse is positioned over it, is called a rollover (it is achieved by using JavaScript, a programming language that most browsers can interpret). The only drawback of these rollover buttons is that they require twice as much data to be transmitted (images for both the "on" and "off" button states need to be downloaded). If you are already using a lot of elements on your page, this might be an issue.

The Studio Archetype Web site was one of the few examples where embossed buttons actually looked good, but most of the time, 3D buttons make a Web site look rather technical. Andreas Lindström, art director of popular sites such as Carnegie Hall (carnegie-hall.org) and Viagra (www.viagra.com), avoids them whenever possible. He prefers more subtle ways of integrating image links seamlessly in the design.

A good example was the old David Bowie Web site, which was designed by Ben Clemens and Marlene Stoffers. The navigational elements were both artsy and an integral part of the design. To ensure that visitors would know where these links were leading, they displayed a text label when the mouse was passed over them. So if you are planning to make the links more an integral part of your design, use the same technique and display some text with the rollover.

Rollovers are not complicated. The only thing you need to know is that if you want to use transparency in a GIF, make sure that the transparent regions are the same for both "on" and "off" images. The browser doesn't refresh the entire display each time a rollover button is triggered; it updates only the parts that change. Therefore, in some browsers and under certain circumstances, some pixels in the transparent areas remain visible.

Another thing you should know is that a rollover doesn't have to trigger a change in the same image; it can change a different image somewhere else on the page. In fact, you can have many image changes triggered by just one event. If you want to do this in GoLive, you'll need a good understanding of JavaScript, because the Rollover element on the Smart tab doesn't allow this (ImageReady, however, can do this. If you create a rollover state for a button, but the changes affect a different slice, ImageReady will save the appropriate JavaScript).

The other way of aiding navigation is to use text hyperlinks: just select the text in your HTML authoring tool (in GoLive choose Special > New Link) and convert it to a hyperlink. Text links let you assign up to three colors: one for the unclicked link (Link), one for every link that has been visited (Visited Link), and one for the moment when the visitor actually clicks on the link (Active Link). When you design your Web page in Photoshop, you want to simulate the look of hyperlinks by placing some text in Helvetica or Arial and choosing "underline" as a style. To get an idea of how the three link colors will look with the rest of the page, you want to have some of the placed text displayed in those colors.

One of the standards in Web design is to have a navigation bar at the bottom of every page. This navigation bar is just made with hypertext links, mirroring the links of the main navigation bar. Users who have scrolled to the bottom of a page then don't need to scroll up again to jump to another page.

Image Maps and Image Tables

Another navigational feature of HTML is image maps. These are images in which certain areas have been designated as hot spots, or hyperlinks. Hot spots can be any shape, from rectangular to elliptical to polygonal, and you can knock out areas of a shape that's a hot spot. ImageReady and GoLive both support image maps (to create an image map in ImageReady, use the Image Map tools in the toolbox), but I recommend you use GoLive unless you need to be able to work with high precision.

Image maps are great, especially if you want to create clickable areas that require polygons (a common use is to allow the user to select a state by clicking on a map of the United States). But image maps don't support rollovers, and since rollovers are so popular these days, Web designers often use image tables instead. The basic idea is to slice up an image into pieces and to drop each piece into the appropriate cell of an invisible table so that the image appears to be one large image in the browser. Besides being able to make each slice a link, you can optimize every slice in the table separately. There are other advantages of image tables: If you want to animate part of a larger image, you can slice it and put it back together in an image table.

POP-UP MENUS

The last navigational element that I want to mention is a pop-up menu. Its advantage is that it can be extended without having to change anything in the design and it uses up the least amount of space. For example,

the first version of the Viagra Web site utilized the pop-up menu for the site navigation. Pop-up menus give your site a somewhat innovative touch and feel.

After reading this chapter, you should be somewhat familiar with some of the most important elements of Web design. In the next section of this book, you'll find all the information on how to create these elements in Photoshop. The last portion of this book will then show you how to get your design into your HTML authoring tool.

HOW TECHNOLOGY IMPACTS DESIGN

As somebody who has done both desktop publishing and Web design, I'm fascinated by the parallels and the direct impact that technology has had on both. I remember, for example, when QuarkXPress, back then a popular page-layout program, introduced gradients in one of its updates. The next month you could go to the newsstand and see which magazines were done in XPress because designers were of course tempted to use this new feature for their designs and used gradients as backgrounds. A few months later gradients disappeared. Now you rarely see them anymore. Designers quickly realized that this feature doesn't necessarily make for a better design and focused again on the fundamentals. On the Web, you could see a similar trend. After designers explored textured backgrounds, animations, and other features, they came back to the very basics: good design. So my recommendation is to stay away from special effects; all you need for a great Web site is a great visual idea.

Metaphors

The goal in using a metaphor is to give a site a central and consistent visual theme. Finding and creating a metaphor is not easy, because not every Web site is suitable for this. Very often you see metaphoric icons used for navigational elements, such as a mailbox for email, but this doesn't really qualify as a metaphoric Web site, where all of the graphics and text leverage some appropriate, figurative concept. An example of a Web site that used a metaphor tastefully and effectively was the Arkansas Web site. This site used a table with several objects to represent the different areas of the site. Another example was the Web site of the German Youth Hostels; it used a backpack and its contents to do the same job.

Web sites that use metaphors are certainly more visually interesting than sites that just use text links or buttons, but at the same time, if you overdo it or if you use an inappropriate metaphor, you run the risk of crossing the line between good and bad design. Using metaphors for your interface design is—in my humble opinion—also a little outdated. There was a time in the short history of Web design when the visual aspect was more important than the functionality or usability of a Web site. Back then, a visually stunning Web site could get a lot of press, which was good in terms of Web site traffic; today you rarely see metaphors used anymore.

On the old Arkansas Web site (www.arkansas.com), all objects on the table represent an area of the site. When the mouse was moved over an item, text appeared to indicate where the link was leading.

INTERVIEW WITH ANDREAS LINDSTRÖM

Andreas Lindström, a native of Sweden who has been living and work-ing in New York for several years now, has achieved something that only a few designers can claim: he has developed a totally unique Web design style. His work for Carnegie Hall and the Viagra site, among others, carry his signature. He is one of the best-known and most in-demand Web designers in New York today.

How did you get into Web design?

I attended a special high school for design in Sweden, and was lucky to get a job offer from an advertising agency in Malma, Sweden, right after my graduation. So instead of going to college I went directly to work, which I think is an advantage.

learning about this new medium and how to push the limits. It was a great experience.

You designed the Lost Highway site, which is a good example of your style, because it used large, dimmed images in the back- ground combined with smaller

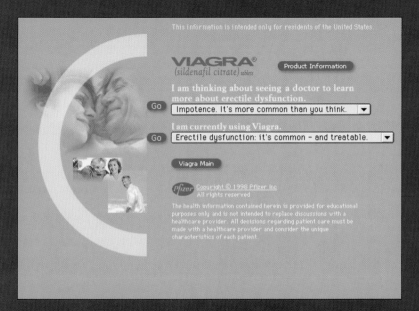

Pfizer, the company that manu- factures Viagra, hired Nicholson NY to do a Web site for their cus- tomers. Andreas Lindström was art director of this site: "The color combination in this Web site is based on the printed brochure, other than that the design is very different. The main navigational element is a pop-up in which the visitor can select the information that he is interested in. This has the ad- vantage that the site can easily be extended and at the same time the design remains very clean and clear. To align the ele- ments on the first page with the background pattern we used JavaScript to compensate for the browser offset."

I learned so much at that time that after five years I felt that Malma was a little bit too small for me. I wanted a bigger challenge, so I applied to the Parson School of Design in New York, and was accepted. After I fin- ished there I started to work in the print field. When the Web started to happen, I got in contact with Avalanche, a company that was just starting up in New York. They did cutting edge stuff on the Internet, and I worked there for two years,

images in the foreground. What can you tell me about the site?

I think the use of large images in combination with smaller images creates a real dimension and depth to the page. For example, on the Lost Highway site I used a large face that blended into the black back- ground, and in the foreground I placed smaller images of the actors in the series. This created tension and depth at the same time.

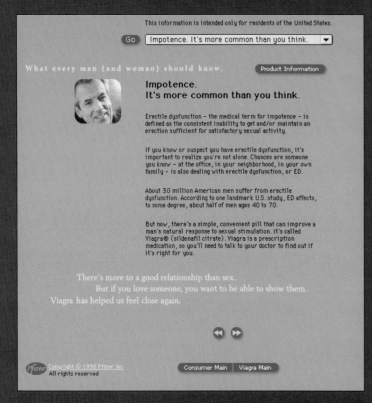

There are quite a lot of Web sites for movie companies in your portfolio, for example the Polygram Filmed Entertainment Web site.

Yes, that was actually the first Web site I created. I used film props to create the tone of the site, and tried to associate various objects with different sections. This is one of the few sites where we actually had a real photo shoot, and didn't have to use stock photos. I think you end up with a much better result that way, because it gives you control over the outcome and you can get closer to your vision as a designer. The same applies to the Carnegie Hall site, where we had a photographer come in and shoot pictures. It made a big difference in the quality of the design.

You also worked for Nicholson in New York. What are some of the projects you did there?

The first site I did as art director for Nicholson was a site for Sony, a business solutions site. We had to create a site that could handle something like 50,000 products. The important thing was to consider Sony's brand, which has a very clear look, as well as creating a navigational system that could pull all this information together—so whatever search results you would get, it would fit into the template we created. Another project was a Web site that was part of IBM's e-business

What was really neat about this site was the navigation elements that we came up with. The site didn't have traditional navigation. Instead of buttons or any other kind of visual indication of where to click, we based the navigation on how the story of the movie was going. We also linked the pages so that you would get more images if you clicked on an image, and you would get more text if you clicked on a text link. Since every visitor has individual preferences, I thought this was a great way of giving them a choice.

campaign. We did that in conjunction with a company called Video Surf that sells videotapes online. It was just a demonstration of how e-business works, an opportunity to see e-business in action. The site reflected the advertising campaign that was going on at that moment, as well as taking you through a couple of IBM pages and a contest.

Another big project was the official Viagra Web site. I think it has a very unusual and appealing charm. We used a very simple user interface with a very unconventional navigational system. Instead of using traditional buttons and links, the main navigational element is a pop-up menu. I was almost surprised that a customer like Pfizer agreed to do it, since big corporations lean more and more toward standard sidebar navigation.

That indeed is the overwhelming trend. When you develop a Web site, how do you approach the navigation?

Personally, I wish clients would experiment with a few more navigational possibilities. I try to break out of that standardized sidebar concept as often as I can by creating navigation elements in different places, or by trying to come up with different page layouts. Usually clients prefer the standardized model, because they have seen it so often, so most of the time it's a battle. My overall goal

is to develop very clear navigation. I prefer to avoid designing with buttons, although they have become such a standard that sometimes I have to use them. Buttons are not necessarily the worst choice, but

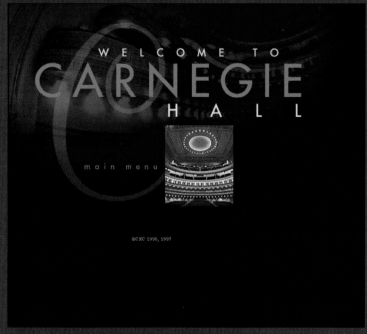

I prefer to use them more delicately, maybe as a subtle sub-element.

When you start a project and get the outline, how do you come up with a concept and a site design?

Generally I sit with the client and show them different kind of designs and see what they like; it's important to find that out. Then, after we have established the creative direction, I experiment with different kinds of imagery. I usually do sketches by hand and try to develop two or three different solutions—solutions that might work together, because sometimes you show the client three solutions but they may like certain things here and there, and want to pick pieces from different solutions. At least that's been my experience.

The history of Carnegie Hall is presented on its own page.

How do you think Web design is going to change the development of new technologies?

Since most of my clients are corporations, I really have to keep the low-end user in mind. I still do my designs so they will be compatible with older browsers, because a lot of people are not using the latest versions. Of course I would love to experiment with the high end, but now that I'm mostly working on corporate Web sites, I have to stay away from really fancy design features.

What do you think the future of the Web will be?

I think the Web will merge with television. Interactive TV is definitely where the Web is going, and I'm really looking forward to that, since in the future, bandwidth will allow for different kinds of design and functionality.

Another thing that's important, particularly when you create a Web site for a location, is to go to that location, which is what Avalanche did for the Carnegie Hall Web site. I walked through the aisles and halls, listening to the noises and trying to visualize sound as a color. Colors and images are my strength, and I try to use these elements for my designs.

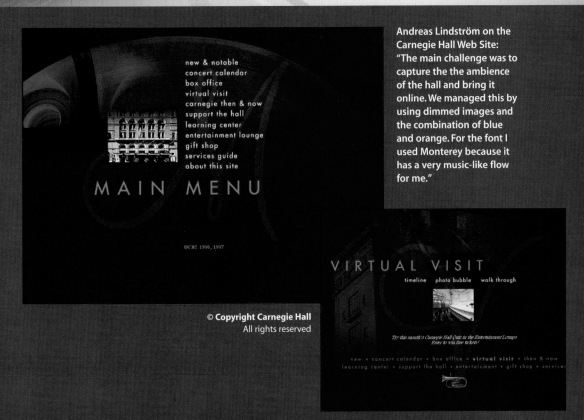

Andreas Lindström on the Carnegie Hall Web Site: "The main challenge was to capture the the ambience of the hall and bring it online. We managed this by using dimmed images and the combination of blue and orange. For the font I used Monterey because it has a very music-like flow for me."

What's your vision of a Web site without any limitations?

It would be like interactive video, where everything is in motion all the time, almost like a computer game. I can see that being used in very interesting ways in corporate Web sites, when they finally get there.

The Web is so serious right now, it's not as experimental as it was in the beginning. Now it's all corporate—I'm really waiting for the next step, because at the moment everything looks the same.

THE WEB GALLERY

Being a Web designer has one advantage: the source of inspiration is right there—accessible 24/7. And becoming a great Web designer involves studying and learning from others. This little Web gallery shows some of the Web sites that I find remarkable for one reason or another. Unfortunately the Web has no memory; many of the pages shown here could be different or gone altogether by the time this book is published.

All Web sites are copyrighted by their owners and were printed with permission. To submit your Web site to be published in one of my books, send me an email at MBaumgardt@Mitomediabooks.com

ARKARTS.COM

museum **shop**

ARKANSAS ARTS CENTER

the collection

General Information
Calendar of Events
The Collection
  Overview
  Drawing Collection
  Objects in Craft Media
  Special Collections
  Collection on Tour
Exhibitions
Education
Children's Theatre
Membership
Museum Shop
Restaurant

HOMEPAGE
CONTACT

☐ **DRAWING COLLECTION**

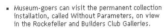

◀ CLICK ON A THUMBNAIL
  TO VIEW IMAGE

At the Arkansas Arts Center's Arkansas Museum of Art, a drawing is defined as a unique work of art on paper in any medium. Thus, in addition to the traditional drawing media-pencil, charcoal, ink, pastel, watercolor and silverpoint-works on paper executed in acrylic, oil and collage are included. This expanded definition of drawing is mandated by postwar artists who have continually sought new ways to challenge the language and hierarchies of traditional artistic disciplines.

In a museum where drawing is given priority over painting, you might expect a more rarefied and subdued atmosphere. This is certainly true from a preservation point of view, since sensitivity of paper to light and changes in temperature and humidity require lower levels of illumination and short-term installations. The familiar expectation that drawings tend to be smaller - allowing for closer inspection to appreciate the subtleties of the materials and the nuances of execution - is well met at the Arts Center. However, our enthusiasm for drawings shows many other facets of drawing - expressions that are large-scale if not monumental; painterly and mixed media approaches; and the confrontational, where subtlety gives way to powerful expressions.

It is the quality of a work on paper that is paramount. Townsend Wolfe explained it best in an introduction to an early collection catalogue.

A unique work on paper can provide us, the viewers, with spiritual and intellectual experiences as profound as one can have in the world of art. A drawing not only shows us the search, but can often be the promised land as well, giving insights and visions not always reachable in other mediums. The touch, sensitivity and decisiveness of the artist are by necessity of one mind in statement on paper. The errors or missed conclusions become part of the beauty and truth of the vision.

To study the drawing collection further, you have several choices.

- Museum-goers can visit the permanent collection installation, called Without Parameters, on view in the Rockefeller and Builders Club Galleries.

- See the newest additions in the Stella Boyle Smith Gallery.

- The public can visit the Ottenheimer Gallery. Here you'll have access to research EmbARK, our collection management software.

- Scholars can schedule a visit to the Donald W. Reynolds Center for Drawing Research and Education to study drawings that are not on view.

- You can join The Collectors Group, a membership organization that focuses on collecting drawings.

- All are invited to purchase catalogues of the collection in the Museum Shop.
  And you can see highlights of the drawings collection below. When you select a work, you'll see enlarged images and interpretive material.

The Arkansas Arts Center, designed by Christopher Stashuk, is a wonderful example of how the right color combinations can set the tone. Almost minimalistic in its concept, the design doesn't try to compete with the exhibits, still the Web site comes across as very rich. Above is the main page for one of the exhibitions; each of the miniatures on the page above leads to one of the exhibits (see left page). On the very right, you see the online museum store. It is also a good example of keeping the design clear and straightforward.

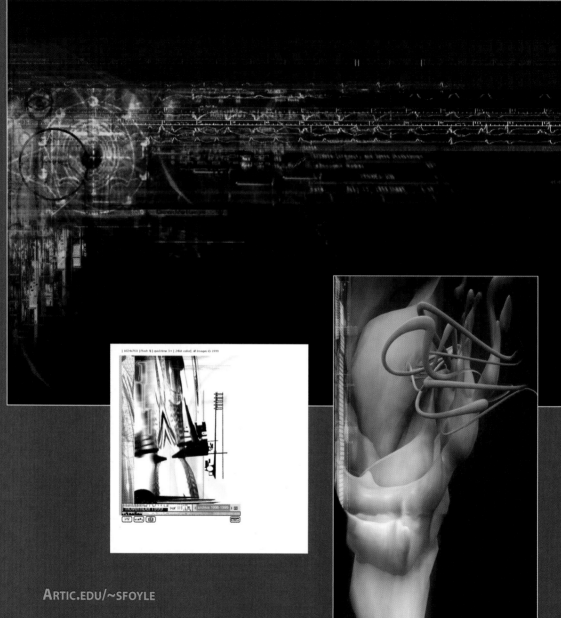

| 1024x768 | Flash 5| quicktime 3+ | 24bit color| all images © 1999

ARTIC.EDU/~SFOYLE

The work of Sean Patrick Foyle is nothing less than remarkable. His pieces of online artwork, done with Flash and 3D software, are a must-see! Several animated layers create an animated texture that draws the viewer in. While the site lacks a clear concept and navigation (it takes a while to explore it), it is worth the effort just to marvel at it.

CIA.COM.AU/DFM/TINTIN

Up for more inspiring artwork? Justin Fox worked in Web design for many years and uses a subdirectory of his Web site to host some of his work and writing. His views and his approach to design are a great break from the mainstream.

CONTEMPT.NET

"Advertising may be described as the science of arresting the human intelligence long enough to get money from it", says a quote on the Web site of the Contempt Web design company. It is apparent that this motto reflects the program on their own Web site: every reload of the main page shows a different image and the quotes change constantly to keep the viewer's attention.

DIGITALWHIPLASH.COM

Another design studio, but with a unique style (in particular when it comes to their own home-page). The coloring is unusual: bright, almost neon-like colors over black.

portfolio.web

FUSION MEDIA GROUP
a new vision in design

"I see Fusion Media Group as cutting edge. The next generation of web developers using some of the latest technologies to develop content and presentations for clients who wish to have an innovative and progressive look but retain functionality."

-- Eric Josue
producer, new media

E 3 DIREKTIV
avant garde media

The animation studio division of the Fusion Media Group, specializing in Shockwave Flash. A two time Macromedia Shocked Site of the Day, and Flash Leading Edge Partner, demonstrates with this site, what can be accomplished with online multimedia.

objective: creation of a showcase site to demonstrate the studio's abilities in multimedia and web design.

contribution: complete site design, sound foleying, and programming.

"IF IT LOOKS AND SOUNDS PRETTY COOL, IT PROBABLY IS." JAK.O.T

E3 DIREKTIV
avant garde media

visit the site

BRAIN INTERNATIONAL

BRAIN INTERNATIONAL

This is a merger of two medium sized software companies in Germany, which combined to form the 8th largest software developer in the country. Offering solutions for medium sized businesses, the merger was an event to be marked with collateral marketing efforts, and a launch party. Originally the companies were known as Rembold & Holzer, and BIW Systemhaus, and together formed Brain International.

objective: to create a visually attractive and modern site, in German language, to co-incide with collateral marketing efforts abroad. The look and theme, was to maintain a consistent "look and feel" to their other materials, as well as offer multimedia and cutting edge graphic and HTML.

contribution: complete site design, shockwave flash, music & sound creation, and support programming.

visit the site

portfolio.web

E3DIREKTIV.COM

It sometimes doesn't take much to make an impression: the Web site of the design company E3 Direktiv features a simple but very elegant intro. A black sphere rolls from the back to the front, opens up, and four "baby" spheres fall out to create the four dots of the main navigational elements. Done in Flash, this animation captures the visitor's attention every time.

E 3 DIREKTIV
avant garde media

THE DIREKTIV   CREDITS

LABORATORIE   PORTFOLIO

news   email

a **FUSION** MEDIA GROUP company

E 3 DIREKTIV-AVANT GARDE MEDIA

HOTSPRINGS.ORG

This site stands out because of its tasteful color combination and the use of rounded corners in the tables. Since HTML doesn't allow for rounded table cells, these rounded corners are all images that were placed inside the cells to create that appearance.

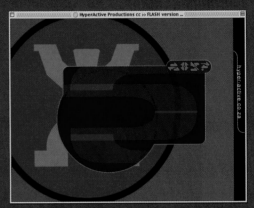

HYPER-ACTIVE.CO.ZA

You just have to love the funky design of this Web design agency in Cape Town, South Africa. The site features Flash and HTML versions, both nice to look at and with bold coloring. The HTML version proves once again that great design doesn't require you to pull any HTML stunts: the complexity of the HTML page comes from a large background image that uses a dimmed version of the logo. The navigational buttons are made of one transparent GIF image that uses an image map.

HyperActive Productions cc is a young, multi-talented company in the visual field of digital communications. We specialise in all forms of digital media ranging from presentations to the Internet to video production. Our vision is to be at the forefront of technology to give our clients the best quality and service with regard to all their communication needs.

We offer the following services to our clients :

Maintenance and development of high-end **Internet and Intranet** sites which includes :

• Information distribution • Banners on the Internet • On-Line Advertising & Shopping • Database access • Computer-based training via the Internet including video clips.

We produce **hybrid CD-Roms*** to include all the elements of :

• sound • video • graphics and text for entertainment, education and communication purposes.

*Our CD-Roms are cross-platform (Macintosh and PC) with access to the Internet if required.

We do **business presentations** on computer or onto CD-Rom.

• A great way to present your service or product • can be customised for speaker support, or as a standalone presentation.

Our **video production** covers :

• television • commercials • launches • corporate videos.

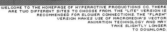

WELCOME TO THE HOMEPAGE OF HYPERACTIVE PRODUCTIONS CC. THERE ARE TWO DIFFERENT SITES TO CHOOSE FROM. THE "LITE" VERSION IS RECOMMENDED FOR SLOWER CONNECTIONS. THE "FLASH" VERSION MAKES USE OF MACROMEDIA'S VECTOR ANIMATION TECHNOLOGY AND MAY TAKE SLIGHTLY LONGER TO DOWNLOAD.

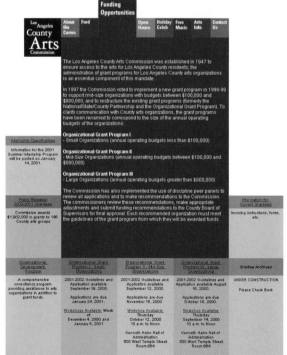

LACOUNTYARTS.ORG

Color and simplicity are the key with this Web site. The designer Linda Chiavaroli hand-coded the HTML instead of using an HTML authoring tool. To convert the text and headlines into images, she used Photoshop.

If the artist Mondrian had created a Web site, it might have looked much like this. The main page consists of one large table with many cells, some of which are merged to create larger squares.

JIONG.COM

Instead of just creating a portfolio, the designer Jiong Li made his art part of the Web site. If you click on the splash screen, another browser window that contains a simple horizontal frameset pops up. The icons on the bottom lead the viewer through five sections of the Web site; the background color of the frame that is hosting them always blends with the artwork in the frame above.

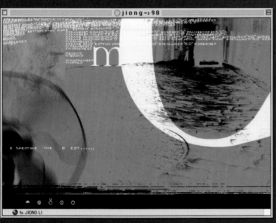

IDEO.COM

"It is impossible to get out of a problem by using the same kind of thinking that it took to get into the problem" says a quote by Albert Einstein on the IDEO Web site. How committed the designers at IDEO are to coming up with new ideas and solutions is apparent if you look at their home page.

The top and right screenshots show how the designer used the center space for the local navigation. The portfolio (bottom) extends the design to the right.

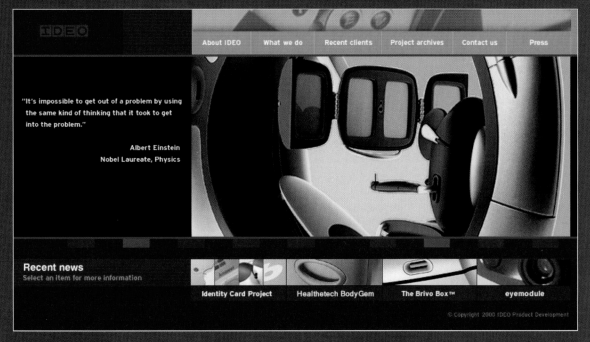

The main page shows how great Web design can look despite its limitations: using just images in tables, the design makes great use of the space.

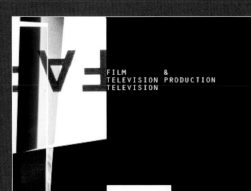

FILM &
TELEVISION PRODUCTION
TELEVISION

idolescence

developed and supervised production of an original half-hour
comedy pilot for the MTV television network's 1999 season.
factoid #1: thematically recalled the WB's *grosse pointe*. factoid
#2: 30 minutes of television equals 22 minutes of production!

TOTAL MEDIA BARRAGE: CORPORATE CLIENTELE. ADVERTISING.
PRINT AND PUBLICATIONS. MUSIC VIDEOS. TELEVISION
PRODUCTION. SOUND DESIGN. WWW PRODUCTION. TYPOGRAPHY.
INDUSTRY DOCUMENTATION AND CONSULTING. SOUNDPROOF
MAGAZINE.

STRIPED GUITARS AND SEVEN UNIQUE FOREIGNERS. MY TONGUE
IS A PAPERCLIP.®

LOWCULTURE.COM

LowCulture.com is yet another design company's self-promotion site.
Using a frameset, the navigation is
placed in the bottom frame. The navigation itself is unique: the links are
made of text that was rendered as
images. Since these links are not
placed within a table, they reflow
when the size of the browser window
changes.

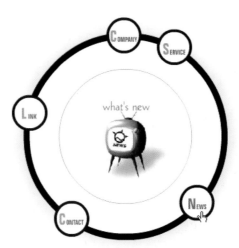

we can do

Neostream Interactive invites you in a dimensionless journey into the unforseen era of multimedia design.

The boundless potential of the Internet will be brought to life through our storm of ideas and creativity.

Experience for yourself what can be achieved with the mind.

NEOSTREAM.COM

Neostream is an interactive media design agency based in Sydney, Australia. The site, which uses a combination of HTML and Flash, has received a couple of awards.

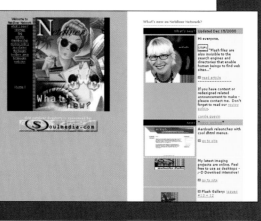

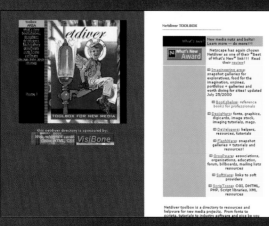

NETDIVER.NET

Netdiver (http://netdiver.net) is a Web resource for the new media community. The most remarkable part of the Web site—in terms of design—is the illustration for each section.

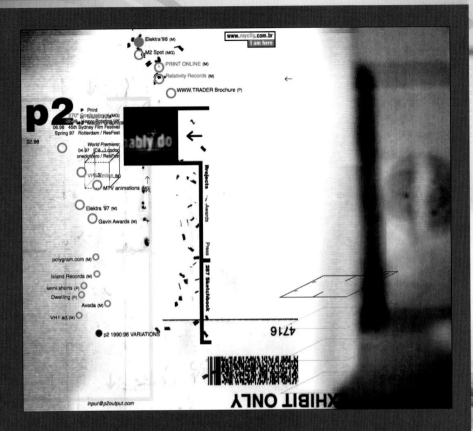

P2OUTPUT.COM

This Web site looks very edgy and artsy, mostly because of the background images. These are mostly blurred and give the design some depth, but unfortunately, if you get to the level of the portfolio examples, the site loses its edge.

ANTIDOT.DE/EYESAW

The German designer Dirk Uhlenbrock is not only very talented, but also very generous. Every three months, he publishes a new issue of Eyesaw in which he gives away his font creations for free (a must-have for any designer who loves funky type). The Web site is also stunning and comes with an unusual design concept: the navigation bar is in the middle of the page (in a frameset). Clicking on one of the buttons (which represent the issues) changes the page in the top frame; the links in the top frame then control the page at the bottom. As in a children's book, this creates a great number of possible combinations. It should come as no surprise that the Art Directors Club awarded this site the Silver Medal in the Interactive Category in 1999.

Stepping backward in time: each issue of the Eye-saw is accessible via the navigation bar in the middle of the page. The issues are displayed in the top frame, the bottom frame displays the content.

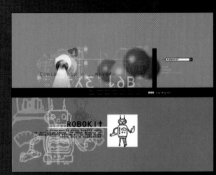

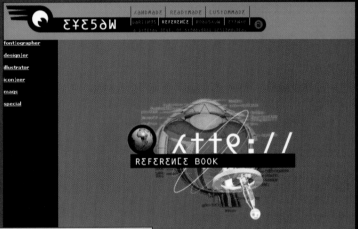

Still available on the site are the old issues (with the old design). Though not as innovative in their design as the current one, they are still very inspiring.

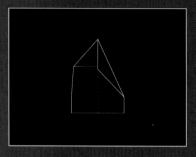

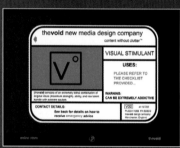

THEVOID.CO.UK

Done almost entirely in Flash, the Web site of The Void New Media company in the UK has received a lot of recognition for its design (Cool Site of the Year winner, Shocked Site of the Day, Cool Homepage Site of the Week). The design builds on a pill package as a metaphor and it is prescription-free.

RONCHAN.COM

Chances are that you have seen this fabulous illustrator's illustrations somewhere, either in a magazine or on a book cover. The design of his site reflects his style. The Flash intro in particular is worth watching (the animation is like the opening of a movie from the Sixties).

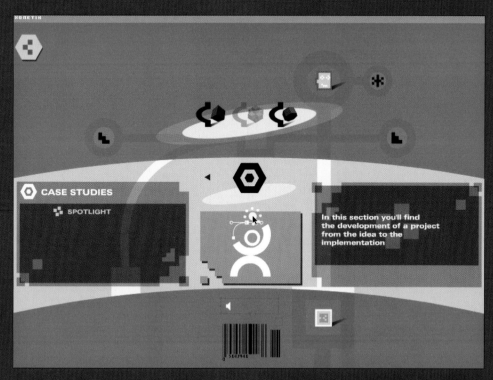

XONETIK.COM

This site apparently is a work still –in progress, because more than half the content is still missing. Another drawback is that the navigation is not very intuitive (to fully understand it, you have to read the help). But these things aside, the site has many interesting ideas.

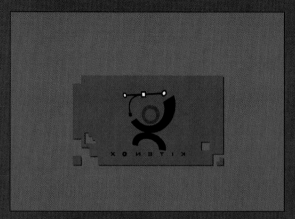

Umbra.com

This online store for designer stuff has two interesting features: the navigation on the left uses a little square to indicate in which section the visitor is currently. At the same time, bringing the mouse over one of the sections will reveal a submenu. When the visitor has chosen an item, a small pop-up menu will allow him to change colors (which are then displayed simultaneously).

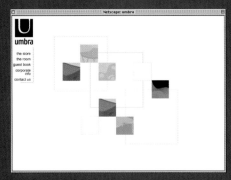

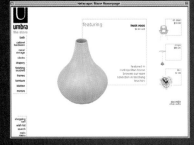
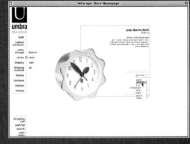

c ur ious [1] [2] [3]

WIDESHOT.COM

Nomen est omen: wideshot.com expects users to have at least a 21-inch monitor to view the displayed artwork.

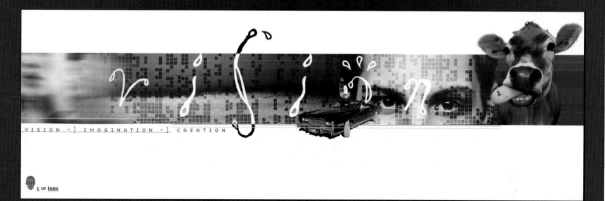

PHOTOSHOP

Illustration: **Antony Kyriazis** from the CD **OnyFrax**

TECHNIQUES

In the beginning of Web design, many designers created their mock-up designs in an HTML authoring tool. That approach seemed logical to the designers who made the transition from desktop publishing to Web design. After all, they were used to designing in layout programs. It didn't take long, though, for designers to realize that this process was too tedious, and they started to do the design process entirely in Photoshop. This made it easier to make changes and create different versions of the design. Sometimes, though, those Photoshop design presentations look so realistic that many clients get the impression that they are seeing the final product, making the design process more difficult. So surprisingly, many of today's designers very often go back to their roots and work with plain paper in their brainstorming meetings with clients. Using scribbles has the advantage of letting you develop different ideas even quicker. Then, after you and your client have worked out a basic concept, it's time for you to start up Photoshop. In this chapter you will learn all the basic techniques you'll need to create a Web site quickly and efficiently in Photoshop.

THE INTERFACE BLUEPRINT

Before you start designing however, there are a couple of other things to consider, particularly if you work with a team of designers. Andreas Lindström, art director for Qwest, who has created many award-winning Web sites, came up with the concept of using an *Interface Blueprint Layer* to avoid the common out the groundwork for the style guide. Andreas Lindström now uses IBLs for all his interface developments. It is placed on the top layer of the Photoshop file, and set to 80 percent transparency so that the underlying design matches the IBL measurements. After the client signs off on the visual direction of a Web site and the design director approves the IBL, it is then distributed to the teams involved in the

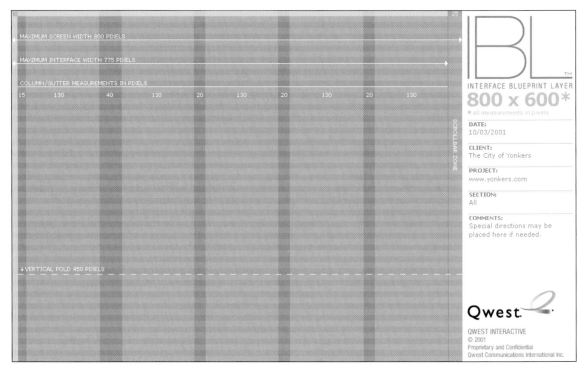

Andreas Lindström, art director at Qwest, created the concept of the Interface Blueprint Layer. Here is an example as it was used for the Yonkers.com project.

issue of inconsistencies, which can easily happen when many designers work on a Web site simultaneously. The Interface Blueprint Layer (IBL) is a single-layered image file that helps deliver a solid, well-designed interface. This idea is really not new; all newspapers and magazines are designed around an invisible grid system, which is used to ensure that the intended design and layout stay consistent throughout the publication. The Interface Blueprint Layer is simply the adaptation of this to Web design.

The IBL functions as a "guide of measurements" throughout the production cycle as well as laying

production. Their responsibility is to make sure that the alignments of the interface are followed according to the IBL. Once the design is finalized and passed on through the next steps of the production cycle, the IBL is also emailed to the individuals who need it. When the Photoshop file is sliced and put into code, the IBL is a great reference to ensure that the integrity of the design is maintained.

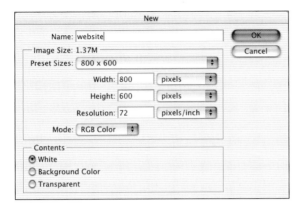

THE RIGHT DOCUMENT SIZE

The important thing in the beginning is to decide on a maximum document size. I suggest that you use 800 by 600 pixels because this is currently the most common monitor size/resolution. If you wanted to play it safe, you could stick to the 640 by 480 monitor resolution. The advantage of a smaller document size is that the page doesn't take up the user's entire screen. Also, text is easier to read if the page width does not exceed 640 pixels. If you want to, you can always change your document size with the Image Size and Canvas Size commands.

CHANGING THE CANVAS SIZE

Changing the canvas size allows you to add or remove space around an image. To enlarge the canvas size, simply enter the new width or height in the Canvas Size dialog box (Image > Canvas Size) and choose where you want that space to be added by clicking on the squares in the Anchor section. The selected square indicates where on the enlarged canvas the original image will be placed. For example, if you change the width of the canvas and select the leftmost square, the original image will go on the left and the additional pixels will be added to the right of the image.

You can use the same technique to crop your canvas size: Simply reduce the number of pixels listed under Width or Height and click OK. Alternatively, you can use the Crop tool in the toolbox, but the Canvas Size command has the advantage of letting you crop the image to a specific dimension by entering a numerical value. You can also enter a specific dimension with the Crop tool, but personally I find that to be cumbersome—you have to enter the dimension in the options bar and then select the area in your document. Using the Crop tool is helpful if the cropped area is asymmetrical, but most of the time all you need to do is to crop a little space on one side or the other. In my opinion, the Canvas Size command is the easiest way to do that.

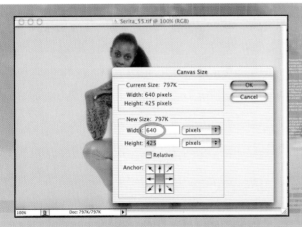

Canvas Size allows you to increase or decrease the measurements of the canvas.

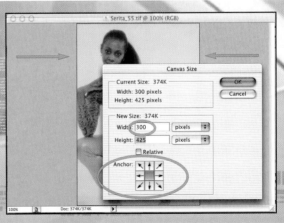

It is important to set the Anchor, which gives Photoshop a reference to where the pixels will be added or substracted.

CHANGING THE IMAGE SIZE

As you are working on the design, you'll frequently need to scale or crop images (or entire designs). The command for changing the image size is Image > Image Size, and it is pretty straightforward: the dialog box displays the width and height of your work area. You can change its dimensions simply by entering new values (make sure the units are set to pixels). To the right, you'll see a chain icon that indicates which parameters are linked, depending on whether you have selected the Constrain Proportions and/or Resample Image options at the bottom of the dialog box.

Constrain Proportions ensures that if the width is changed, the height changes accordingly (and vice versa). Unless you plan to intentionally distort the image, perhaps as a special effect, this option should always be checked. The Resample Image option ensures that Photoshop resamples the image if you make any changes in its resolution. You can choose Nearest Neighbor, Bilinear, or Bicubic.

The Image Size dialog box also displays a value for resolution. Ideally, this value should be set to the screen resolution of 72 dpi, but this is more or less a cosmetic task. To a browser or HTML authoring program, it makes no difference whether the resolution of an image is set to 72, 85, or 255 dpi. To the browser, a pixel is a pixel—it will always display the real size of the image. I mention this because it is different from desktop publishing, and a lot of designers who come from that field ask this question.

Most often you will want to resize an image by a certain percentage. Instead of doing this by calculating pixels or inches, use the Units pop-up menu to change units to percent. Now all you need to do is enter the percentage reduction you want. For best results, use "round" values like 25%, 50%, 200%, and so on.

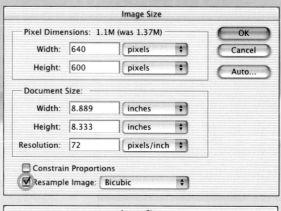

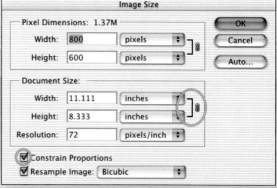

The Image Size dialog box allows you to shrink or enlarge an image. Resample Image ultimately determines the quality of the result and the Constrain Proportions option ensures that the proportions are kept.

Fixing Images

Except for navigational elements such as buttons, most images on the Web are photos. Unfortunately, very few Web site projects have big budgets to hire a professional photographer. Most Web designers have to rely either on stock images or on photos supplied by the client, and these sometimes need some fixing and cleaning up. The good news is since most images on the Web are very small in size, fixing images is rather easy. In fact, because images usually get downsized anyway, many of the imperfections are minimized and thereby resolved. For those spots, stains, and scratches that didn't disappear, here are some of the main techniques to improve an imperfect photo.

ELIMINATING NOISE AND SCRATCHES

Print is much more forgiving of small imperfections (on a pixel level) than a monitor is, so one of the first steps in preparing a photo for the Web, regardless of whether it will be saved as a GIF or a JPEG, is to get rid of noise and scratches. Noise in a photo can come from the film itself or from a bad scanner, and it can impact your file size when you save as GIF (depending on your settings) or JPEG. The less noise you have, the better compression you will achieve. Photoshop provides not one but three filters designed to reduce noise. Each one employs a slightly different approach.

The **Despeckle** filter reduces noise by subtly blurring the image while preserving areas with strong contrasts. In other words, **Despeckle** blurs only those pixels with minor differences in color, so contours don't become fuzzy. Unlike the standard **Blur** filter, which affects everything in the photo (making it look out of focus), **Despeckle** prevents your photo from losing too much quality. For smoothing gradations or blended color areas in an image with strong contrasts, the **Despeckle** filter is the way to go. You can apply it more than once until you get the desired blurring effect. It's great for small amounts of noise, but if the contrast of the noise is very high (for example, if there was dust on the photo you scanned), you may not get the result you want. In that case, try the Median filter.

The **Median** filter adjusts the brightness of adjacent pixels by interpolating their color values while disregarding all the values beyond a certain threshold. It works a lot like the **Despeckle** filter, except that **Median** interpolates, while **Despeckle** blurs. You use a slider to select the range of pixels that you want Photoshop to interpolate; it's best to stay between 1 and 3 pixels. Since a GIF compresses more efficiently if several pixels on a horizontal row have the same color value, this filter can be particularly handy if you are preparing GIFs.

The **Dust & Scratches** filter lets you designate the size of the dust and scratches that you want to eliminate by using the **Radius** slider. If you set the slider to 1 pixel, only one-pixel scratches will be corrected; all larger scratches will be ignored. Use the **Threshold** slider to define the degree of contrast that Photoshop should use to distinguish a scratch.

Here's a little buying tip: Logitech® Pocket Digital™ is for people who want to capture spontaneous moments, but don't want to carry a bulky camera. Although it measures a scant inch thick, Logitech Pocket Digital camera can hold up to 52 images at up to 1.3 Megapixel resolution. It has a built-in lithium polymer battery that automatically recharges through the USB cable each time the camera connects to the PC during picture download. Since Web design doesn't require high-res images, this camera is perfect to create your own stock photo library of objects and textures. I find some of the best objects at flea markets and in store windows.

Here are a couple examples of how a photo with dust and scratches can be repaired. In the original photo (on the left) there are very heavy scratches that were treated with the Despeckle filter. Even though they have almost vanished, you still can see parts of the scratches (right). In cases like this try using the other filters that are mentioned here.

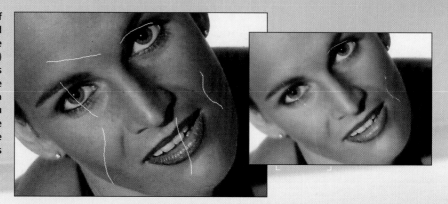

With the Median filter you can achieve quite impressive results. As you can see in this example, all scratches were eliminated with almost no traces.

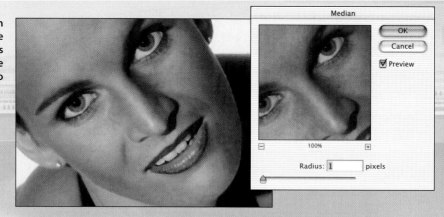

The Dust & Scratches filter lets you use the Radius slider to define what will be treated as dust. The Threshold slider adjusts the filter's sensitivity to contrast and saturation changes. One side effect of this filter is that it blurs the image; to avoid a serious loss of quality, use this filter on selected parts of the image.

Sharpening an Image

Sometimes dust and scratches are not the problem, but the photo lacks sharpness or is out of focus. Photoshop provides a set of filters to enhance sharpness; they are all gathered in the Filters menu under Sharpen. The most useful filter in this collection is **Unsharp Mask**, which lets you set the precise amount, radius, and threshold for sharpness enhancement. You can watch the effect of adjusting these parameters by checking the Preview box. If you plan to save the image as a JPEG, you should use this effect sparingly because JPEG's compression algorithm actually works best on slightly blurry images.

Fixing Larger Areas and Problems

Filters will not always do the job, so you might find yourself having to fix an image manually. One of the best tools for this is the **Clone Stamp** tool, which applies the pixels from one part of the image to another. To use this tool, you have to first show Photoshop which area of the image should be the source. You do this by holding the Option key (Macintosh) or Alt key (Windows); the cursor changes to a crosshair with which you click in the image. After releasing the Option/Alt key, you can start painting in a different area of the image and Photoshop will copy the pixels from the source area.

The **Clone Stamp** tool is amazing; with a little experience, you can easily erase large areas of an image (even a person) or correct major problems and scratches. It offers a couple of important options. If you need to cover a large area of your image with a certain texture, deselect the **Aligned** option. Now every time

In order to use this snapshot of a blimp for a Web site, the current advertising needs to be removed. It would be difficult to do this with the Clone Stamp tool because there is not much that can be used as a source, but it can be done using the Healing Brush. Since the Healing Brush adapts the pixels to the background pixels, their brightness matches that of the background.

you release the mouse button, you can move the **Clone Stamp** tool to a new position, and when you click in the image, Photoshop will copy the pixels from the same source. If the **Aligned** option is selected, the distance between the source and the destination will always be the same (this distance is determined the first time you click in the image). Select the **Aligned** option when you are duplicating an element in an image. In addition, the options bar allows you to specify the blending mode, opacity and flow. If you are working with several layers in your document, select the **Use All Layers** option. Deselect this option if you want to work only on the currently activated layer.

One disadvantage of the **Clone Stamp** tool is that it duplicates the source pixels exactly, which can be a problem if you have to correct an area of your image for which you don't have a texture that matches in brightness or color. A typical example is having to fix a person's skin, but the area to fix is in shadow. This is where the **Healing Brush** comes in. Think of this tool as the **Clone Stamp** tool with texture and lighting adjustment. Any pixel that you paint with this tool will adapt to the pixels that it is painted on, meaning that the painted pixels are mixed with the ones of the background. As with the **Clone Stamp** tool, you have the options of setting a blending mode or selecting **Aligned** (see above). The **Healing Brush** can also use a pattern as a source, which is a great way to blend patterns with the background.

If you have larger areas to fix, the **Clone Stamp** or **Healing Brush** tools can be cumbersome. For those scenarios, the **Patch** tool might be the perfect choice.

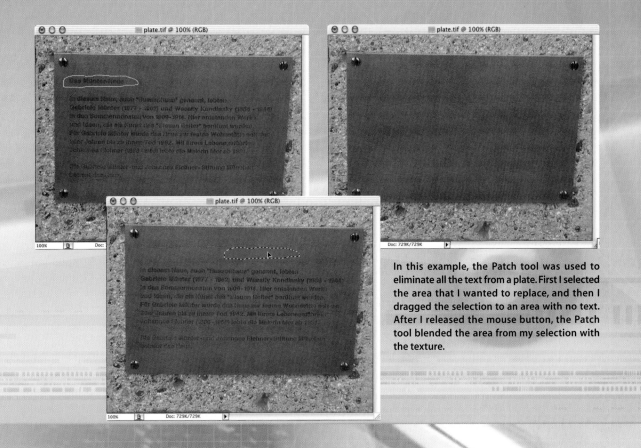

In this example, the Patch tool was used to eliminate all the text from a plate. First I selected the area that I wanted to replace, and then I dragged the selection to an area with no text. After I released the mouse button, the Patch tool blended the area from my selection with the texture.

The **Patch** tool can be seen as the combination of a selection tool and the **Healing Brush**. When you select the **Patch** tool, you first draw a selection tool around the area that you want to fix, and then you drag the selection to a part of the image with a similar texture. The part of the image where you drop your selection will then be copied to the target area and adjusted so that it blends smoothly (if you have the **Patch: Source** option activated in the Options bar). What I like about the **Patch** tool is that the original selection stays active, so you can keep dragging it to different source areas in your image until the part is completely fixed. And, like the **Healing Brush**, the **Patch** tool allows you to apply a texture or pattern to the area.

Here's a tip on how to quickly create a pattern to fix up an area: Make a rectangular selection of a texture that you want to apply, then choose the **Filter > Pattern Maker** command. In the **Pattern Maker** dialog, click the **Generate** button, and in the Tile History area (on the right side of the dialog), click the disc icon (Saves preset pattern). Now close the dialog and go back to the **Patch** tool; select an area in your image, choose the pattern in the pop-up menu, and click the **Use Pattern** button. The pattern tiles seamlessly (thanks to the **Pattern Maker**), so you don't run the risk of seeing any edges, and the texture will blend right in with the background.

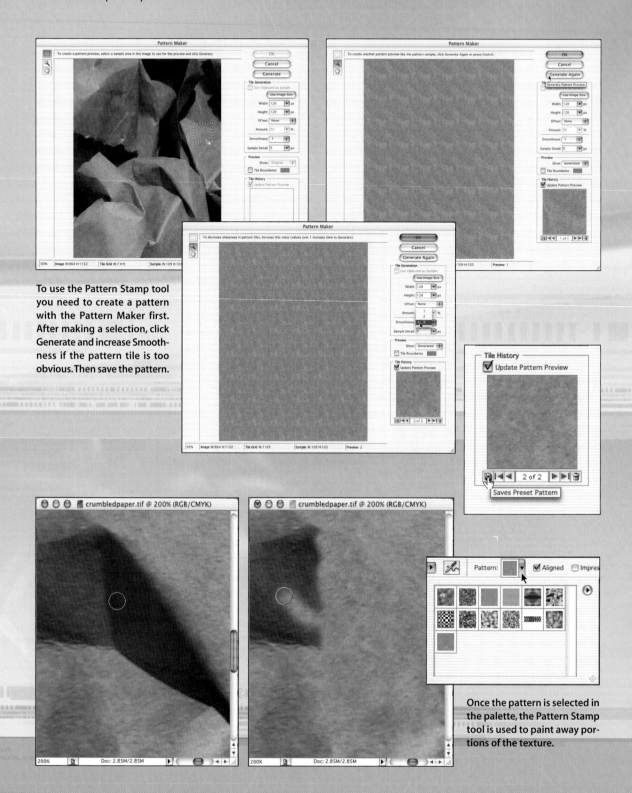

To use the Pattern Stamp tool
you need to create a pattern
with the Pattern Maker first.
After making a selection, click
Generate and increase Smoothness if the pattern tile is too
obvious. Then save the pattern.

Once the pattern is selected in
the palette, the Pattern Stamp
tool is used to paint away portions of the texture.

Color Manipulation and Correction

Most of the color-correction and manipulation tools can be found in **Image > Adjustments**. Many of the correction tools, when used to an extreme, can also manipulate the colors. Although not all the commands are equally important, and many of them can be used in various ways, I want to give you an overview and visual guide to the commands in the Adjustments menu and how they are commonly used.

Image > Adjustments >	Manipulation	Correction
Levels	-	By setting the highlights and shadows in an image, you can maximize the photo's dynamic range.
Auto Levels	Adjusts each color channel to the maximum dynamic, which shifts the colors in a color image. Can result in interesting color changes.	Sets highlights and shadows automatically. Works as a correction tool only with grayscale images. When used on RGB images, the result is usually a color shift.
Auto Contrast	-	Increases the contrast in grayscale and RGB images automatically.
Auto Color	-	Adjusts the highlights and shadows based on the actual pixels in the image (not the histogram or the channels).
Curves	Can be used for some dramatic color changes. Many effects—for example, most techniques for chrome—are based on the creation of curves.	Allows for more precise control over the tonal range than just highlights, midtones, and shadows. Pros usually use Curves as the main tool for color corrections.
Color Balance	-	Allows you to change the overall color mixture by shifting the Red, Green, or Blue value.
Brightness/Contrast	-	Adjusts the Brightness and Contrast values by the same amount. Not the best choice for corrections because it can cause loss of details.
Hue/Saturation	Can adjust the entire image or just an individual channel. It is a great tool for changing the color of an object or giving dull digital photos more saturation.	Is not usually used for color corrections.
Desaturate	Can be used to make a grayscale image out of an RGB image without having to switch to grayscale mode.	-

Here is a list of all the commands in the Image > Adjustments menu and how they can be used (list continues on next page).

Replace Color	Can replace a particular color. It is the perfect tool for changing the color of an element in an image.	-
Selective Color	-	Make color adjustments by selecting a part of the spectrum and then changing the color mixtures.
Channel Mixer	-	Can be used to create grayscale images, giving you precise control over the amount of color in each channel. In CMYK mode, it is also a great tool to do some color corrections.
Gradient Map	Creates wonderful color effects by replacing each pixel of the spectrum with the colors of a gradient. Very useful for compositions.	-
Invert	Works best with grayscale images. Inverting RGB images usually produces somewhat unappealing colors.	-
Equalize	-	Use this command if the scan is too dark overall.
Threshold	Produces a black-and-white version of the image. Can be used as the basis for other effects or compositions.	-
Posterize	Creates interesting color shifts and also reduces the image to large flat areas of color.	-
Variations	-	Easy tool for color corrections because it displays thumbnails. Not the best choice for precise color correction.
Layer Modes	Determines how the color values of two layers interact. Great for any photo composition.	-

Layer Modes is not part of the Image > Adjustments menu, but it is listed here since it is essential for creating photocompositions and for some other design techniques.

ADJUST THE TONAL RANGE

It would be great if every image was perfectly scanned, but the reality is that even with stock images you don't always get the best quality and you end up having to do some adjustments. Photoshop offers a wide range of adjustment commands. Every time you use one of these commands, however, the color values are permanently altered. In addition, all of these com-

Levels: When you select the Levels command (**Image > Adjustments > Levels**), Photoshop creates a histogram of the image. That means it looks at each pixel's brightness value and presents this information in a graph. This makes it easy for you to see the kinds of visual information in your image, but more importantly, **Levels** lets you extend the tonal range of the image. If the majority of your image's tonal values are in the range of 20 to 80 percent, you can expand those

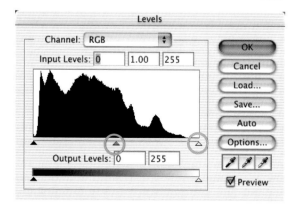

An image before and after adjusting the Levels.

mands create a rounding error, which can add up when you make many color corrections. When you do color corrections, it is better to use Adjustment layers. The mathematical algorithms of the adjustment layers are combined and then applied to the image pixels once, which reduces the rounding error.

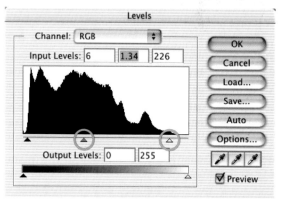

values to the full range of zero to 100 percent, which will instantly give your image much more contrast and detail. To stretch the histogram of an image to the maximum amount, simply adjust the black and white Input Levels triangles to the left and right of the histogram. Click OK, and the shadows and highlights will be adjusted. The triangle in the middle sets the value for

50 percent, meaning it will indicate the middle of the tonal range. Checking the Preview box lets you see the effect of the sliders interactively. Once you click OK, call up Levels again to see how the tonal range has been stretched.

Auto Levels: The Auto Levels command sets highlights and shadows for each color channel individually. This is different from setting the highlights and shadows for the RGB channel and it usually results in a color shift. This can sometimes be a nice effect, especially if you are creating a photocomposition.

Auto Contrast: Use this command to adjust the overall contrast and mixture of colors in an RGB image. It makes the lightest pixels appear lighter and shadows

appear darker. Auto Contrast does not adjust the channels individually (all channels are set identically), so it does not introduce or remove color cast.

Auto Color: Use Auto Color to adjust the contrast and color of an image. It does this not by analyzing the channels' histograms, but by looking at the actual image and then setting the highlights and shadows and neutralizing the midtones.

Brightness/Contrast: This command offers one slider for Brightness and one for Contrast. The simplicity of this command is also its problem: Unlike Curves and Levels, this command makes the same adjustment to every pixel, which can easily result in a loss of detail in the image.

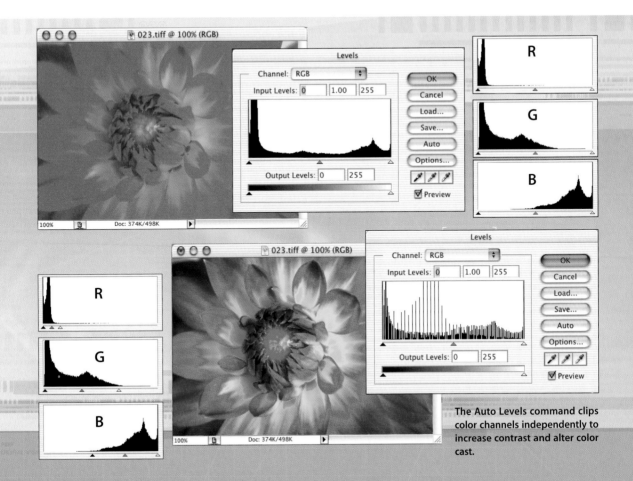

The Auto Levels command clips color channels independently to increase contrast and alter color cast.

CORRECTING COLORS

One of the common tasks in Photoshop is color correcting photos. If the photo wasn't shot in a professional studio, the images often have color shifts as a result of variations in lighting conditions. Daylight, for instance, brings out different color frequencies than fluorescent light, and you have to correct those color differences in Photoshop.

Photoshop offers several commands aimed at color correction, including **Color Balance** and **Variations**. Both do exactly the same thing, but their approaches and interfaces are different. The Color Balance command (**Image > Adjustments > Color Balance**) allows you to change the color via three sliders, while in the Variations command (**Image > Adjustments >** **Variations**), you work with a preview in which you see several variations of the same image and select the one you like the best. Both functions shift the image color toward the value on the opposite side of the color wheel, so to correct a red tone in your image, you would add more cyan; to compensate for too much green, you would shift toward magenta; and to correct for blue, you would add yellow.

Even though the **Variations** command seems more intuitive, you can actually get a more precise result by using **Color Balance** because it lets you set the value for each color between 0 and 100. The Variations dialog gives you only six possible alternatives. The only tricky part of using **Color Balance** is deciding which color needs to be shifted, but once you have determined that, making the actual correction is simple: Just

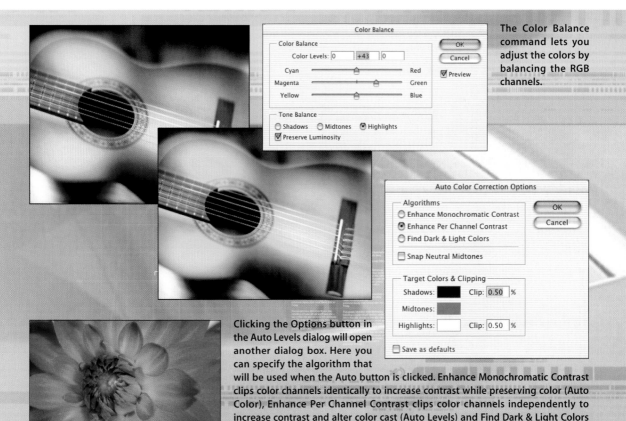

The Color Balance command lets you adjust the colors by balancing the RGB channels.

Clicking the Options button in the Auto Levels dialog will open another dialog box. Here you can specify the algorithm that will be used when the Auto button is clicked. Enhance Monochromatic Contrast clips color channels identically to increase contrast while preserving color (Auto Color), Enhance Per Channel Contrast clips color channels independently to increase contrast and alter color cast (Auto Levels) and Find Dark & Light Colors analyzes the image to find dark and light colors, which are used for the shadow and highlight colors (Auto Color). In this image you see the result of Auto Contrast.

STEP BY STEP: SETTING HIGHLIGHTS AND SHADOWS WITH THE CURVES COMMAND

The Curves command, like the Levels command, allows you to set the highlights and shadows—a great starting point for any other color adjustments. Here's how you do it:

1 Before setting the highlights and shadows, it is helpful to use the Threshold command to locate those areas in your image. Open the Threshold dialog and drag the Threshold slider all the way to the left. The remaining black areas in your image are the ones that contain the darkest pixels in your image.

2 Now drag the Threshold slider to the right to locate the highlights in your image. Then click the Cancel button (you used the Threshold command only to help you locate the highlights/shadows).

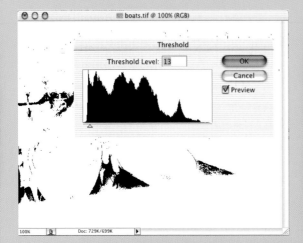

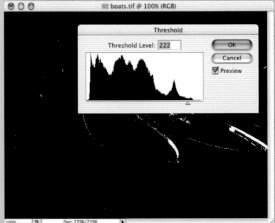

3 Open the Curves command (preferably as an adjustment layer). With the black eyedropper (Set Black Point) click in the image where the Threshold command located the darkest pixels.

4 Then use the white eyedropper (Set White Point) to set the lightest area. If you now switch to the different color channels, you can see how the curves for each channel have been adjusted.

5 Pick a midtone with the Set Gray Point eyedropper. When you click with this tool in the image and keep the mouse button pressed, you will see a circle that moves along the curve, indicating where the current pixel is on the color spectrum. After releasing the mouse button, your image should be adjusted. You can fine-tune it by adding additional points on the curve.

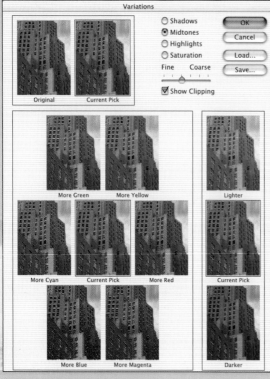

The Variations command, and the Before and After images.

move the appropriate color slider in the correct direction. (For instance, if the image has too much yellow, then move the Yellow/Blue slider toward blue.)

If you are using the **Variations** command to correct colors, adjust the Fine/Coarse slider until one of the previews is the right color; click on it, and it becomes the new Current Pick, with new variations around it.

Another great tool for color correction is the **Hue/Saturation** command (**Image > Adjustments > Hue/Saturation**). The two color bars at the bottom of the dialog box help you understand what you are doing by showing the color spectrum and how it is changed. Using the Hue slider, you can rotate the color wheel and shift the colors in your image dramatically, which is sometimes a great way to create the basis of a photocomposition. When trying to optimize your image, you want to focus on the **Saturation** slider. This slider makes dull colors just pop out. And if the image is too dark, use the **Lightness** slider to brighten it. However, the true power of the **Hue/Saturation** command lies in working with individual color ranges. If you switch to one of the color ranges in the Edit pop-up menu, you can change the **Hue**, **Saturation**, and **Lightness** for a specific range. If you are not quite sure which range to pick, just click in the image with the **Eyedropper** tool. An adjustment slider will appear at the bottom of the **Hue/Saturation** dialog box. If you keep clicking with the **Eyedropper** tool in different areas of your image, you will notice how that slider moves according to the color in the spectrum (the **Edit** pop-up will also change to reflect that). If you need to alter a wider range of colors, use the Eyedropper tool with the plus sign or simply drag the range sliders (the vertical bars that surround the dark gray area). You can also move the triangles to adjust the color fall-off and then use the **Hue**, **Saturation**, and **Lightness** sliders to change the colors.

If working with the **Hue/Saturation** command doesn't seem intuitive to you, consider using the **Selective Color** command for making color corrections. It's similar to the **Hue/Saturation** command in the way that it allows you to specify a color range. The main advantage over **Hue/Saturation** is that it allows you to correct the image by using the process colors cyan, magenta, yellow, and black. Most designers who come from desktop publishing are more familiar with defining colors this way, so using this command can make life a little bit easier.

Probably the best tool for color correction, however, is the **Curves** command. As with the **Levels** command, you can adjust the entire tonal range of an image. Instead of just three variables (highlights, shadows, midtones), the **Curves** command allows you to adjust up to 15 points along a zero-to-255 scale. **Curves** can also be set individually for each color channel, which gives you the most precision of all the correction tools. To set a point on a curve, simply click on the curve and drag the point to the desired location. To remove a point, drag it away from the curve.

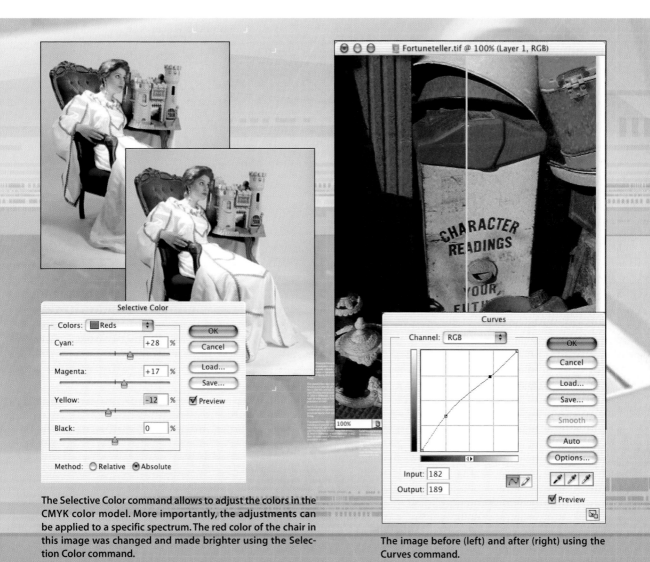

The Selective Color command allows to adjust the colors in the CMYK color model. More importantly, the adjustments can be applied to a specific spectrum. The red color of the chair in this image was changed and made brighter using the Selection Color command.

The image before (left) and after (right) using the Curves command.

STEP BY STEP: FIXING DIGITAL PHOTOGRAPHS

While pictures captured by digital cameras usually don't suit the high-resolution requirements of print publishing, they are more than sufficient for Web design—and for Web designers who don't have the budget for photo shoots, digital cameras are essential. They also free designers from copyright issues involved with stock photo CDs, which are not always royalty-free and sometimes have restrictions for online publishing. So it's no wonder that the digital camera industry is booming and that digital cameras have become quite affordable.

The biggest problem with digital cameras is that their CCD (which captures the image) creates a digital grain when the shot is not well lit. If you downscale the image and save it as JPEG, this might not be much of an issue, and using the Hue/Saturation and Levels commands may be enough to fix the image. But if the image is used as a background, you have to salvage the picture with a regimen of blurring, sharpening, and blending, as follows. (This trick was developed by Deke McClelland, author of *The Photoshop Bible*.)

1 Adjust the Levels: Almost every picture taken with a digital camera needs some adjustment. Adjusting and balancing the brightness and contrast of an image is best done with the Levels command. The Levels dialog box displays a histogram of the image's highlights and shadows. Slide the black and white triangles to adjust them manually. The most important option is the middle slider, which allows you to change the midtones.

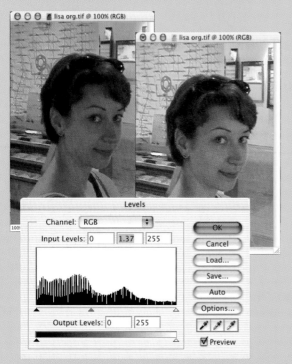

2 Copy the layer by dragging it onto the **New Layer** button at the bottom of the Layers palette (alternatively, select everything and copy and paste it to a new layer). Now use the **Hue/Saturation** command and increase the **Saturation** up to the point where the grain comes out and looks really extreme (move the slider up to between 60 and 80 percent).

3 Smooth the grain with a combination of **Median** and **Gaussian Blur** filters, and enhance the edges by using **Unsharp Mask**. Start with **Filter > Noise > Median** with a radius of 3 pixels; increase this value and reapply the filter until the artifacts are smoothed. (The image will look blurry, but that's okay because you will regain the focus later with the **Unsharp Mask** filter.) But first use **Filter > Blur > Gaussian Blur** with a value of 1 pixel to smooth the image even further. When the edges are completely softened, it's time to regain some of the edges by using **Filter > Sharpen > Unsharp Mask**. Set the **Radius** to the same value that you used in the **Gaussian Blur** filter and set the Amount to 500 percent. This exaggerated value compensates for the extensive blurring that happened earlier. The result will probably look different from what you had expected. That will change, however, when you blend the two layers.

4 Blend the layers and add finishing touches: By lowering the **Opacity** level in the **Layers** palette, you can blend the two layers. The actual opacity can be 5 percent or even less if the original photo was in good shape. Problem images require higher **Opacity** levels but it should not exceed 50 percent. It's easy to get carried away and end up with an image that looks artificial. The goal is to get a natural-looking image that doesn't reveal its digital origin. Flatten the layers when you're done and apply color and focus adjustments as you would if this image had been scanned from film.

STEP BY STEP: CHANGING THE COLOR OF A SOLID-COLORED AREA

One of the most common tasks you'll have to perform when designing Web pages is changing the colors in your design. There are several scenarios you might run into. You might have to change the color of a shape layer, for example, but you can easily do that by double-clicking on the Shape Layer thumbnail and then picking a new color in the Color Picker. A little bit more difficult is changing the color of a rasterized layer.

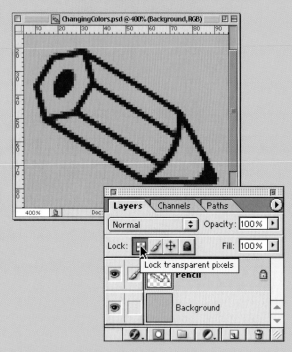

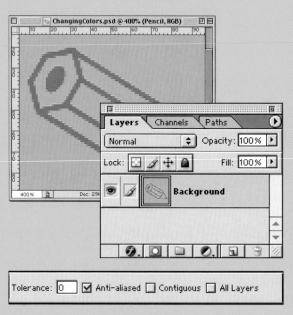

1 If you have a solid-colored area that is on its own layer, activate the layer that contains the object you want to color. Make sure the **Lock transparent pixels** option is selected in the **Layers** palette.

3 Choose the **Paint Bucket** tool and click on the graphic; it will be filled with the new color. If the graphic is on the same layer, the process is slightly different. To try this, merge all the layers using the palette pop-up. Use the Anti-aliased option, otherwise the pixels at the edges will not be filled. But even with the Anti-aliased option, the result might not be as good as before.

2 Double-click on the color field in the toolbox to open the **Color Picker**, and change the color. Select the **Only Web Colors** option if you want to select a color from the Web color palette. If you want to start out with the color of your object, use the **Eyedropper** tool and click in the image (it now becomes the foreground color in the toolbox). Most importantly: make sure that the **Anti-aliased** and **Contiguous** option are deactivated.

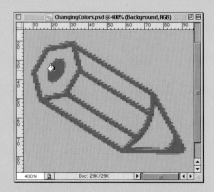

STEP BY STEP: REPLACING THE COLOR OF AN OBJECT

If you come from the world of desktop publishing, this technique may be completely new to you, but if you do Web design, this trick can save you the cost of an entire photo shoot, since it lets you reuse one element of a photo over and over again. For example, imagine that you want to use paper clips in different colors as navigational elements. One way to do this would be to get these paper clips and have them shot by a photographer (well, with paper clips you could also simply scan them, but this is just an example, so bear with me). Alternatively, you could use an element from a stock art photo CD and change its color.

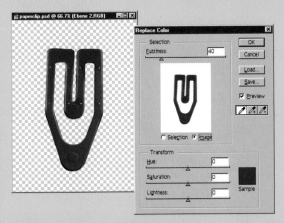

1 To change the color of an object, such as this paper clip, choose **Image > Adjustments > Replace Color**. Select the **Preview** option in the **Replace Color** dialog.

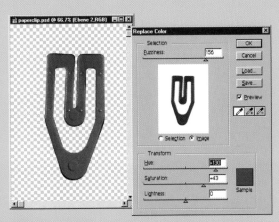

2 Using the Eyedropper tool, select a hue that is between the darkest and lightest color value of the object. Then use the Fuzziness slider to adjust the tolerance (in this case it was changed to 156). You can select additional colors by using the Eyedropper tool with the plus sign until the entire object is selected.

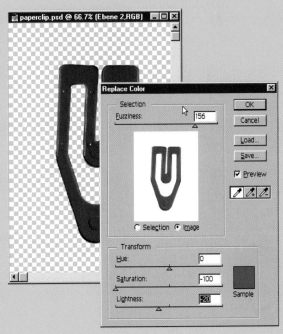

3 Once all the colors in the paper clip are selected, use the Hue slider to shift through the color spectrum. If the preview is activated, you can see how the changes affect your original image. To get white and black, and various levels of gray, set the Saturation slider to -100. You can then set the brightness of the black (to gray) with the Lightness slider.

Compositing and Designing

Many Web sites use a photocomposition as an eye-catcher, including some graphics, solid-colored areas, and text. You create a photocomposition in Photoshop by stacking layers on top of each other and then having them fade into each other, blending the colors. You don't need to be a Photoshop whiz to master these techniques, but you do need to know the basics of the Layers palette.

WORKING WITH THE LAYERS PALETTE

You can open the Layers palette via **Window > Show Layers**. When you start a new document, you will usually see only one layer (the background layer), but as soon as you paste something from the clipboard into your new document, it becomes an additional layer. You can easily see the layers because each layer displays a little thumbnail of the layer content. You can also use the **Layers** pop-up menu, accessed from the triangle in the upper-right corner of the palette, to create new layers. A third way to create a layer is by clicking the **Create New Layer** button at the bottom of the palette. You can hide a layer or make it visible with a click on the eye icon next to the layer listing.

Moving and positioning layers: You can arrange your layers using the **Move** tool, which is located in the upper-right corner of the toolbox. First activate the layer in the **Layers** palette, then select the **Move** tool, click on the image, and drag the layer to the desired position in the palette. To move several layers at once so they keep their relative position, click in the second column of the **Layers** palette (next to the eye icon) and a chain icon should appear. Now the layer is linked to the currently selected layer and you can treat the two layers as a group.

If a new layer is larger than your background layer, it won't get truncated if you move it outside the document area. Even if you flatten multiple layers to one layer, they will keep the measurements of the largest one. Since those hidden image areas can add to your file size, you may want to crop some of your layers to save on memory and disk space. To do that, use the **Crop** tool to select the entire image, then double-click inside the rectangle and all your layers will be cropped.

The Layers palette with the different types of layers (from top to bottom): Gradient, Pattern and Color (with a shape layer mask). Beneath that is an adjustment layer and the background (image)

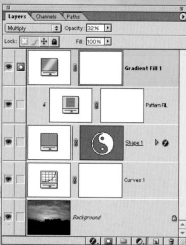

There are different previews available in the Layers palette. To switch among them, select Layers Palette Options from the palette's pop-up menu. You can select one of three preview sizes or you can turn off the preview altogether.

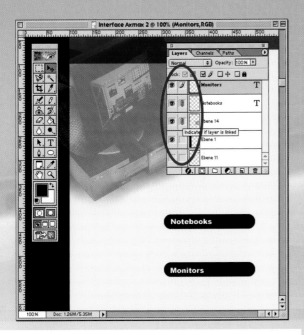

In order to move several layers at once, click on the Link icon in the Layers palette.

Selecting layers quickly: If you work with the **Layers** palette frequently, sooner or later you will find it tedious to have to select a layer in the palette before you can move and drag it. This process is not very intuitive, especially if you have used a graphics program such as Adobe Illustrator where you can simply click on an object to make it active. You won't find the same convenience in Photoshop, but you will find something that comes close: If you select the **Move** tool and hold down Command (Mac) or Ctrl (Windows) and click on the object you want to move, Photoshop will automatically select the object's layer. The currently activated layer will be displayed at the top of the document window.

Sometimes there are just too many layers on top of one another, which makes it hard for you (and for Photoshop) to be clear about which layer you want. In this case, select the **Move** tool, Control-click (Mac) or right-click (Windows) in the image, and choose the layer you want from the floating context-sensitive menu that appears; in this case, it's a list that identifies all of the layers that contain pixels under the current pointer location. Context-sensitive menus are available for almost all of Photoshop tools. If you're

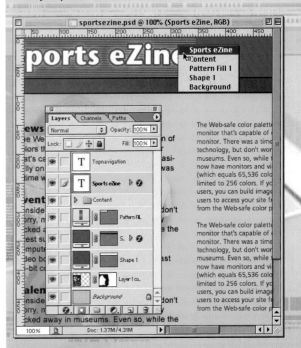

Control-click (Mac) or right-click (Windows) in the image, and choose the layer you want from the context-sensitive menu.

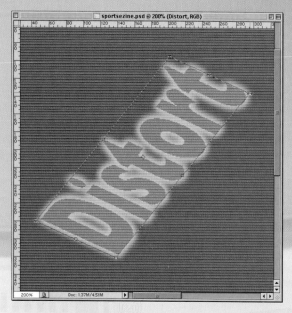

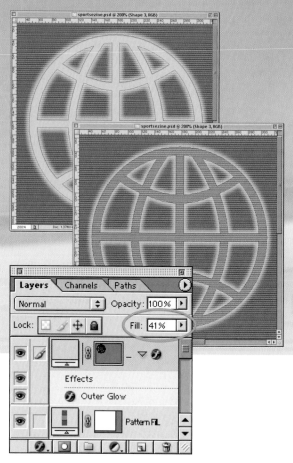

With the Free Transform command, a layer can be distorted in any way from scaling to skewing.

using the **Pencil** or **Paintbrush** tool, for example, you can Control- or right-click to select a different brush shape and size, as well as select a blending mode.

Scaling, rotating, and skewing a layer: If all you want to do is change the size of one layer, use **Edit > Free Transform**, which allows you to not only scale the layer, but also rotate and skew it. To scale a layer, move one of the corners or side handles (for proportional scaling, hold the Shift key). You can rotate the layer by bringing the cursor close to the frame (not the handles), and when the cursor becomes a bent arrow, click and rotate the layer. Skew a layer by pressing Command (Mac) or Ctrl (Windows) and dragging one of the corners. To finish the task, double-click inside the frame.

Layer Transparency

Layers can have an opacity level of 1% to 100%. You can use the **Opacity** slider in the **Layers** palette to select how much the current layer will be blended with the layers underneath it.

In order to make a layer transparent without affecting the layer effects, use the Fill slider.

Partial transparency with layer masks: Sometimes you want to make a layer only partially transparent—this is where you can use layer masks. To add a layer mask to a layer, select the layer and either choose **Layer > Add Layer Mask > Reveal All**, or click on the **Add Layer Mask** button in the **Layers** palette (the second from the left). A new (white) area should appear next to the layer thumbnail in the palette. You will see a chain symbol between the icons, which works just the same as it does with linked layers. Click on the symbol to group or ungroup the layer mask and the layer. Ungrouping the layer mask allows you to move the layer mask independently from the layer.

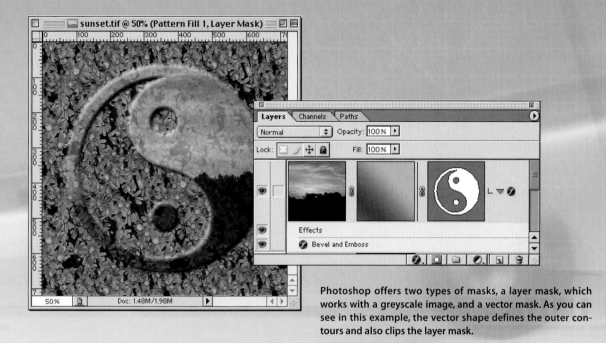

Photoshop offers two types of masks, a layer mask, which works with a greyscale image, and a vector mask. As you can see in this example, the vector shape defines the outer contours and also clips the layer mask.

To make part of your layer transparent, select the **Brush** tool (or any other appropriate tool), click on the layer mask icon in the palette (it should acquire a heavier border and the color fields in the toolbox should switch to black and white) and start painting onto the layer mask. To see any effect, you have to use the right color: Black represents 100% transparency; if you want to make parts of your image transparent, be sure you select black when painting. The inverse is also true: If some parts of the layer are too transparent, you can use white to make them more visible. By the way, you can view the layer mask by clicking on the icon in the palette while pressing the Command (Mac) or Alt (Windows) key. This can come in handy when placing text in the layer mask.

Fill opacity: Adobe introduced layer effects to make it easy to create standard effects like drop shadows and glows. But because the Opacity command affects the entire layer, including layer effects, Adobe added a second opacity command: the Fill command, which makes the content of the layer transparent without affecting the layer effects. This is important if, for example, you want to create a glass effect in which the layer is supposed to be semitransparent but the shadow that this object might cast is unaffected.

Preserving the transparent areas of a layer: For many design tasks that involve layers, you may want to leave the transparent parts untouched. To make sure the transparent area is not affected by any filter or command, check the **Lock transparent pixel** check box in the **Layers** palette—everything that is completely transparent will be protected. Let's say, for instance, you want to change the color of an area with the **Fill** command. If the **Lock transparent pixel** option is not selected, the **Fill** command will fill the whole layer, but if it is selected, the color will fill only the part of the layer that has pixels (including any anti-aliased edges).

Blending Layers
The color blending modes are essential for photocompositions. Blending modes are nothing more than

algorithms (mathematical calculations) that determine how the color values of one layer will blend with the color values of the layer beneath. If you used only transparency to blend layers into each other, photo-compositions would be not very exciting because the result would be more or less predictable. But blending modes are like a box of chocolates: You never know what you are going to get. Even after years of using them, sometimes all I can make is an educated guess and often I end up just flipping through the blending modes and trying each one out.

Some blending modes, however, do produce some predictable results. If, for example, you use **Multiply** with a layer that has white areas, they will disappear and show the exact colors of the underlying layer.

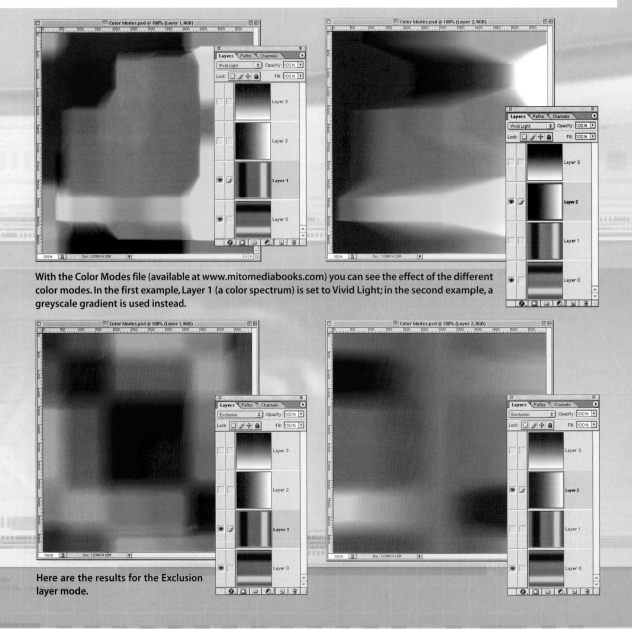

With the Color Modes file (available at www.mitomediabooks.com) you can see the effect of the different color modes. In the first example, Layer 1 (a color spectrum) is set to Vivid Light; in the second example, a greyscale gradient is used instead.

Here are the results for the Exclusion layer mode.

Layer Modes	Effect	How to work with them
Normal **Dissolve**	Doesn't depend on the underlying image.	
Darken **Multiply** **Color Burn** **Linear Burn**	Darkens the underlying image.	Painting with white will not affect the underlying image. Any color darker than white will darken the image. The exception is the Darken mode, which will only affect the underlying image if the color on the active layer is darker than the color in the underlying image. Linear Burn works much like Color Burn but has a greater tendency to make the underlying image pure black.
Lighten **Screen** **Color Dodge** **Linear Dodge**	Lightens the underlying image	Painting with black on an active layer—using one of the lighten modes—will not change the underlying image. Any color that is lighter than black will lighten the underlying image. One exception is the Lighten mode, which will only affect the underlying image if the color on the active layer is lighter than the color in the underlying image. Linear Dodge works much like Color Dodge but has a greater tendency to make the underlying image pure white.
Overlay **Soft Light** **Hard Light** **Vivid Light** **Linear Light** **Pin Light**	Adds contrast to the underlying image.	Painting with anything brighter than 50% gray will brighten the underlying image; anything darker than 50% gray will darken the underlying image. Think of the contrast modes as the combination of the Lighten and Darken modes. Hard Light, for example, is a combination of Multiply and Screen (anything brighter than 50% gray will act like Screen; anything darker, like Multiply). Pin Light mode is a combination of the Darken and Lighten modes. Vivid Light is a combination of Color Dodge and Color Burn; use this to have the underlying colors affected as much as the brightness. Linear Light is the combination of the Linear Dodge and Linear Burn modes, which is useful if you need a higher contrast than what you get with Hard Light or Soft Light.
Difference **Exclusion**	Compares active layer to underlying image.	Difference will subtract either the blend color from the base color or the base color from the blend color, depending on which has the greater brightness value. If you use white, the colors of the underlying image will be inverted; using black will have no effect. Exclusion works similarly but produces less contrast. Using it on white and black has the same effect as Difference.
Hue **Saturation** **Color** **Luminosity**	Applies the qualities (Hue, Saturation, Color, or Luminosity) of the active layer to the underlying layers.	Hue uses the hue of the active layer and blends it with the luminance and saturation of the underlying image. The same principle applies to Saturation. It uses the saturation values of the active layer and blends it with the luminance and hue of the underlying image. Color uses the luminance of the underlying image and combines it with the hue and saturation of the active layer. This is a great way to color monochrome images because the gray levels in the image are preserved. Luminosity keeps the luminosity of the active layer and blends it with the hue and saturation of the underlying image. The effect creates the opposite result of Color.

Anything that is black (or just very dark) will not be affected. This can be useful sometimes, such as when you have a black-and-white scan that you want to merge with the background. Just the opposite is **Screen**, which makes dark colors disappear and show the background while white (and light) areas are unaffected.

Difference is another frequently used blend mode. If you use **Difference** on a layer filled with white, it will invert the colors on the layer beneath. Black (and darker) areas don't do the opposite, in case you were wondering. They darken the picture but mostly keep the colors the same. **Difference** can create interesting color effects; use the **Opacity** slider to watch how the effect changes (with the other blending modes, **Opacity** doesn't really have much of an impact on the look, but with **Difference**, it's completely different).

If blending modes are so unpredictable, you might be wondering how you work with them. I can only give you some suggestions on how I approach a photocomposition. Once I add a new layer I go through all the blending modes and make a mental note of which ones produce an interesting result. Depending on how many blending modes I liked, I just create several copies of the layer and assign to them the blending modes that appealed to me. Then I hide all of them except the first one on which I want to work. For that layer I create a layer mask and start masking everything that I don't like. After I am done with one layer, I activate the next one and work again with a layer mask to determine which parts I want to keep. At the end I have several layers that blend together and create a rich texture or background that I can then use as a starting point.

By default, Photoshop creates a new shape layer every time a new shape is drawn. To add another shape to the currently active layer, the Add option must be selected in the options bar.

SHAPE LAYERS

Before Adobe introduced shape layers, every rectangle, circle, or polygon had to be either drawn with the **Path** tool (and then converted into a selection so that it could be filled) or imported from a graphics program like Illustrator. This was quite a hassle, and it didn't give the designer much flexibility to just experiment in Photoshop. Now with shape layers, designers can work almost as they would in Illustrator.

You create a shape layer using the **Custom Shape** or **Pen** tool. By default, Photoshop creates a new layer every time you create a shape with the **Custom Shape** tool, but you can also draw multiple shapes in a layer and specify how overlapping shapes interact. Select the layer to which you want to add a shape and then choose the **Add**, **Subtract**, **Intersect**, or **Exclude** option in the options bar. If you need to combine several shapes on one layer into one shape, switch to the **Path Component Selection** tool (the mouse arrow) and select all the shapes that you want to combine. You then have the same options that you have with the **Custom Shape** tool, with the addition of the **Combine** button.

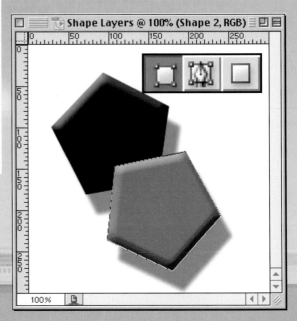

When you create a shape, it is automatically filled with the current foreground color. Since a shape layer is a fill layer linked to a vector mask, you can easily change the fill to a different color, a gradient, or a pattern by editing the shape's fill layer. To change the color of a shape you need only double-click on the shape layer's thumbnail in the **Layers** palette and choose a different color from the color palette that appears. If you want to fill a shape layer with a pattern or gradient, use the commands in **Layer > Change Layer Content**.

You can also edit the shape's vector mask to modify the shape outline and apply a style to the layer. To modify the outline of a shape, click on the vector mask thumbnail of the shape layer in the **Layers** palette or **Paths** palette. You can then use the **Custom Shape** and **Pen** tools to work on the paths, very much like you would work in Illustrator or any other graphics program.

You can also rasterize a shape layer to use a filter on it by choosing **Layer > Rasterize**. If you want to rasterize all vector layers at once, use **Layer > Rasterize > All Layers**.

Photoshop includes a library of custom shapes.

The Preset Manager allows you to create your own favorite selection of shapes.

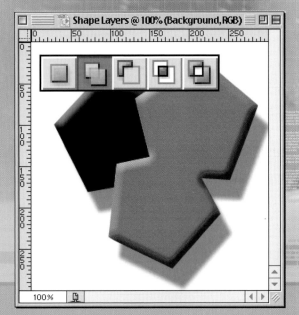

USING ILLUSTRATOR WITH PHOTOSHOP

With Photoshop's ability to work with paths and vectors, you don't need Illustrator at all anymore, except maybe for some particular effect like creating text along a path (and Photoshop even offers the **Warp Text** feature, which can probably handle most of your needs). However, if you need to create more complex vectors graphics you still have to use Illustrator. Fortunately, Adobe has done a remarkable job of making both programs work together.

There are basically three choices when importing vector graphics from Illustrator: They can be imported as pixels, paths, or shape layers. However, these choices are available only if you use the clipboard to copy and paste the element, which requires that you have Illustrator installed on your computer. If you don't, you can convert the Illustrator file only by opening it in Photoshop. Photoshop can open native Illustrator files (they don't need to be in any special format); just use the **Open** command and look for the file on your hard drive. The **Rasterize** dialog box will appear, letting you enter the resolution and dimensions. (The values that are already filled in are the current values of the document, but you can scale an illustration simply by entering new dimensions.) Rasterizing an Illustrator graphic in Photoshop—rather than rasterizing and exporting it from Illustrator—has the advantage that transparent areas stay that way (when converting them in Illustrator they are rendered to white).

Using Illustrator's **Export** command, you can also export an Illustrator file as a Photoshop file with its layers intact. (You probably take this for granted, but it actually wasn't implemented until Illustrator 8.0. Before that, getting multiple layers into Photoshop was labor intensive.) In the **Export** dialog box, select the Photoshop format from the pop-up menu and name the file. In the **Photoshop Options** dialog box that appears, set the resolution to 72 dpi and check the **Write Layers** box.

Rasterizing an EPS: Most graphics programs let you save image files in an editable EPS format, making it

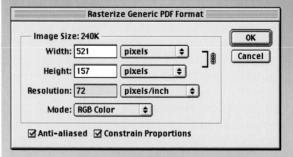

When opening an Illustrator file, Photoshop rasterizes it. Changing the Resolution has no effect on the size at which the illustration is later displayed. To scale an illustration during import, change its dimensions.

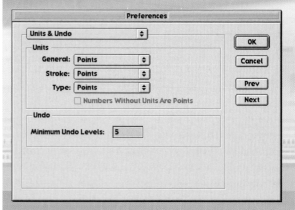

Use points as your unit in Illustrator—every point will translate to one pixel when you're importing an element into Photoshop.

You can even use elements and designs created in a layout program like QuarkXPress or Adobe InDesign and import them into Photoshop. Just save the page as an EPS and open the file in Photoshop.

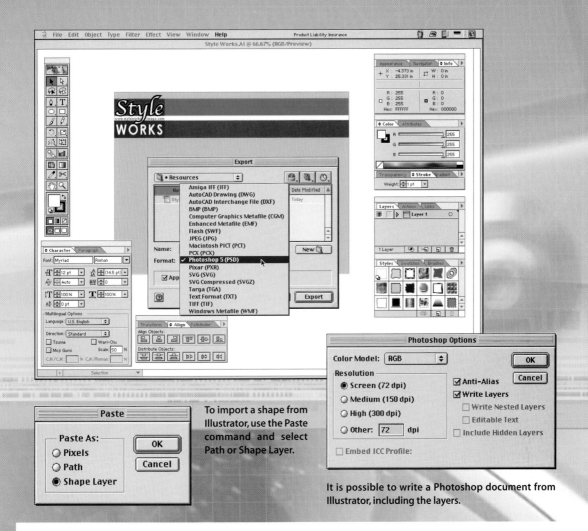

To import a shape from Illustrator, use the Paste command and select Path or Shape Layer.

It is possible to write a Photoshop document from Illustrator, including the layers.

possible to have illustrations generated in one graphics program transfer easily to another. In most cases, you'll find this option listed in the Save dialog box or as an Export command. Photoshop can even interpret an EPS file that was created in QuarkXPress—it doesn't always work, and you may end up with unexpected results, especially if the layout includes both images and text. If you want to rasterize an Illustrator graphic, it is important to design the graphic in Illustrator already in the size that you later need in Photoshop (1:1 scale) because changing the size of a layer in Photoshop compromises its quality. Because one point is equal to one pixel in Photoshop, it's a

good idea to choose points as the general unit in Illustrator (or any other graphics program, for that matter). You'll find these settings in Illustrator in **Edit > Preferences > Units & Undo.** If you'd rather specify something in points, you can always enter "pt" when you create an object using a dialog box. (Press Option (Mac) or Alt (Windows) and click with the tool inside the work area. Illustrator will display a dialog box for numerical entry.) This way, an object created in points in Illustrator will have the same size in pixels in Photoshop.

DESIGNING TEXT

I won't go into much detail on how to work with the **Type** tool. Besides creating labels for buttons, you'll need the **Type** tool only if you want to render some headlines as images or if you need to simulate HTML text for your mock-up. To simulate HTML text, simply draw a text frame with the **Type** tool and set the anti-aliasing to **None**. Other than that, working with this tool is straightforward and explained in the manual.

Filling text with an image: Photoshop's Clipping Groups feature, which allows you to mask the content of one layer with another, is very helpful for creating type that contains a photographic image or a texture. This feature is great for using texture or a photo to fill type because you don't have to convert your text layer to a bitmap layer, and you can still edit the text.

To fill a text layer with the content of a photo layer, the photo layer has to be above the text layer. If that is not the case, then move the layer in the Layers palette by clicking on the layer and dragging it to the right position. To convert the text layer to a **Clipping Group**, bring the cursor over the line between the two layers and press the Option (Mac) or Alt (Windows) key. The cursor will change to two overlapping circles to indicate that you can now click to create a **Clipping Group**.

You'll see the result right away: you can now move the two layers independently using the **Move** tool. To move both layers together, link the two layers by clicking in the second column (next to the eye icon). A chain icon will appear.

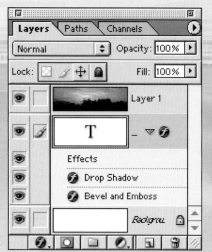
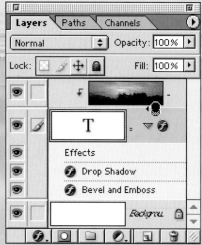

The Clipping Group feature allows Photoshop to use a text layer as a mask. In order to clip an image with a text layer, the image layer needs to be above the text layer. While holding the Alt/Option key, click on the line between the layers.

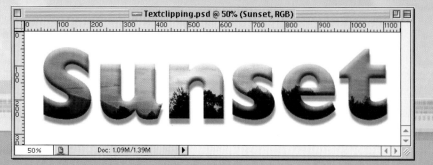

The last feature that I want to bring to your attention is Photoshop´s ability to warp text layers. This allows you to distort a type layer into an arc or a wave. The best part of this feature is that you can change the warp style very easily, freeing you from the need for a graphics program. This feature's only restriction is that it doesn't work with faux bold formatting and fonts that do not include outline data (such as bitmap fonts). To use this feature on a text layer, activate the text layer and then click on the **Warp Text** button in the options bar or choose **Layer > Type > Warp Text**. Select the orientation of the warp effect (horizontal or vertical) and specify the amount of warping and distortion. If you want to change back to the original layer, choose **None** from the **Style** pop-up menu in the **Warp Text** dialog box.

The Warp Text feature in Photoshop allows you to create many text effects that would be difficult to create in a graphics program. The best part is that the text is still editable.

Effects and Tricks

Most Web sites use a photocomposition, some solid-colored areas, and maybe some simple effects like a drop shadow or bevel. These effects used to require a good understanding of Photoshop's Channels and other more advanced features, but since Adobe introduced layer styles, even special effects such as chrome, glass, and plastic are just a couple of clicks away. In this section, I want to show you some popular effects that can be easily modified for your own Web site.

WORKING WITH LAYER STYLES

Adding a layer style is as easy as selecting a layer and choosing a style from the **Layer Style** pop-up in the lower part of the **Layers** palette. You can also add a style by choosing **Layer > Layer Style**. In the left part of the **Layer Style** dialog box that appears is a list of all the effects that can be used. When you select one of the styles in the list, you'll see more details about the effect. You can also change the settings of the styles. One big advantage of layer styles is that they aren't applied permanently—you can modify or remove them at any time. Here's an example of how to create some beveled buttons using layer effects:

1. Create a new layer in the **Layers** palette, and then draw a shape with the **Rectangle** tool (or any other shape tool). Now choose **Layer > Layer Style > Bevel and Emboss** to open the **Layer Style** dialog box. Here

you can adjust light opacity as well as many other parameters.

2. You define how to combine the light reflections with the layers using the **Highlight Mode** pop-up. You should already be familiar with these modes—they are the same ones that are in the **Layers** palette. To see the light reflections clearly, choose **Normal** or **Screen**. You can choose a color for the highlights by clicking on the color field next to the **Highlight Mode** pop-up menu. You can also define a custom value for **Opacity**.

3. For the Shadow Mode, choose **Normal** or **Multiply**. As with the **Highlight Mode**, you can choose a shadow color.

4. Depth and **Size** options set the intensity and width of the bevel. If you're using several objects with layer effects, select the **Use Global Light** option. This way you can change the effect angle for all the layers at once.

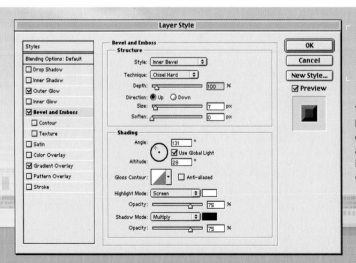

The Layer Style dialog box lists all the available effects on the left side. To activate an effect, you must check it. To edit the effects, select one in the listing.

5. Perhaps the most important settings for **Bevel and Emboss** are in the **Style** pop-up: **Outer Bevel, Inner Bevel, Emboss, Stroke Emboss**, or **Pillow Emboss**. **Outer Bevel** and **Inner Bevel** will produce standard buttons, while **Emboss** will process all the edges, making the button appear to be carved out of the background. This can be a very appealing effect when combined with text. Another great feature is the **Gloss Contour** effect, which is in the **Shading** section of the dialog box. This determines the shape of the bevel.

If you know that you will need a specific combination of styles more than once, save it as a style by clicking on **New Style** in the **Layer Style** dialog box. All the styles are listed in the **Styles** palette (**Window > Styles**) and you can switch styles by simply clicking on them. Often after applying a style to a layer you'll want to scale it using **Layer > Layer Style > Scale Effects**. Every style can look different depending on whether you apply it to a thick or thin graphic, a bold or light-weighted typeface, or a large or small photo.

To deactivate an individual style, click the eye icon next to the style name in the **Layers** palette or double-click the layer effect in the **Layers** palette and the **Layer Style** dialog box will appear. Here you can uncheck the effect to deactivate it, but there is even a quicker way if you need to delete just one style: Click the effect in the menu while pressing the Option (Mac) or Alt (Windows) key.

To customize or fine-tune the appearance of layer styles, you can convert the layer styles to regular image layers. This allows you to enhance that layer by applying filters or painting directly onto the layer. Converting a layer with its effects is a one-way process (you can't go back and change any of the layer styles), so you want to do this only with a copy of the layer. Choose **Layer > Layer Style > Create Layers** and the effects will be converted to individual layers. The original layer becomes the clipping layer of a clipping group.

CHROME

You can do a lot more with layer styles. With a little know-how you can easily create chrome, metal, and plastic effects. These are probably not effects that you need every day as a Web designer, but they are a good way to learn how to work with layer styles to create your own effects. To follow this example, just create a new document and place a bold typeface (such as 48-point Gill Sans or Helvetica) on a layer and give it a drop shadow.

Bevels like this one would not be possible without the Contour effect: it lets you assign a separate bevel shape to the contour.

Bevel and Emboss
Structure

Style: Inner Bevel

Technique: Chisel Hard

Depth: 100 %

Direction: ● Up ○ Down

Size: 4 px

Soften: 0 px

Shading

Angle: 120 °

☑ Use Global Light

Altitude: 30 °

Gloss Contour: ☑ Anti-aliased

Highlight Mode: Screen

Opacity: 75 %

Shadow Mode: Multiply

Opacity: 75 %

Contour
Elements

Contour: ☑ Anti-aliased

Range: 50 %

Color Overlay
Color

Blend Mode: Screen

Opacity: 100 %

Gradient Overlay
Gradient

Blend Mode: Normal

Opacity: 100 %

Gradient: ☐ Reverse

Style: Linear ☑ Align with Layer

Angle: 138 °

Scale: 100 %

Here is an overview of all the styles that make up the chrome effect.

The next step is to give the layer a bevel (**Layer > Styles > Bevel and Emboss**). Use Technique: **Chisel Hard** with a sine-shaped **Gloss Contour**, which will start to give the layer a metallic look. What will make the biggest difference, though, is a grayscale gradient. Select **Gradient Overlay** in the **Styles** list and double-click on the gradient to open the **Gradient Editor**. Here you can switch the **Gradient Type** to **Noise** (keep the **Roughness** at its default setting of 50 percent). Since the gradient still has color in it, you'll need to make it grayscale by selecting the **Restrict Colors** option and switching to **Color Model: HSB**. Now move the white triangle of the **Saturation** slider (S) to the left. This takes all the color out of the gradient. If you just want to make the gradient lighter, you could use the **Brightness** slider (B) and drag the black triangle to the right. The gradient looks best with an angle of 140 degrees. Since chrome often has a slight touch of blue, use a **Color Overlay** style with a bright cyan color. It's important here to set the **Blend Mode** to **Screen**, so the blue tint shows up only in the darker parts of the effect and not in the white highlights.

To get an even more realistic chrome effect, use a texture that gives the reflections more complexity: Fill a new 200-by-200-pixel document (grayscale mode) by choosing **Filter > Noise > Add Noise** and setting the options to **Uniform** and **Monochromatic**. The Amount needs to be very high, and the image (after clicking OK) needs to be blurred by choosing **Filter > Blur > Gaussian Blur** (use a **Radius** greater than 5 pixels). Since there is not much contrast, choose **Image > Adjust > Auto Levels**. Then store the result as a pattern via **Edit > Define Pattern**. This pattern can be used in the layer styles in the **Texture** option (part of **Bevel and Emboss**; use very little **Depth** and scale the texture with **Scale**).

Another style that works great for chrome effects is the **Satin** effect. Try experimenting with a white color and the **Screen** mode. For a contour, experiment with the "Rounded Steps" shape, which is one of the presets. But the most important element of every chrome effect is the **Gloss Contour** in the **Bevel and Emboss**

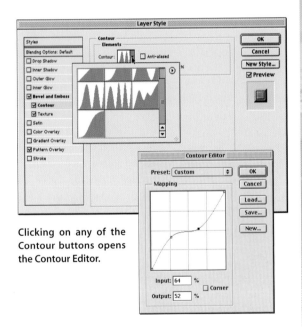

Clicking on any of the Contour buttons opens the Contour Editor.

dialog box. If the chrome doesn't look right, create your own customized **Gloss Contour** by clicking on the thumbnail. The **Contour Editor** will appear, in which you can add points to the curve by clicking on the curve itself, then dragging the points to create several waves.

This image illustrates the power of layer styles. All of these effects, done with layer styles, are from *Adobe Photoshop Elements One-Click Wow,* by Jack Davis and Linnea Dayton, the authors of *The Photoshop Wow! Book.* It's an indispensable book to have if you are interested in mastering layer styles. The book comes with a CD-ROM full of ready-to-use layer styles.

WHITE CHROME TYPE

Here's a step-by-step guide on how to create a white chrome effect that works particularly well for large type or logos, especially for a logo on a splash screen (it won't really work with small elements). I saw this technique in an issue of *Photoshop User* magazine, whose editor, Scott Kelby, writes the *Photoshop Down & Dirty Tricks* books.

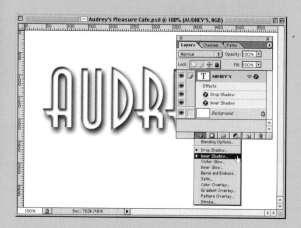

1 Create a new RGB document in Photoshop (for example, 600 by 400 pixels and 72 ppi). In this example, the font I used was ITC Anna (200 pt.). In the **Layers** palette, choose **Drop Shadow** from the **Layer Style** pop-up menu; set the **Distance** to 9 and the **Size** to 13, and click OK to apply. Switch the foreground color to white and fill your type with the foreground color by pressing Option–Delete (Mac) or Alt-Backspace (Windows). Viola! The color of your type has changed to the color of the foreground color. That's a pretty neat trick that can easily be used in a variety of ways.

2 Click on the **Layer Style** pop-up menu and choose **Inner Shadow**. Don't make any adjustments to the default settings—don't click OK yet because we are also going to use the **Satin** style. Choose **Satin** from the **Styles** list on the left to make its options visible. Lower the **Distance** setting to 2 and the **Size** setting to 5, then click on the downward-facing triangle next to the **Contour** setting to bring up the **Contours Library**. Choose the contour (from the default set) that has two steep hills (Ring Double). The type already looks good, but it has the appearance of dark chrome. We are going to change this into a white chrome by selecting the **Anti-aliased** checkbox and deselecting the **Invert** checkbox. Now the type looks like white chrome. Click OK.

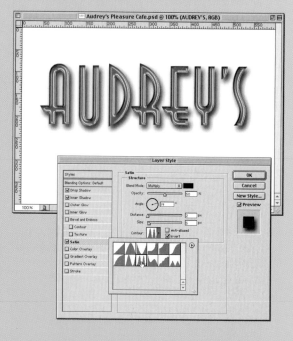

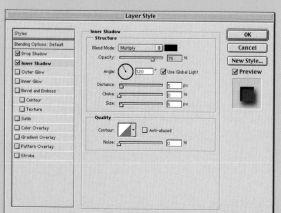

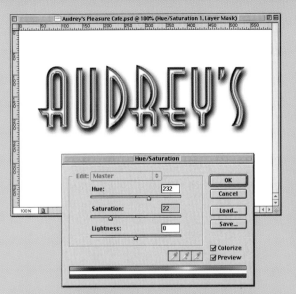

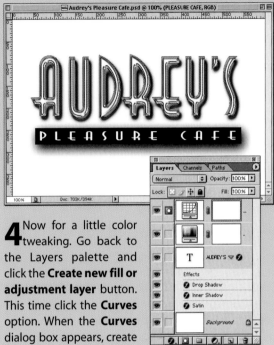

3 Right now you have a good-looking white chrome effect. It would be fine to stop here, but why not bring some color into the equation? Let's start by clicking on the **Create new fill or adjustment layer** button at the bottom of the **Layers** palette (third from the right) and choosing **Hue/Saturation**. When the **Hue/Saturation** dialog box appears, click the **Colorize** checkbox in the lower right of the window, increase the **Hue** to 232, and decrease the **Saturation** to 22. A blue tint has now been applied to your chrome effect. After clicking OK, you can double-click the adjustment layer in the **Layers** palette to bring up the **Hue/Saturation** dialog box whenever you want to adjust your settings.

4 Now for a little color tweaking. Go back to the Layers palette and click the **Create new fill or adjustment layer** button. This time click the **Curves** option. When the **Curves** dialog box appears, create the curve shown in the example here. Click toward the left side of the chart and a black point will appear. Drag that point upward to the position in the example to form the first "slope." Then click at the top of your new curve and a new point will appear. Drag that downward to the position shown. Add one more point to the right and drag it upward, re-creating the curves shown before you click OK. If you want to, you can now merge all the layers into one: Hide the background from view by clicking the eye icon to the left of the background layer. Only your type and adjustment layers are now visible. Now go to the pop-up menu on the top right of your **Layers** palette and choose **Merge Visible** to merge all these layers into one before you make the background layer visible again.

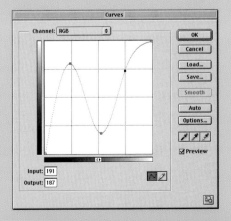

BRUSHED METAL

Finding a texture that doesn't interfere with text and actually enhances the design isn't easy. Sometimes it is easier to create a texture, such as brushed steel, directly in Photoshop. Here's how:

1 Create a new file that measures 100 by 100 pixels. This document needs to be filled with a neutral gray. Add noise with the **Add Noise** filter (**Filter > Noise > Add Noise**). Choose the **Monochromatic** option and use an amount around 10 percent.

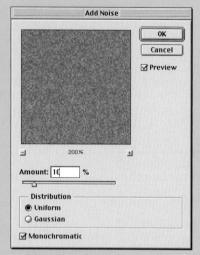

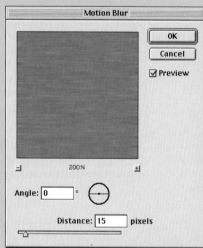

2 With **Motion Blur** (**Filter > Blur > Motion Blur**) the noise will turn into fibers when you're using a blur of 5 to 20 pixels (any angle is OK, though 0 to 20 degrees seems to look the most realistic). Use **Filter > Sharpen > Sharpen** to make the fibers come out more (usually one application of this filter is enough). Lastly, use the **Offset** filter to shift this texture by 50 pixels horizontally and vertically (with the option **Wrap around**) and then use the **Stamp** tool to erase the edges.

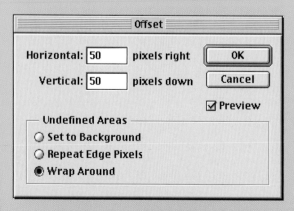

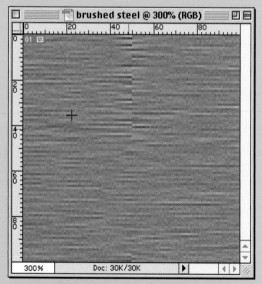

You'll need to fix the edges of the brushed-steel texture, like any other texture.

RUNNING LIGHTS EFFECT

One of the things that make New York so exciting is the lights on the signs on Broadway. You, too, can create the effect of running lights. (This is another inspiration I got from *Photoshop User* magazine.) There are a couple of things that make this technique effective, one of which involves some mathematics. But don't worry, it is just a simple matter of dividing two values.

1 Create a new document (**File > New**) and pick a value for the dimension that is divisible by 10 pixels. Let's make, for example, a 400-by-200-pixel document and fill it with black by selecting a black foreground color and then clicking with the **Paint Bucket** tool on the document.

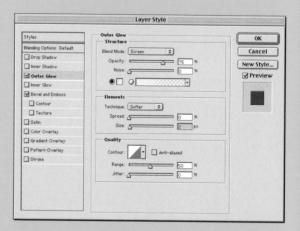

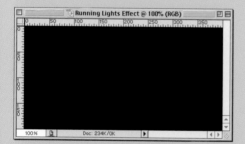

2 We are now designing the light bulb that we are later going to use as a fill pattern. Create another new document (**File > New**) and this time enter 10 by 10 pixels as the dimensions. This time we are not filling the background because we will later want to have the light bulb surrounded by transparent pixels. Therefore, we need to place the light bulb on a new layer. With the **Shape** tool, draw a circle in the middle of this document. The circle shouldn't fill the entire space so that we can later add some **Outer Glow** effect.

3 In order to make the light bulb a pattern you have to first rasterize the shape layer by choosing **Layer > Rasterize > Shape**; otherwise, Photoshop will gray out the **Define Pattern** command. Hide the background layer by clicking the eye icon so that we can later use layer effects on the light bulbs. Now try this little trick to keep the shape layer and still be able to define a pattern: just select the background layer (which is a pixel layer) and Photoshop will allow you to use **Edit > Define Pattern**.

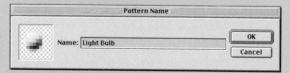

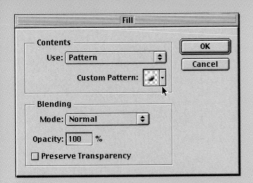

4 After you have named that pattern, switch to the main document and create a new, empty layer. Fill this layer with the light bulb pattern by choosing **Edit > Fill** and then choosing **Use Pattern**. In the **Choose Pattern** menu, select the pattern that you saved earlier. Your document should now be filled with light bulbs. Next, apply the **Outer Glow** and the **Bevel and Emboss styles**.

6 Now start typing your text (black on white) in the document. Since the document is so small, you have to use a small font size. It's also very important that you set the anti-aliasing method to None. That's right! No faded edges. We need clear and crisp contours! You can already see what fonts might work better than others because of the different font thickness. I picked an Arial font for this example, but this technique also produces nice results with a smaller font size.

5 We now need to create the text that is going to mask a portion of the lights. Since we need to do this in another document, create a new document, but this time the dimensions are determined by our target document and our pattern document size. The formula is "Final Document" divided by "Pattern Size." In our case, this is 200 by 400 pixels divided by 10 pixels, which leaves us with a text document size of 20 by 40 pixels.

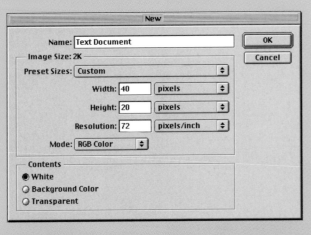

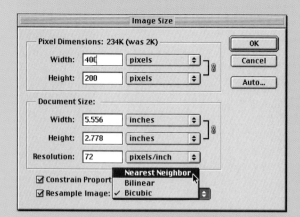

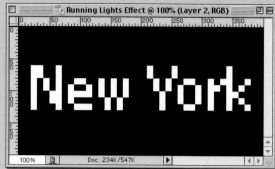

7 After placing the text, we need to flatten the image to rasterize the text layer. Now scale the image to the size of the other document. Use **Image > Image Size** and—most importantly—select the **Resample Image: Nearest Neighbor** option. This will ensure that no anti-aliased edges will appear after the scaling (as they usually do with the default setting of **Bicubic**). The last step before copying this document over to the other is to invert it so that we actually have white text on a black (**Image > Adjustments > Invert**).

You are basically done—unless you want to also animate the lights. If you want to animate the running lights, working with a layer mask is not the best way. Instead of using a layer mask, paste the contents of the clipboard into the document as a regular layer. With the **Multiply** mode, you can blend out all the unwanted lights. To animate the lights, you could just keep pasting different layers into the document and then switch among them in ImageReady.

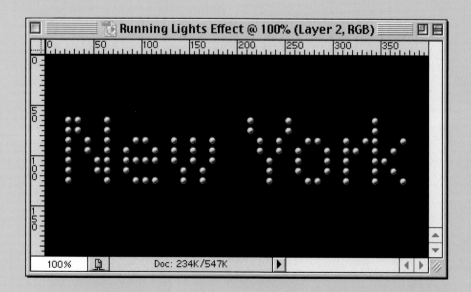

EFFECTS FILTERS

With layer styles, creating special effects in Photoshop has never been easier. However, there are many Photoshop plug-ins available that do the most amazing things.

Alien Skin Splat!

Splat! is Alien Skin Software's latest addition to its Photoshop plug-in line. The interface looks very much like Alien Skin's Eye Candy 4000 interface, but Splat's approach is different. Splat comes with 200 MB of frames, textures, edges, borders, and more that can be applied to your image. Here are some of the effects:

- Frame adds mattes and frames to any photo or rectangle. Included in the package are 100 frames that include things like wood frames, Dover, and geometric borders.
- Resurface allows you to choose and apply one of 100 high-resolution surface textures, including paper, concrete, leather, stone, metal, and wood.

- Edges adds decorative edge effects such as torn paper and pixelated edges to your image. This effect also works great with text.
- Fill Stamp fills any selection with objects. For example, you could have text filled with leaves or buttons. These stamps can be adapted to any shape, can tile seamlessly, and can be colorized to match your image.
- Border Stamp does the same thing as Fill Stamp, except that it applies the stamp to a border.
- Patchwork re-creates images as mosaics. There are only four variations: ASCII text art; light pegs (which can be used to create the running light board that I showed you before); ceramic tile; and cross-stitch, which looks like woven textile.

Splat can easily apply textures and borders like this leopard frame or these coffee beans to the text.

Below: images can be converted through the Patchwork filter.

Increasing Distortion levels makes the S adhere to the contours created by the surface texture.

Alien Skin Eye Candy 4000

Alien Skin's Eye Candy boasts a huge variety of effects and a simple user interface, making it one of the most popular collections of filters for Photoshop. The 23 filters include a couple of filters that Photoshop also has, such as the Bevel Boss filter. Here are some of the filters that are unique to Eye Candy 4000:

● Antimatter is similar to inverting an image. The difference is that the brightness gets inverted without affecting hue and saturation values. This can be a great effect for inverting a button for a JavaScript rollover.
● The Chrome filters that Eye Candy offers produce even more realistic chrome effects than Photoshop. The main reason for this is that Eye Candy comes with some reflection maps, which are images that are mapped on the selection, which greatly improves the effect.
● The Corona filter creates solar flares, gaseous clouds, and other astronomical effects.
● The Drip filter turns text and images into dripping paintings.

● The Fire filter lets you create flamelike effects. You can also choose the color scheme.
● With the Fur Filter you can create some hairy effects: fuzzy texture, wavy curls, and long strands that look like hair.
● The Glass filter makes it easy to simulate clear and colored glass. Eye Candy simulates refraction, light filtering, and light reflection, among many other commands.
● The Marble Filter can be used to create marble textures that can be seamlessly tiled.
● The Jiggle filter creates randomly spaced bubbling and distorts the image.

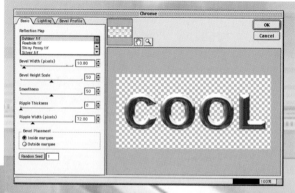

The Fire filter lets you create flamelike effects and the Drip filter turns text and images into dripping paintings. Here is also an example of the Smoke filter and the Jiggle filter, which creates randomly spaced bubbling that distorts the image.

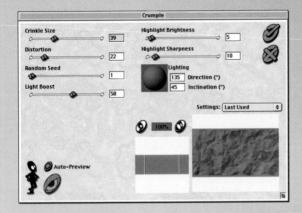

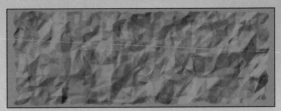

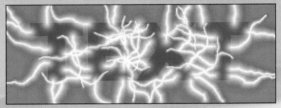

These are just some of the filters that ship with Xenofex: Crumble, Electrify, Distress and Television.

Alien Skin Xenofex

Alien Skin's Xenofex is a collection of 16 filters for Photoshop (all of them in the Alien Skin interface design). Some of the effects include Crumple, which gives a layer the look of crumpled paper, and Television, which gives an image the appearance of being viewed on a television screen. Many filters can create some interesting background images or logos. Other effects, such as the Electrify filter, can make for some nice animations. One filter even simulates the stain left by a coffee cup.

Here's a list of Xenofex's filters:

- Baked Earth creates the appearance of dried and cracked earth.
- Constellation re-creates the image as little points of lights (think star constellation) and even provides a range of kaleidoscopic textures and effects.
- Crumple simulates paper that has been crushed and then partially flattened out again.
- Distress makes the edges of your selection look like they have aged and crumbled away.
- Electrify creates bolts of electricity that branch out from the edges of your selection.
- Flag allows you to map artwork on windblown flags and banners.
- Lightning will create a thunderstorm with lightning in which you can control the length, branching, spread, and color of the lightning.

- Little Fluffy Clouds creates cloud shapes and cloud-like effects.
- Origami will cut your selection into small triangles and swap them, creating the appearance of folded paper.
- Puzzle makes every image look like it's a jigsaw puzzle.
- Shatter breaks up the image like the reflection in a broken mirror.
- Shower Door is a distortion filter that simulates how your image would look viewed through a shower door.
- Television makes your image look like it is viewed on an old television.

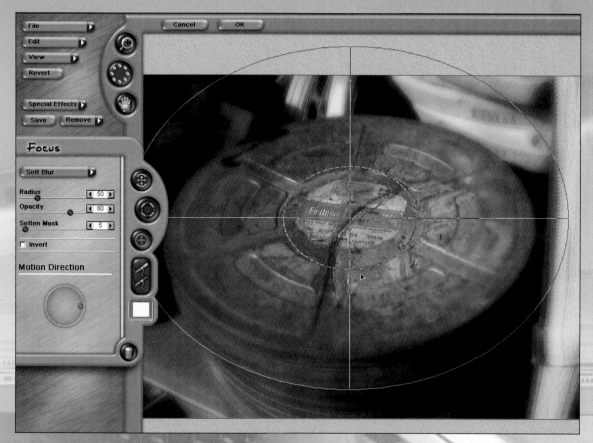

Among its many filters, DreamSuite offers a variety of Blur filters. With the Soft Blur filter, for example, you can create a depth of field effect, which is especially interesting for photographers working with digital cameras.

Auto FX DreamSuite

Over the years I have seen many Photoshop plug-ins, but very few have impressed me as much as Auto FX Software's DreamSuite. Sure, the DreamSuite plug-in is among the more expensive plug-ins, but DreamSuite is more like a program that disguises itself as a Photoshop plug-in. This becomes very clear the first time you start the plug-in because it takes over the entire screen. The interface makes it fun to toy around with the images, even though it's sometimes hard to find all the relevant values. But once you take the time to familiarize yourself with the interface, you will be amazed what you can do with this plug-in.

Here's what I think are DreamSuite's best filters:

- 35mm Frames puts your photos in 35mm slides. You can even create collages of your work—a useful feature when creating a Web site for a photographer or an image gallery.
- Instamatic surrounds your photo with a photorealistic instamatic frame.
- Chisel will create a bevel effect that goes far beyond what you can do with Photoshop's layer styles, since Chisel lets you apply hammered, chipped, and dented textures.

Here's an example of the Liquid Metal filter (Gold) and the Dimension X filter, which creates different bevels with glassy reflections.

- Liquid Metal is a collection of metals like chrome, liquid mercury, and melted gold.
- Crackle simulates photorealistic aged-photo cracks and crackled surfaces.
- Metal Mixer blends metal surfaces together, which is useful in creating any metallic surface.
- Crease lets you bend and crease a photo. DreamSuite will "fold" the image along a line that you paint into the image.
- Photo Border will stylize borders around your photo.
- Cubism adds artistic cubed shapes to photos and backgrounds.
- Photo Depth adds depth to photos by fraying, denting and, crimping.
- Deckle rips and tears your photos to give them a torn deckled crimping.
- Photo Tone will create blended sepia tones, focal glows, and mottled backgrounds.
- Dimension X offers a dozen unique depth bevels, shading, and glassy reflections.
- Putty allows you to bend, twist, enlarge, push, reshape, squish, and re-form your image with Bezier tools.
- Focus simulates soft focus, zoom, rotated, and motion focus effects. This filter is perfect to add depth of field to digital images.
- Ripple creates photorealistic ripples, waves, and water surfaces.
- Hot Stamp adds blends and melded glows to type and graphics.
- Tape offers several types of masking tape, including transparent, duct, and sports.

custom made furniture
We make furniture for your home or office

individual design
You have total control of how it looks

outstanding quality
By using the best materials and craftsmen

TUTORIAL: CREATING A PHOTOCOMPOSITION

Many Web site designs are a combination of one or more photos and graphical elements. In this tutorial I'll show you some of the basic techniques for working with layers and layer masks to create such photocompositions.

1 Create a new document that is 630 by 440 pixels. The design is compact, almost like a CD-ROM interface, because the Web site doesn't have much content to display, and what content there is will later appear in a frame.

If you paste the images into the new document, they will be placed on a new layer automatically. If you use the Free Transform command, the layers are scaled and arranged.

2 The background is composed of four images. You can import the images for the photocomposition by opening the images and drag them with the Layer Select tool over to the other document, or you can import them by selecting everything (**Select > Select All**) and copying to the clipboard. When it's pasted into a new document, the image will automatically be placed on a new layer. Since all the images are too big, they need to be scaled and placed with **Edit > Free Transform**.

The photocomposition consists of four images. The photos were taken by Tom Behrens.

3 You'll need to use layer masks to blend the four layers into each other. To create a layer mask for an activated layer, use the **Layer > Add Layer Mask > Reveal All** command. Then use the **Brush** tool with the **Airbrush** option and a black foreground color to paint the areas of the layer mask that should blend with the layer below.

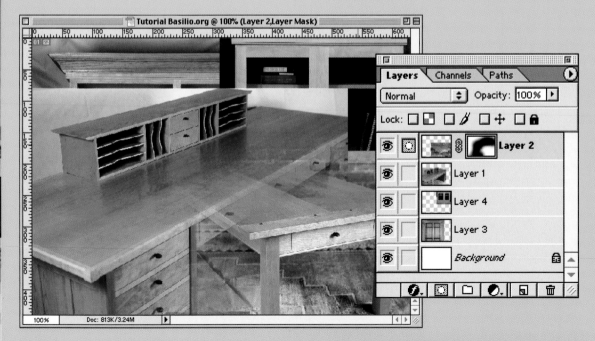

The background layer is filled with orange.

After all the layer masks are in place, change the blending mode to Overlay (and Darken for the layer with the desk).

4 You need to fill the background layer with a color—#FF9933, a bright orange—by clicking on the foreground color in the toolbox and selecting it in the **Color Picker**. Select the background layer and fill it with the **Paint Bucket** tool. Then select all the other layers and change the blending mode to **Overlay** (only the layer with the desk is set to **Darken**). Now, all the layers blend together with the orange background. You can adjust their overall opacity using the **Opacity** slider in the **Layers** palette. You may need to do some more work on other layer masks, because now areas that were covered by the layer above might be visible.

The background is basically finished. To organize the layers, create a new layer set by clicking on the folder icon at the bottom of the Layers palette. Drag all the layers into this folder.

5 Lastly, you'll create the text layers and buttons. For the text layers, use the **Type** tool and click on the document. Some of the text layers use the **Outer Glow** effect so that they'll stand out more. Create the navigation buttons at the top and the bottom by drawing the shapes on their own layer with the **Rectangle** tool (the blue color is #333366, the brown #660000).

In the final Web site, the text was animated with GoLive's **Open DHTML Timeline Editor**. If you want to experiment with this feature, you can take advantage of a new command that GoLive offers: **Photoshop layers to floating boxes**. To do this, save a copy of the file, delete all the unnecessary layers (the buttons, for example), and flatten the images with the background color. GoLive will place every one of the text layers in a new layer automatically so that they're ready to be animated.

You can download the files for this tutorial (and the others in this book) at www.mitomediabooks.com.

If you're interested in seeing the final result, check out www.basilio.org.

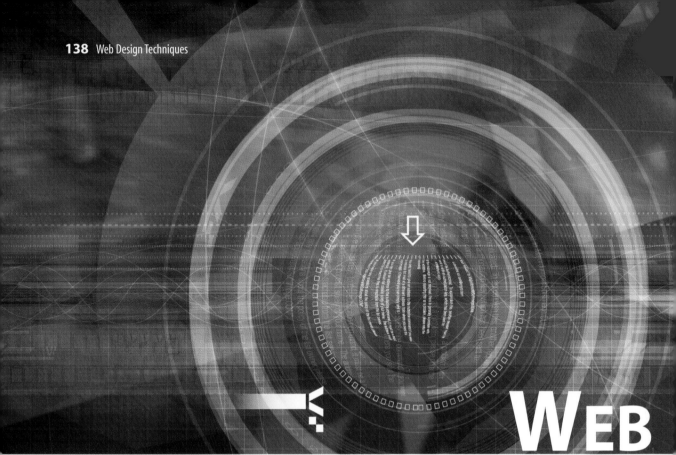

Illustration: **Bradley Grosh/Antony Kyriazis** from the CD **Fuse**

A4
ᙧO∃ᒐTITLE03

DESIGN TECHNIQUES

I remember the first time I saw a Web site that used a sidebar for navigation. It took me quite some time to figure out how it was done; I finally realized that it was a background image. Not long after that, Web sites with sidebars were popping up everywhere; it seemed that every site on the Internet was using them. Over the years, Web designers have come up with different techniques to make the best of the limitations that HTML imposes on them. This section of the book gathers all these tricks. From creating seamless background tiles to GIF animation to working with the Web-safe Color palette, you will learn everything you need to know to create your own award-winning Web site.

Optimizing Photoshop

Photoshop has come a long way: For years it was the image editing program of choice for print designers, but over the years it has also become the primary tool for many multimedia and Web designers. Because of its "print" history, not all the default settings in Photoshop are optimal for Web designers. In this chapter you will learn how to optimize Photoshop for your work. One day Photoshop might allow us to save different preference settings so all preferences can be changed with the click of a mouse button, but for now we have to do it manually.

OPTIMIZING THE COLOR PICKER

You are probably familiar with Photoshop's **Color Picker,** which you can access by clicking on the colors in the toolbox. This **Color Picker** shows you color values of several color models at once. Choosing colors from the Web–safe Color palette used to be tedious because you had to enter the numerical RGB values, but then in Photoshop 5.5 Adobe introduced a little enhancement that makes it easier to select only

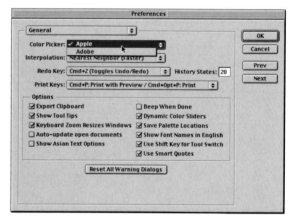

If you want to work with a different color picker, you can switch to Apple (or Windows) in the Preferences dialog box.

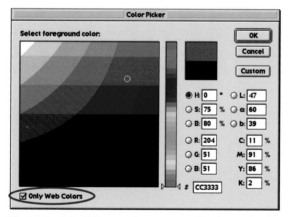

The Adobe Color Picker now features an option that makes the selection of Web-safe colors much easier.

Web–safe colors: the **Only Web Colors** option will limit the color spectrum to the 216 colors of the Web-safe Color palette. Still, if you want to work with an alternative color picker, you can select Apple or Windows (depending on which platform you work in) in the Preferences (**Edit > Preferences > General**).

It's very useful to know that you can change the perspective from which you look at the color spectrum—just click on one of the radio buttons next to the value fields and the spectrum in the Color Picker

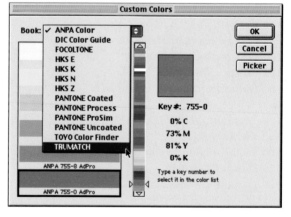

You can select Pantone Colors via the Custom Color Picker.

will change accordingly. And if you ever need to match a color on your Web site with the spot color of a company logo on printed material, for example, click the Custom button in the Color Picker.

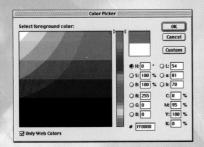
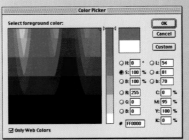
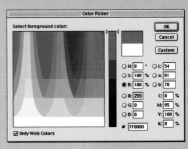
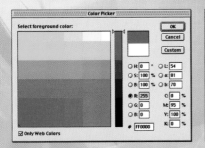
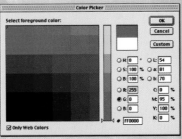
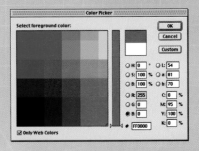
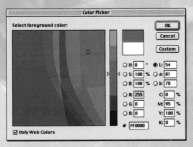
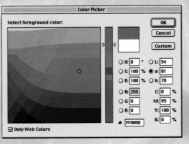
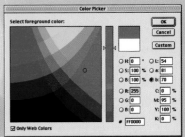

The Adobe Color Picker lets you look at the colors in the spectrum from different perspectives. In the examples above, you always see the color red, but each time with a different option: in the top row (upper-left corner) the Color Picker shows red with respect to Hue. But it can also show the color red to Saturation (upper middle) and Brightness (upper right). In the middle row you see the color as slices of the color cube. The slider next to the Color Picker field represents the edge of the color cube. Last but not least, the bottom row shows red in the LAB color model. The ability to change the angle on the color spectrum is very helpful when you are trying to pick color combinations.

Using the Right Interpolation Mode

When you scale images in Photoshop, the pixels and their colors are adjusted using one of three methods: **Bicubic, Bilinear,** or **Nearest Neighbor**.

Photoshop defaults to the **Bicubic** method because it usually gives you the best result when resizing an image. In this method, Photoshop analyzes the values of adjacent pixels and calculates the middle value between them (when sampling down) or creates additional intermediate colors (when sampling up).

However, the **Bicubic** creation of colors may create a problem if you want to work with GIFs or colors from the Web-safe Color palette. Imagine, for example, that you have created an illustration using only colors from the Web-safe Color palette, but when you resize you

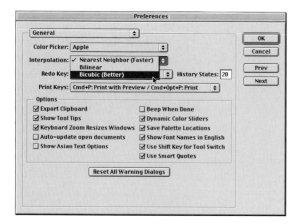

There are several interpolation methods in Photoshop. Although Bicubic is the default setting, it is better to use Nearest Neighbor when creating GIF images.

get a lot of non-Web-safe colors at the edges that will ultimately dither on monitors with 256 colors. Moreover, these additional colors may have a dire impact on how well the image compresses. Therefore, use **Bicubic** only for photos that are to be saved as JPEG images. Any illustration that you plan to publish as a GIF is better resized using the **Nearest Neighbor** color adjustment. If you resize using the **Resize** command, you can select the method in the dialog box, but if you use the **Layer Scale** command, Photoshop automatically uses the default method set in **Preferences**.

The **Bilinear** method works similarly to the **Bicubic** method, but according to the Photoshop manual, it uses a simpler algorithm and is therefore less accurate. Nonetheless, my experience has been that the Bilinear method is better for images with strong contrasts. The side effect of the **Bicubic** method is a blurrier picture, as you can see in the example with the character "T," where it creates something of an aura, while the **Bilinear** method creates a blend. The bottom line is that if you resize a graphic that you later want to save as GIF, use the **Nearest Neighbor** interpolation method so that you end up with fewer additional colors in your image. While this may seem like a minor

point, it is much better to do it right in the beginning than to try to fix it later when you index the image.

THE INFO PALETTE

The **Info** palette shows the color value of a pixel at a specific position of the cursor, updating the position and the value as you move the cursor with the mouse. Open the **Info** palette from the **Window** menu, then click and hold on the cross icon in the bottom-left corner, and select **Pixel** from the pop-up menu. The two eyedropper icons in the upper part of the palette allow you to display two different color modes (RGB and CMYK, for example). You can select the settings for these the same way as you did the units—click on the icon to display the pop-up menu with your choices. Make sure that you select the **Web Color** mode for at least one of the displays; this shows the hexadecimal values (HTML) of a color and also—if the image is indexed—its position within the color look-up table (CLUT; more info on this in the Optimizing and GIF chapters).

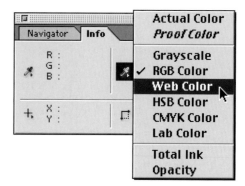

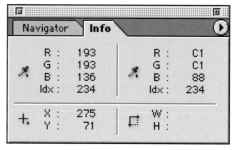

PHOTOSHOP'S INTERPOLATION METHODS

 The original 2-by-2 pixel image (left) was enlarged by 1000 percent using Photoshop's three interpolation methods. The effect can be seen in the three images below : with Bicubic and Bilinear scaling, Photoshop introduces additional colors to smooth out the appearance of your image. Only with Nearest Neighbor does the enlarged result look like the original.

In general, Bicubic gives you the best results—but not necessarily in every case. The top two images here compare Bilinear (on the left) and Bicubic (on the right). You can clearly see that the blurring effect is much stronger in the image scaled with Bicubic, but Bicubic also produces halo effects in images with sharp contrasts. And while Bilinear (bottom left) creates a blend between only two colors, the Bicubic method (bottom right) generates even more colors. My advice: If you are scaling up an image by a fairly large percentage, you are better off using Bilinear for all images where two solid colors are adjacent, as in this example. If you are scaling up by a smaller percentage, you probably won't even notice the difference between the two methods.

Bicubic

Bilinear

Nearest Neighbor

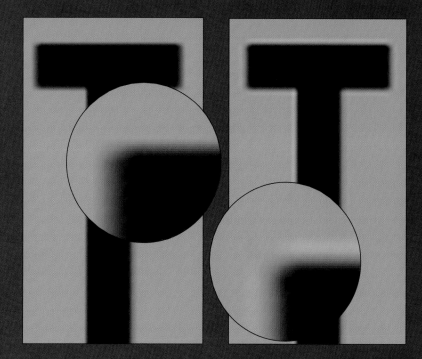

RULERS IN PIXELS

The most important unit in Web and multimedia design is the pixel, so it makes sense to set the preference unit for **Units & Rulers** to pixels. If the ruler is not visible in your document, select **View > Show Ruler** to make it appear.

GUIDES AND GRIDS

Using guides and grids makes it much easier to slice up an image. Slicing is a common technique for exporting pieces of an image and putting them back together in a table using an HTML authoring tool. Depending on the color of your image, you might want to adjust the color of the guides and grids to make them more visible. You can do this in **File > Preferences > Guides & Grid**.

LOADING THE WEB-SAFE COLOR PALETTE

You want to use as many Web-safe colors as possible in your illustration, because you don't want colors to dither on monitors that display only 256 colors. Instead of typing in the color values by hand, it is easier to work with color swatches.

You can open the Web-safe color swatches via **Window > Color Swatches**, and then use the palette menu to replace the standard swatches (**Replace Swatches**). In the dialog box that appears, navigate to the Presets folder in the Color Swatches folder (most of the available color swatches are already listed in this menu and you can select them directly).

To select a color from the Swatches palette, click on it. Saving a color is as simple as clicking on an empty field; the tool switches momentarily to the **Paint Bucket** and fills the swatch with the current foreground color that is selected in the toolbox.

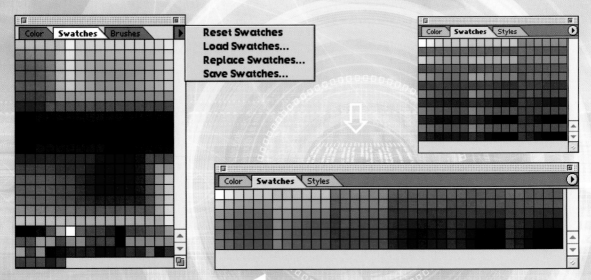

Using Web-safe colors is much easier if you load them into the Swatches palette using the Load Swatches command. You can append or replace the current color swatches with several versions of the Web-safe Color palette. One is called Spectrum (seen here on the left). Since the colors in the Swatches palette always adjust to the width of the palette, you may have to experiment with the width of the palette. For example, in order to see the Spectrum palette as you can see it here, the width is adjusted to 16 swatches. On the right the Web-safe Colors Swatches palette is set to a width of 36 swatches; on the right (top) it is set to 18 swatches. While both widths give you an idea of how the colors relate to each other, the bottom example is clearly more intuitive: every 6-by-6 pixel block represents a slice of the Web-safe color cube.

GAMMA

As you probably know, the brightness of a monitor is measured on a Gamma scale. If you have worked in desktop publishing before, this would have been of little concern to you. After all, the end product is paper, and all that matters is the right calibration of the monitor with respect to that. With Web design this is different; the medium is the monitor, and since Macs and PCs use different Gammas, the image you optimized for one platform may look too bright or too dark on the other. The differences in Gamma between the two platforms is roughly 10 percent (the Macintosh Gamma is 1.8 and the Windows Gamma is 2.2). As a rule of thumb, if you work on a Macintosh make your images a little brighter with **Image > Adjustments > Brightness/Contrast** than you normally would; on a PC make them a little darker.

If you want to have more precise control, you can simulate how your images will look under a different Gamma. Both ImageReady and Photoshop can emulate the Gamma of Macintosh and Windows systems. In Photoshop, use **View > Proof Setup** to switch between **Windows** and **Macintosh RGB**. In ImageReady, use **View > Preview** and choose between **Standard Macintosh Color** and **Standard Windows Color**. An alternative is to set the Gamma to 2.0 so that your images look fine on both platforms. To set the Gamma on a Macintosh, use the **Adobe Gamma Control Panel** and enter 2.0 as your custom desired Gamma value. You can always set the value back by selecting Macintosh Default or Windows Default. On a Windows computer, start Adobe Gamma, located in the Control Panels folder. This will start the **Gamma Wizard** utility, which will take you through the process of calibrating your monitor.

If you work on a Macintosh, make your images a bit brighter (around 10 percent) to make them look good in Windows.

Adobe has its own Gamma Control Panel: this panel guides you step by step through the calibration process. If you want to optimize your images for the Web, you need to preview them with a Macintosh and a Windows Gamma, but instead of switching the Gamma in the control panel, I suggest that you use a custom Gamma value (2.0).

The Actions Palette

The **Actions** palette is a very useful tool for large Web design projects. It allows you to record, and automatically repeat, several commands in sequence. You can even assign an action to a key, allowing you to trigger an action with a single keystroke. Actions are great if you have to convert hundreds of images to GIF or if you have to resize images to a specific size. ImageReady's **Actions** palette is similar to Photoshop's, but there are a couple of differences that you should know about. The most important is that ImageReady's **Droplet** and **Batch** commands are in the **Actions** palette's menu, while Photoshop has them in the **File** menu (**File > Automate**).

Droplets are little scripts that can be placed on the desktop that will automatically process any images that you drag onto them. They still require that the original program be installed and they will start ImageReady automatically if the application is not already open. But other than that, they are self-running and don't require a knowledge of the software. This is very handy if you have repetitive tasks to do. **Droplets** are a great alternative to the **Batch Processing** command. For example, if you have images that need to be resized and that are all spread out in different folders, all you need to do is open the folders in List view, select the images that you want to process, and drag them onto the droplet icon. (Unfortunately, this procedure doesn't work in Windows.) The images are opened automatically and saved in their original folders. This is a little different from the **Batch Processing** command, which will only process all images within a folder. Using droplets, you can perform some standard tasks directly from the desktop without having to open up files in ImageReady.

Photoshop's **Actions** palette has a feature that ImageReady lacks: **Button Mode**. Open the Actions

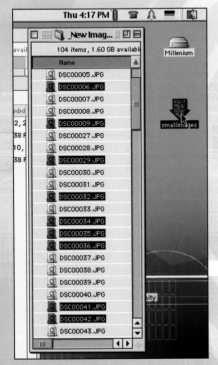

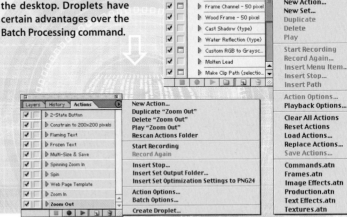

Here you can see how different images in one folder are dragged onto the droplet on the desktop. Droplets have certain advantages over the Batch Processing command.

ImageReady's Actions palette (left) and Photoshop's Actions palette (right) are almost identical in their functionality. However, Photoshop has its Droplet and Batch commands in the File menu, while ImageReady has them in the menu of the Actions palette.

palette from the **Window** menu in Photoshop. To switch to **Button Mode**, click on the palette menu (the triangle in the upper–right corner) and select this command from the options in the menu. If you would like to trigger an action with a keystroke, go back one step (deactivate the **Button Mode**) and then double-click an action to open up the **Action Options** dialog box. Here you can set the color and the key combination for the action, which is particularly helpful when you use the **Actions** palette in **Button Mode.**

To record an action, work with the palette as if it were a tape deck, using the buttons at the bottom of the palette (in Windows, change from **Button Mode** back to **List** view to see these controls). The red circle is for recording, the square stops the current recording, and the triangle plays back the action. Before you start recording, click on the icon that looks like a sheet of paper to create a new action; otherwise, you will record over an existing action.

Toggle Dialog On/Off

When you record an action, you also record the settings in dialog boxes. To use an action flexibly, for different images, it is important to be able to adjust the settings in a dialog box.

For example, if the **Gaussian** blur filter is used in an action, it will probably be necessary to adjust the value for each image individually. To allow for this, you need to open the action by clicking on the little arrow in the **Actions** palette and then toggle the dialog box on (in the second column, next to the checkmarks). Another good example is if you copy a selection to the clipboard and you then want to paste it into a new document. Photoshop usually uses the exact dimensions of the image in the clipboard when creating the new document (which is good). But if this procedure is part of a recorded action, it will use the dimensions of the document that was used when the action was recorded (which is not so good). You can avoid this by locating the

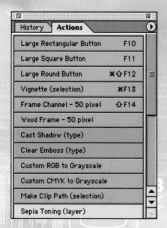

The Actions palette in Button Mode. The actions are represented by buttons instead of in folders. Here's the main difference: in Button Mode, one click is enough to start the action. You also can see the key combination that triggers the action in the Action Options.

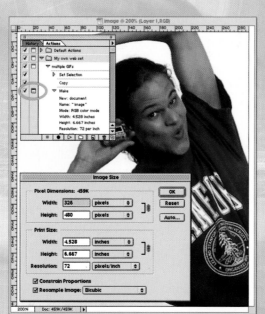

Sometimes when dialog boxes are recorded in an action, you may need to use the "Toggle dialog on/off" switch so that you're able to change some settings. For example, whenever this action plays, it will stop at the New command and display the dialog box to allow the user to set the image size manually. If the dialog weren't toggled on, the Photoshop action would always use the dimensions of the image that was used originally to create this action. So using Toggle is a way to use this action flexibly for images of different sizes.

New command in the action and toggling the dialog on. When you run the action again, Photoshop will open the **Image Size** dialog box, fill in the current dimensions, and wait for you to confirm them. By the way, you can also activate the modal control for all dialog boxes at once within an action. Just click next to the **Toggle** dialog on/off icon beside the action entry in the palette.

Inserting Stops

If you want to create an action that allows you to make some manual changes with one of the tools, such as creating a selection with the **Lasso**, you must insert a stop in the action. You can choose this command from the **Actions** palette menu. Select the step after which you want to insert a stop, and choose **Insert Stop**. In the dialog box that appears, you can enter a comment to remind you what you are supposed to do. You will probably want to write something like "Select the part of the image that you want to copy." Later on, the action will display the dialog box with a Stop button for you to confirm the stop. Once you are done, a click on the **Play** button in the palette will pick up where the action stopped.

Because it might not always be necessary to make changes, you can select the **Allow Continue** option in the **Stop** dialog box. Then, in addition to the **Stop** button, you will get a **Continue** button, which will save you the hassle of clicking the **Play** button in the **Actions** palette.

Recording Paths in Your Action

Paths are an alternative to Alpha channels as a way of creating selections. They can also be used as layer clipping paths or even when making a fill. If you create an action that requires a certain path and that should work with different documents, make sure that you have copied this path to the clipboard before you start recording the action. Suppose you want to create an action that builds a rounded button in a document. Start recording your action, select the path in the **Paths** palette, and use the **Insert Path** command from the **Actions** palette menu (in the upper-right corner of the palette). Now, when you apply the action in another document, the path will be pasted into the document.

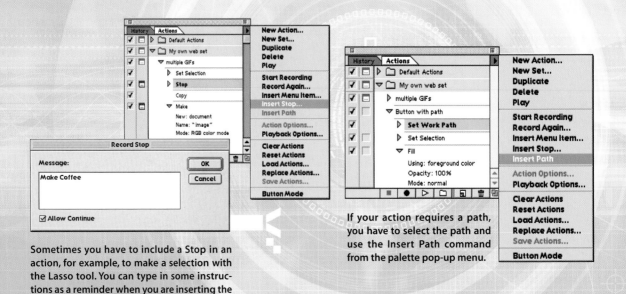

Sometimes you have to include a Stop in an action, for example, to make a selection with the Lasso tool. You can type in some instructions as a reminder when you are inserting the Stop command.

If your action requires a path, you have to select the path and use the Insert Path command from the palette pop-up menu.

Batch Processing

One of the best features of the **Actions** palette is the ability to apply an action to several images automatically. This is called batch processing, and it is particularly useful for Web designers, as they often have to convert several images with the same settings. To activate batch processing, first create the action that you want to apply, then choose **File > Automate > Batch**. The **Batch** dialog box displays all the sets and actions listed in the **Actions** palette. Pick the right set and action and then—by clicking on Choose—select the folder (for Source) containing the images you want to be processed.

The **Override Action "Open" Commands** option is only important if your action actually has an **Open** command. (Note: It is usually better to open an image before you start recording an action.) If you have no embedded **Open** command, this option must be deactivated! I emphasize this because people often overlook this and many have been frustrated because batch processing displays an error alert. By the way, the same is true for the option **Override Action "Save As" Commands** in the **Destination** section. If you have no **Save As** command embedded in the action, don't activate the **Override** option.

If batch processing doesn't work as expected, use the **Log Errors To File** command. This simple text file contains all the events and errors that Photoshop encounters while running the batch script, which will usually give you enough information to fix the problem.

Photoshop also comes with a set of ready-made batch-processing scripts that are all listed in **File > Automate**. One that might be particularly helpful to you is **Web Photo Gallery**. Just select an image folder and this script will generate a main page with all the images as thumbnails. A click on one of the images will bring you to an HTML page with an enlarged version of the image. Best of all, these pages include all the navigational elements to move parallel between the pages and you can even customize the design.

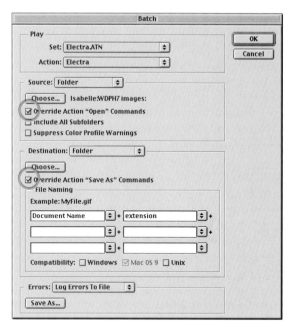

You might think that you're being safe by choosing the Override options regardless of whether the action contains any Open or Save commands, but this will confuse the Batch command and you'll get an error message. Only use the Override option when there is an Open or Save command. For any other errors, check the Error Log to find out where the problem lies.

Web Photo Gallery is a special batch-processing command that makes it easy to display a couple of images on the Internet.

Working with Web-Safe Colors

Color is an essential element of most designs. While using color in print media is relatively easy and uncomplicated, this unfortunately doesn't hold true for Web design. There are numerous pitfalls in using color online: For instance, you have to be prepared to compensate for different color depths on different monitors as well as color shifts between different browsers and different platforms. Problems like these make it a little bit of a challenge to get your Web site to look equally good on every platform. Knowing why color doesn't always equal color, and how you can fix the most common problems is essential to achieving consistently great-looking designs.

COLOR DEPTH

As I've mentioned elsewhere, the most common color problems occur because different monitors offer different color depths. But what does "color depth" actually mean? To answer this question, it helps to look at how a computer stores images in memory.

How Computers Store Information

All computers save information as bits. A bit is the smallest unit of data that a computer recognizes; it means either on or off (or the mathematical equivalent: 1 or 0). All the information on your computer, from software to photographic images, is saved on the hard drive or stored in memory (RAM) in the form of bits. Because you can't do much with just one instance of on or off, a number of bits are combined to form a byte. Eight bits equal one byte, which is able to represent—in different combinations of 1 and 0—up to 16 numbers. This hexadecimal system is represented by the numbers 0 through 9 and the letters A through F.

Color Depth of an Image

To save an image, you have to store the vertical and horizontal position of the pixels as well as their color value. Most image formats use a color depth of 24 bits (or hexadecimal FFFFFF), which allows you to represent 16,777,216 color values (256 levels for each color channel).

Not every monitor or graphics card can display so many colors, so color values may be rounded up or down (when necessary) to the closest equivalent. This causes the color displayed on the monitor to shift. Many graphics software packages try to compensate for this error by using a technique called "dithering" (see the chapter on GIF). But dithering can't change the fact that an image that looked great on your monitor may look terrible on someone else's. The monitor dithering has no permanent effect on the image; the information in the file is still stored with 24 bits of color information, and as soon as you view the image with a graphics card that is capable of displaying all those colors, you'll see the photo in its original quality.

Value	Binary Code	Hexadecimal Code
1	0000	0
2	0001	1
3	0010	2
4	0011	3
5	0100	4
6	0101	5
7	0110	6
8	0111	7
9	1000	8
10	1001	9
11	1010	A
12	1011	B
13	1100	C
14	1101	D
15	1110	E
16	1111	F

WEB-SAFE COLOR PALETTE

The Web-safe Color palette is a collection of colors that look the same on any monitor that's capable of displaying 256 colors—basically on every computer monitor. There was a time when 16-color monitors were considered the latest in technology, but don't worry, most of those machines are safely tucked away in museums. Even so, while the latest surveys show that most home-computer users now have monitors and video boards capable of displaying at least 16-bit color (which equals 65,536 colors), quite a few monitors in the corporate world are still limited to 256 colors. If you expect most of your Web site visitors to be home users, you can build images using thousands of colors, but if you expect some users to access your site from work, you should use as many colors as possible from the Web-safe Color palette.

The Web-safe Color palette actually consists of only 216 colors; the remaining 40 are reserved for the operating system (Windows). Those 216 colors are evenly divided and assigned to different shades and intensities of red, green, and blue. In addition, the palette uses a linear system in which every color value is increased or decreased by 20 percent; this was done largely for convenience, since the resulting hexadecimal values (00, 33, 66, 99, CC, and FF) are easy for programmers to remember. So if you want to create an element in GoLive using a Web-safe color, just use these hexadecimal values (in any combination) and you are sure to get a Web-safe color that won't dither on 256-color monitors.

The linear division of the color space means that the Web-safe Color palette doesn't give you much choice if you want to create, for example, shades of brown or skin tones. The palette would have been much more useful if it had been modeled after the color perception of the human eye; there's no reason not to include different color values, but unfortunately this wasn't considered important enough at the time the palette was devised.

MONITOR COLOR DEPTH

Technically, a computer monitor can display far more than 16 million colors; it's simply a question of how much VRAM (Video RAM) is installed in the graphics card—it also depends on the video card's ability to handle more than 24-bit display. Since the human eye can't distinguish this kind of subtlety anyway, 32-bit video cards use the additional 8 bits to address a transparency channel, also known as Alpha channel.

Bits	Colors
1 Bit	2
2 Bit	4
4 Bit	16
8 Bit	256
16 Bit	65,536
24 Bit	16,777,216
32 Bit	4,294,967,296

THE WEB-SAFE COLOR PALETTE SEEN AS A CUBE

You often see the Web-safe Color palette presented as a cube in which red, green, and blue are placed at three opposite corners. Cyan, magenta, and yellow are dropped in between those colors, and white and black take up the remaining two corners. Most books show the cube in six slices, which, in my opinion, isn't very helpful, because it's very difficult to see the relation of the colors. If you pick a color and want to find a related color, you have to locate it in another slice. Even though this isn't very difficult, it isn't natural either, and it takes up a lot of time.

I wanted to find a way of showing the relationship that each color has to its neighbor, as well as making it easy to find colors with the same quality (light, dark, pastel, and so on). While searching for this new color organization (which I did back in 1997; I published the first edition of this book in 1998), I realized that the best solution was basically to dismantle the color cube rather than slice it. This approach has many advantages: First, it shows the whole spectrum with all the colors and their relationships. Second, it is sorted by brightness and luminance, which makes it a breeze to pick, for instance, two pastel colors with the same quality. I call this the Unwrapped Color Cube chart.

The Web color table, shown as a cube. The eight corners of the cube are occupied as follows: Three corners show the basic colors Red, Green and Blue. Their complementary colors Cyan, Magenta and Yellow are placed on opposite corners. Black and White occupy the remaining two corners. My preferred Web color chart, beginning on page 156, "unwraps" the traditional Web color cube. On the first spread I show the shell, or outer mantle, of the cube, and the next two spreads show the inner, deeper levels of the cube. To find related colors, simply identify the colors in corresponding positions in each chart. Each color field is identified by the hexadecimal and RGB values, as well as by a Web color number (0 to 215). Since these charts were printed in CMYK, they will unfortunately differ from what you see onscreen.

00 FF 00	33 FF 00	66 FF 00	99 FF 00	CC FF 00	FF FF 00
00 CC 00	33 CC 00	66 CC 00	99 CC 00	CC CC 00	FF CC 00
00 99 00	33 99 00	66 99 00	99 99 00	CC 99 00	FF 99 00
00 66 00	33 66 00	66 66 00	99 66 00	CC 66 00	FF 66 00
00 33 00	33 33 00	66 33 00	99 33 00	CC 33 00	FF 33 00
00 00 00	33 00 00	66 00 00	99 00 00	CC 00 00	FF 00 00
00 FF 33	33 FF 33	66 FF 33	99 FF 33	CC FF 33	FF FF 33
00 CC 33	33 CC 33	66 CC 33	99 CC 33	CC CC 33	FF CC 33
00 99 33	33 99 33	66 99 33	99 99 33	CC 99 33	FF 99 33
00 66 33	33 66 33	66 66 33	99 66 33	CC 66 33	FF 66 33
00 33 33	33 33 33	66 33 33	99 33 33	CC 33 33	FF 33 33
00 00 33	33 00 33	66 00 33	99 00 33	CC 00 33	FF 00 33

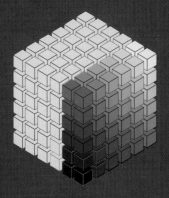

THE WEB-SAFE COLOR CUBE SHOWN IN SLICES

Choose the colors for your design from this table and enter the color values into the program. In Photoshop, you can select the Only Web Colors option in the Color Picker. You can also use the following table:

Hexadecimal		in %	in RGB
00	=	0%	0
33	=	20%	51
66	=	40%	102
99	=	60%	153
CC	=	80%	204
FF	=	100%	255

The hexadecimal color value "CC FF 33" translates to red = 80%, green = 100% and blue = 20%. In an RGB color picker, values are divided into 256 steps, so accordingly, you would need to enter red = 204, green = 255 and blue = 51.

The color fields in this table with white outlines represent shades of gray.

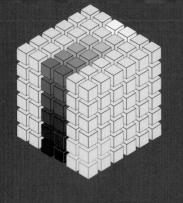

00 FF 66	33 FF 66	66 FF 66	99 FF 66	CC FF 66	FF FF 66
00 CC 66	33 CC 66	66 CC 66	99 CC 66	CC CC 66	FF CC 66
00 99 66	33 99 66	66 99 66	99 99 66	CC 99 66	FF 99 66
00 66 66	33 66 66	66 66 66	99 66 66	CC 66 66	FF 66 66
00 33 66	33 33 66	66 33 66	99 33 66	CC 33 66	FF 33 66
00 00 66	33 00 66	66 00 66	99 00 66	CC 00 66	FF 00 66
00 FF 99	33 FF 99	66 FF 99	99 FF 99	CC FF 99	FF FF 99
00 CC 99	33 CC 99	66 CC 99	99 CC 99	CC CC 99	FF CC 99
00 99 99	33 99 99	66 99 99	99 99 99	CC 99 99	FF 99 99
00 66 99	33 66 99	66 66 99	99 66 99	CC 66 99	FF 66 99
00 33 99	33 33 99	66 33 99	99 33 99	CC 33 99	FF 33 99
00 00 99	33 00 99	66 00 99	99 00 99	CC 00 99	FF 00 99

00 FF CC	33 FF CC	66 FF CC	99 FF CC	CC FF CC	FF FF CC
00 CC CC	33 CC CC	66 CC CC	99 CC CC	CC CC CC	FF CC CC
00 99 CC	33 99 CC	66 99 CC	99 99 CC	CC 99 CC	FF 99 CC
00 66 CC	33 66 CC	66 66 CC	99 66 CC	CC 66 CC	FF 66 CC
00 33 CC	33 33 CC	66 33 CC	99 33 CC	CC 33 CC	FF 33 CC
00 00 CC	33 00 CC	66 00 CC	99 00 CC	CC 00 CC	FF 00 CC
00 FF FF	33 FF FF	66 FF FF	99 FF FF	CC FF FF	FF FF FF
00 CC FF	33 CC FF	66 CC FF	99 CC FF	CC CC FF	FF CC FF
00 99 FF	33 99 FF	66 99 FF	99 99 FF	CC 99 FF	FF 99 FF
00 66 FF	33 66 FF	66 66 FF	99 66 FF	CC 66 FF	FF 66 FF
00 33 FF	33 33 FF	66 33 FF	99 33 FF	CC 33 FF	FF 33 FF
00 00 FF	33 00 FF	66 00 FF	99 00 FF	CC 00 FF	FF 00 FF

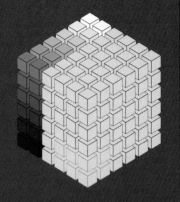

FF FF FF			FF 00 33				00 00 00			
0			215				0			

THE UNWRAPPED COLOR CUBE©

Here is the traditional Web color cube "unwrapped." This is the first mantle of the cube, and inner mantles are on the following pages.

Hex	No.
FF FF FF	0
FF 00 33	215
00 00 00	0
FF CC CC	7
FF FF CC	1
CC FF CC	37
FF 99 99	14
FF CC 99	8
FF FF 99	2
CC FF 99	38
99 FF 99	74
99 FF CC	73
FF 66 66	21
FF 99 66	15
FF CC 66	9
FF FF 66	3
CC FF 66	39
99 FF 66	75
66 FF 66	111
66 FF 99	110
66 FF CC	109
FF 33 33	28
FF 66 33	22
FF 99 33	16
FF CC 33	10
FF FF 33	4
CC FF 33	40
99 FF 33	76
66 FF 33	112
33 FF 33	148
33 FF 66	147
33 FF 99	146
33 FF CC	145
FF 00 00	35
FF 33 00	29
FF 66 00	23
FF 99 00	17
FF CC 00	11
FF FF 00	5
CC FF 00	41
99 FF 00	77
66 FF 00	113
33 FF 00	149
00 FF 00	185
00 FF 33	184
00 FF 66	183
00 FF 99	182
00 FF CC	181
CC 00 00	71
CC 33 00	65
CC 66 00	59
FFoo33	53
CC CC 00	47
99 CC 00	83
66 CC 00	119
33 CC 00	155
00 CC 00	191
00 CC 33	190
00 CC 66	189
00 CC 99	188
99 00 00	107
99 33 00	101
FFoo33	95
99 99 00	89
66 99 00	125
33 99 00	161
00 99 00	197
00 99 33	196
00 99 66	195
66 00 00	143
66 33 00	137
66 66 00	131
33 66 00	167
00 66 00	203
00 66 33	202
33 00 00	179
33 33 00	173
00 33 00	209
00 00 00	215

Conversion Table

Hex	in %	R/G/B	R=MY	G=CY	B=CM
FF	100	255	100%	100%	100%
CC	80	204	80%	80%	80%
99	60	153	60%	60%	60%
66	40	102	40%	40%	40%
33	20	51	20%	20%	20%
00	00	0	00%	00%	00%

000000					00 00 00				00 00 00			
0					0				0			
CC FF FF					00 00 33				FF CC FF			
36					42				6			
99 FF FF	99 CC FF				00 00 66			CC 99 FF	FF 99 FF	FF 99 CC		
72	78				84			48	12	13		
66 FF FF	66 CC FF	66 99 FF			00 00 99		99 66 FF	CC 66 FF	FF 66 FF	FF 66 CC	FF 66 99	
108	114	120			126		114	54	18	19	20	
33 FF FF	33 CC FF	33 99 FF	33 66 FF		00 00 CC	66 33 FF	99 33 FF	CC 33 FF	FF 33 FF	FF 33 66	FF 33 99	FF 33 66
144	150	156	162		168	144	108	60	24	25	26	27
00 FF FF	00 CC FF	00 99 FF	00 66 FF	00 33 FF	00 00 FF	33 00 FF	66 00 FF	99 00 FF	CC 00 FF	FF 00 FF	FF 00 CC	FF 00 99	FF 00 66	FF 00 33
180	186	192	198	204	210	174	138	102	66	30	31	32	33	34
00 CC CC	00 99 CC	00 66 CC	00 33 CC		00 00 CC	33 00 CC	66 00 CC	99 00 CC	CC 00 CC	CC 00 99	CC 00 66	CC 00 33
187	193	199	205		211	175	139	103	67	68	69	70
00 99 99	00 66 99	00 33 99			00 00 99		33 00 99	66 00 99	99 00 99	99 00 66	99 00 33
194	200	206			212		176	140	104	105	106
00 66 66	00 33 66				00 00 66			33 00 66	66 00 66	66 00 33
201	207				213			177	141	142
00 33 33					00 00 33				33 00 33
208					214				178
00 00 00					00 00 00				00 00 00
215					215				215

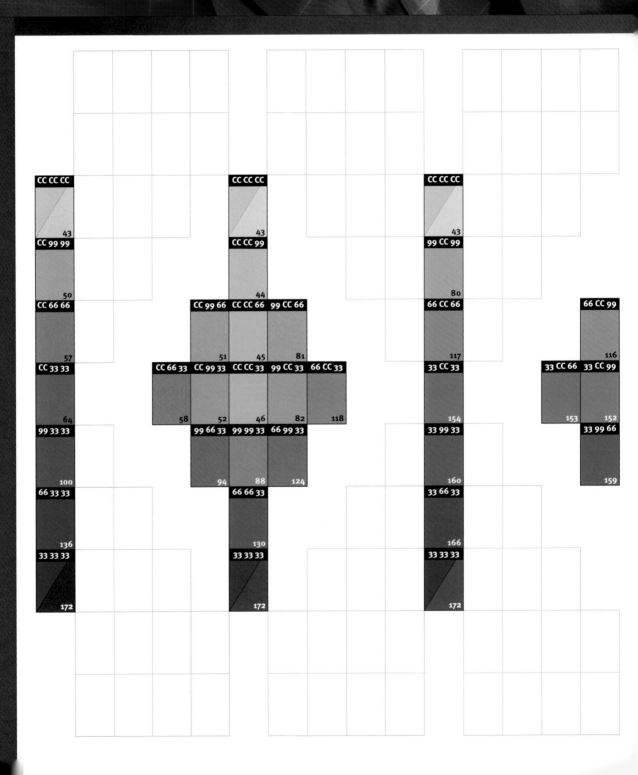

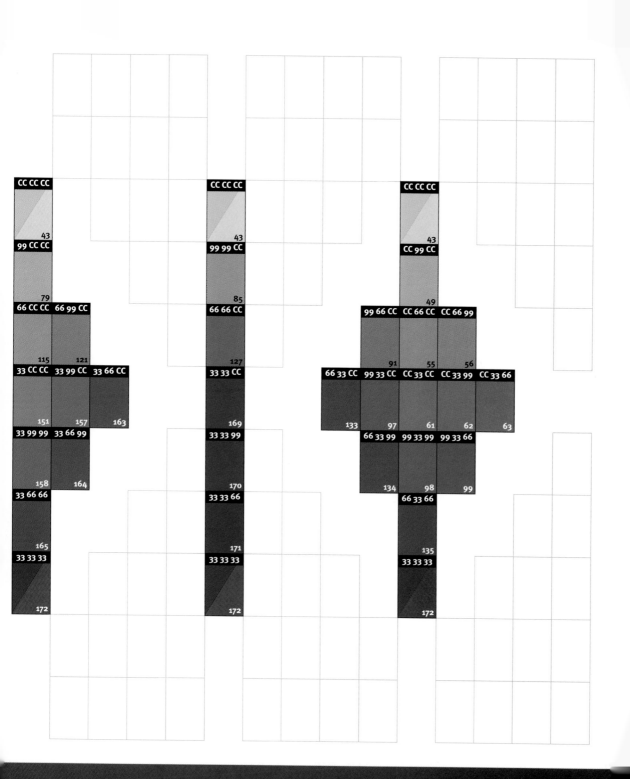

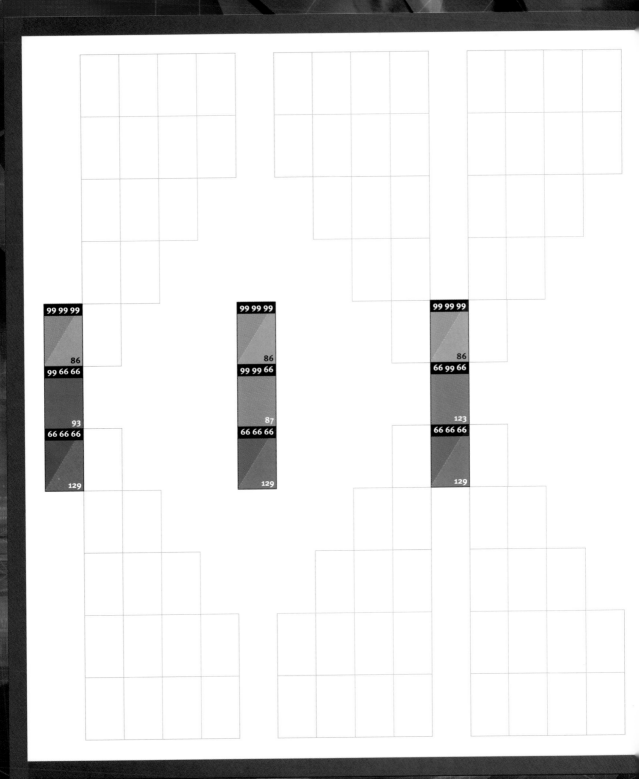

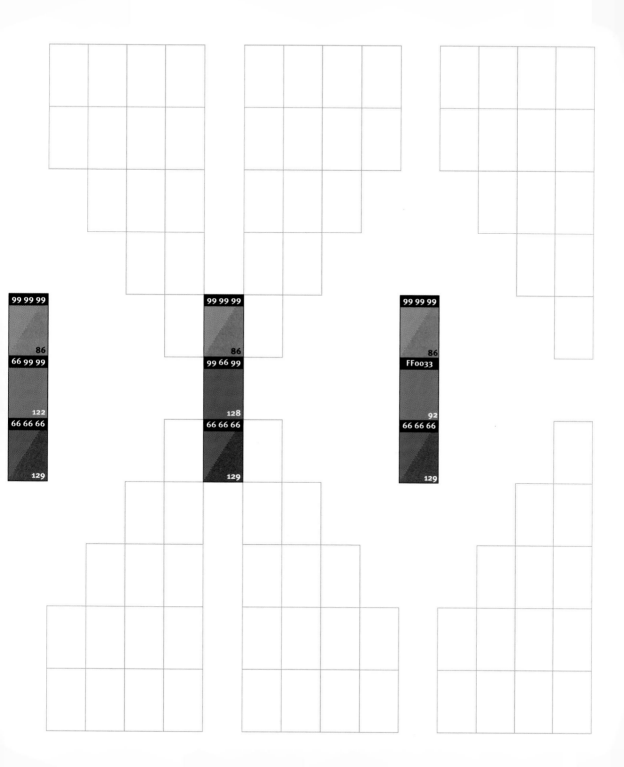

99 99 99
86
66 99 99
122
66 66 66
129

99 99 99
86
99 66 99
128
66 66 66
129

99 99 99
86
FF0033
92
66 66 66
129

WORKING WITH WEB COLORS

When designing a Web site, it's important to work with as many Web-safe colors as possible; this will help you avoid any problems later. This is rather simple when you're designing and colorizing elements, because all you need to do is use the Only Web Colors option in Photoshop's Color Picker. And if you forget to do this, you can always later convert to a Web-safe color when you optimize and export GIF images in the Save For Web dialog box. If, for some reason, you need to use a non-Web-safe color and you want to make sure that it looks good on 256-color monitors, here are a few ways to do so:

Changing to a Web-safe color before exporting

If you have a solid-colored area that you want to change into a Web-safe color, use the Paint Bucket tool. Set **Tolerance** to 0 and pick a foreground color in the toolbox, and then click on the area you would like

to fill. That's it! Well, it would be if you wanted to fill a rectangle or other shape that had only vertical and horizontal edges. More likely, however, you'll want to fill an area with anti-aliased edges, which means that there will be intermediate colors at the edges to blend the element with the background. You can adjust those pixels, too, by checking the **Anti-aliased** box in the **Paint Bucket** options bar. In addition, consider whether the shape that you are filling is on its own layer (with transparency at the edges) or if it is part of a layer with adjacent pixels. If it shares the layer with other pixels, set the **Tolerance** to 0 and check the **Anti-aliased** option. The **Contiguous** option is important if you only want to fill part of a layer. Then there is the Lock transparent pixels option in the Layers palette, which you also need to take into consideration when you want to fill a layer that has adjacent transparency.

To make it a bit easier to understand, I created a little overview that shows you different scenarios. Here

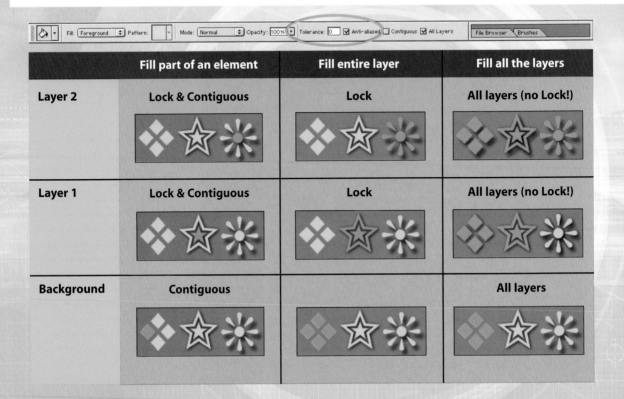

	Fill part of an element	Fill entire layer	Fill all the layers
Layer 2	Lock & Contiguous	Lock	All layers (no Lock!)
Layer 1	Lock & Contiguous	Lock	All layers (no Lock!)
Background	Contiguous		All layers

are the options that need to be selected (Important: **Tolerance** should be set to 0 and **Anti-aliased** should be selected throughout this process, so they're not listed, but are assumed). If you wanted to fill only part of an element that happens to be on its own layer, you can see from the overview (first column) that the Lock option in the Layers palette needs to be activated, as well as the Contiguous option in the options bar. And, of course, you have to select the right layer in the Layers palette before using the Paint Bucket tool.

If you look in the "Fill all layers" column, you will notice that the All layers option doesn't produce the expected result. The reason for this is simply that when you click with the Paint Bucket on the area that you would like to color, Photoshop fills the entire selected area, but any layers above the currently selected layer will still cover the underlying layer. Honestly, this makes no sense to me; it would be better if the appropriate color would automatically fill all the layers, but what can you do?

It is not always possible to use the Paint Bucket to change a color; sometimes there are too many areas to be changed—for example, if text is rendered, every letter has to be changed individually. In that case, choose **Image > Adjustments > Replace Color**. This command, however, will only work with the selected layer.

Changing to a Web-safe color when exporting

It's not always necessary to make a color a Web-safe color before you optimize it as GIF in the **Save For Web** dialog box. Since GIF works with a color look-up table, all the colors in the image are listed and you can easily convert them to Web-safe hues by selecting them and then clicking on the **Snap** button (with the cube icon) at the bottom of the **Color Table** palette. Keep in mind, however, that this method is specifically to convert colors to the Web-safe palette. If you would like to change a color to a shade that's outside of this palette, it's better to use the **Paint Bucket** tool or the **Fill** command.

This is the document that was used for the overview (on the left). Layer 1 and Layer 2 have a slightly different drop shadow, to set them apart.

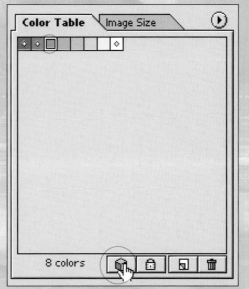

Clicking on the Snap button at the bottom of the Color Table palette converts a selected color to the nearest Web-safe equivalent.

Backgrounds

One very popular HTML function involves filling the background of a Web page with a pattern or image. A lot of Web sites use this trick in one form or the other—it is part of the standard repertoire for any Web designer. There is a catch to using the background function, however. Since the background image is repeated in the browser by default, the same image will display again when the viewer scrolls down or to the right. From the chart, you can see that you may need to make your background image 1,280 pixels wide and at least 1,024 pixels high to ensure that users with larger monitors won't see the repetition. However, because this creates a lot of unnecessary over-head, many designers limit their background images to 800 pixels in width or, even better, they use Cascading Style Sheets. Since Cascading Style Sheets are able to limit the number of repetitions for a background image, the image doesn't have to be very large. If you wanted to have just a small image in the upper-left corner that fades into the background color of the browser, you could use Cascading Style Sheets to reformat the BODY tag and have the background image be repeated only once. Instead of creating an 800-by-800-pixel image, you would need only a 200-by-200-pixel image, a savings of more than 93 percent (working with Cascading Style Sheets is explained in the GoLive chapter).

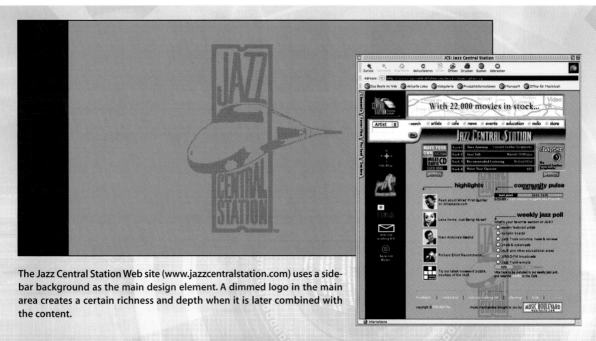

The Jazz Central Station Web site (www.jazzcentralstation.com) uses a side-bar background as the main design element. A dimmed logo in the main area creates a certain richness and depth when it is later combined with the content.

MONITOR SIZES AND THEIR RESOLUTIONS (WIDTH X HEIGHT)				
14"	15"	16"/17"	19"	21"
640x480	800x600 (SuperVGA) 82x624 (Mac)	832x624	1024x768	1152x870 (Mac) 1152x1124 1280x1024

USING LARGE BACKGROUND IMAGES

Andreas Lindström, who created the Web site for Carnegie Hall, has his own special way of using backgrounds in his Web designs. He likes to use dimmed images that blend with the background color, combining them with smaller images in the foreground. This creates an interesting dynamic and lends depth to the Web site. Here's how to dim an image and have it blend with the background:

1. Put the image on its own layer. If your background is already on its own layer, skip this step. Otherwise, create a new layer by clicking on the New Layer icon at the bottom of the Layers palette. Fill this layer with the background color that you want to use, then use the **Layer > New > Layer from Background** command to make this layer the new background layer.

2. Use the Opacity slider in the **Layers** palette to dim your image. However, if you want to make sure that text on top of it will be readable, dimming alone will not guarantee that the background color and the image will blend together sufficiently. Try applying a blending mode to the layer: Multiply, Soft Light, Hard Light, or Luminosity work very well. Another nice effect is to blur the image with Gaussian blur—done to the extreme, this can create a great background texture. But even a little blurring helps to improve the readability of any text. If you want your image be monochromatic, use **Image > Adjustments > Hue/Saturation** and activate the Colorize option. This allows you to change the hue and saturation.

3. Very often you will also want to blend the edges of your image layer with the background color. This is done by applying a layer mask to the layer (**Layer > Add Layer Mask > Reveal All**) and using the **Airbrush** tool with a black foreground color to paint into the layer mask. All the dark areas of the layer mask will be transparent. Use a large brush size with soft edges, and make sure that the layer mask is activated when you paint into the image; otherwise, you will paint over it.

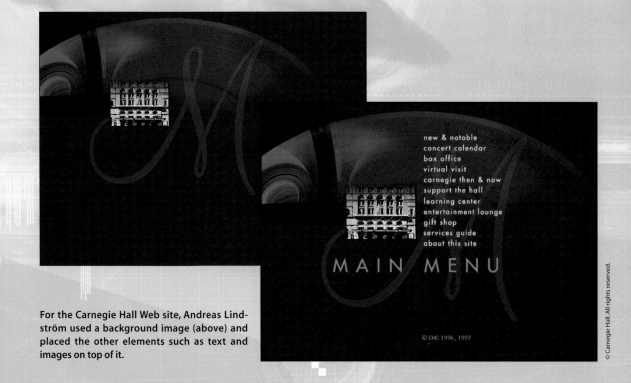

For the Carnegie Hall Web site, Andreas Lind-ström used a background image (above) and placed the other elements such as text and images on top of it.

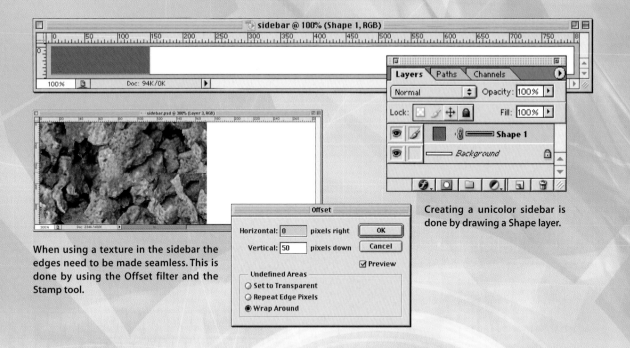

Creating a unicolor sidebar is done by drawing a Shape layer.

When using a texture in the sidebar the edges need to be made seamless. This is done by using the Offset filter and the Stamp tool.

Sidebar Backgrounds

Using a sidebar is still a very popular design concept and all you have to do is color one side of the background. Since the background image is repeated, it can be as small as one pixel in height, resulting in a very small file size.

Using a one-pixel image is a bit extreme, of course, and doing this does have a hidden drawback: It requires a lot of processing power on your visitor's computer, because the browser has to render the background every time the user changes the window size or scrolls quickly down a page. With a background image just one pixel high (and, for example, 800 pixels wide), the browser has to repeat the background more often—while this may not be noticeable on today's computers, that extra demand can slow down the browser on an older, low-end machine. Using a pattern with a height of 40 pixels is less demanding. If you use textures and save the image as a JPEG, use a dimension that is divisible by 8 because the JPEG compression algorithm works with 8-by-8-pixel blocks.

Here's how to create a simple sidebar: Create a new document via **File > New** and enter, for example, 40 pixels for height and 800 pixels for width. Click the foreground color field in the toolbox and choose a foreground color from the color picker then use the **Rectangle** tool to create a rectangle in the left-hand part of the image. Then choose **File > Save For Web**. Since images like this are ideally saved as GIFs, choose a color depth of three bits in the **Save For Web** dialog box. If you need to change the color, just double click the **Shape Layer** icon in the **Layers** palette.

Although the sidebar in the example above is easy to create, it may look rather technical; a sidebar with texture can contribute significantly to the design. To avoid unwanted visible breaks at the edges, the upper and lower edges of the image should fit seamlessly.

Here's how to create a sidebar with texture:
1. Create a new document and place a background or texture on the left side of the image. Choose the **Offset** filter (**Filter > Other > Offset**).

Sidebars don't necessarily have to be boring. In this example the logo and the buttons extend the white stripe from the background. This breaks up the repetitiveness of the background texture.

2. For Vertical: Pixels Down, enter half the height of the sidebar and activate the **Wrap Around** option. This ensures that image elements that disappear at the bottom will reappear at the top. Check the **Preview** option to see the effect before clicking OK.

3. Now remove the edge in the image. Depending on the image itself, either the **Smudge** tool or the **Rubber Stamp** tool will be most appropriate. Generally, the Rubber Stamp tool is more suitable for retouching. With the Option (Mac) or Alt (Windows) key pressed, click on the image region you want to use as a source. Release the key and click in the image where you want to fill in the information you've just picked up. As you move the tool around, you will see a

cross following your movement; it marks the spot that you clicked on the first time while holding the Option/Alt key. To get the best results, you will have to change this point frequently; otherwise, you will still see an edge.

4. After the image has been smoothed out to create a seamless transition, use the **Offset** filter to convert the image file back to normal. (Enter a negative value and use the **Wrap Around** option.) The exported image will appear in Navigator or Explorer as one big background.

TEXTURE BACKGROUNDS (WALLPAPER)

Using texture backgrounds can sometime make text difficult to read, but there are a lot of good examples of Web sites where designers avoided this by using textures with subtle colors. You will also want to use a pattern that's large enough to make the continuous repetition less obvious. There are two ways to create a seamlessly tiling background: One is the "old" way, where the edges are touched up with the Stamp Tool; the "new" way is with the Pattern Maker. Since the old way gives you a little bit more control over the outcome, let's start there first.

1. Load a file with a texture, and use the **Crop** tool to select the region that you'd like to use (crop by double-clicking inside the selection). Open the **Offset** filter and enter approximately half the pixel size of the image in the vertical and horizontal boxes. Activate the **Wrap Around** option to make sure moved image elements reappear on the opposite end.

2. In the center of the picture, you will now see the image break in the shape of a cross. It needs to be removed with the **Rubber Stamp** tool (or, in some cases, with the **Smudge** tool). Hold down the Option (Mac) or Alt (Windows) key, and click on the image spot you want to use as a source. Release the Option/Alt key and paint over the image break (a copy of the source area will be used). You might have to constantly change the source for the **Rubber Stamp** tool to get the result you want, but in the end you should have an area that shows no more edges. You can use the **Offset** filter one more time to double-check that there are really no more visible edges, or you can just move the pattern into its original position by entering a negative offset with the same values that you used before.

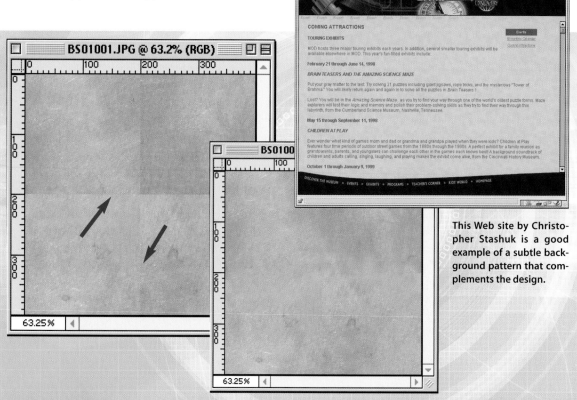

This Web site by Christopher Stashuk is a good example of a subtle background pattern that complements the design.

CREATING TEXTURES WITH THE PATTERN MAKER

Photoshop also offers a feature to create patterns from selections automatically. The **Pattern Maker** feature is not intended to be an alternative to the technique explained before. Rather than just blending the edges of a selection to make them appear seamless when they're tiled, it rearranges the pixels in a selection into a completely new pattern. **Pattern Maker** lets you produce textures that look very organic. For example, if you design a Web site with a stone texture background, you might want to create buttons or other elements that blend right in.

To work with the **Pattern Maker**, open an image and choose **Filter > Pattern Maker**. With the selection tool in the upper-right corner make a selection of the area that you would like to use as the basis for the pattern. You want to use an area that has subtle color changes, or the results will not be usable as a background (although there are some exceptions to this rule). There are a couple of key values that determine the outcome: **Image Size, Smoothness**, and **Sample Detail**. The default setting for the image size is 128 by 128 pixels. It might seem logical to have the image size be approximately the size of the selection, but there is truly no benefit to making the image size smaller, since the tiling can easily become noticeable. There is also no need to change the **Smoothness** slider unless you see edges within the created pattern. In that case, increase the **Smoothness** to 3, and the next pattern you create will have less prominent edges. If your selection contains details that are cut up in the pattern, increase the **Sample Detail** slider to the approximate size of the detail.

Finally, click **Generate** and the **Pattern Maker** will fill the area with the pattern. Keep clicking the **Generate** button until you see a pattern that you like, then click the disk icon to save the pattern permanently. Photoshop stores up to 20 patterns automatically. You can flip through them using the arrow key.

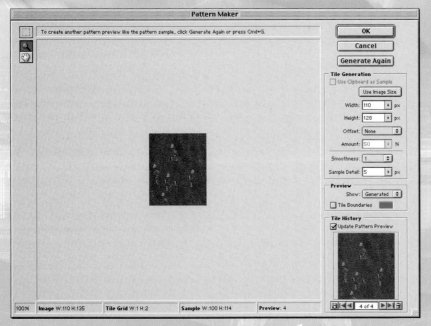

After you create a texture with the Pattern Maker you can use this texture to fill a selection and then prepare it like you would any other pattern.

Transparency

To create lines and edges that are not perfectly vertical or horizontal, Photoshop employs an approximation based on the available resolution. To get the best result, Photoshop uses a technique called anti-aliasing, in which pixels at the edges of an object are smoothed to blend with the background.

The intermediate colors that anti-aliasing creates are a problem only if you are planning to use transparency with a GIF. If the image is viewed on a browser in front of the same color as the transparency color, you won't have a problem because the edges are already anti-aliased to the right color. But if you change the background in the browser at some point, your image may show a halo at the edges. Fortunately, Photoshop offers you a great way of dealing with this problem.

USING TRANSPARENCY WITH SOLID-COLORED BACKGROUNDS

The best way to demonstrate transparency is with an example that you are very likely to run into: rendering a headline as an image. To make sure the text image displays correctly in the browser and blends perfectly into the background, it is important that before you render the text, you use a background color that's as close as possible to the one on your Web page. To accomplish this, follow this procedure:

1. Create a new document, select a foreground color (which will be the font color), and click on the working area with the **Type** tool. Photoshop will automatically create a new layer. Choose a typeface and point size in the options bar and select the **Anti-Alias** option.

2. Since you want the background to be transparent, hide the background layer by toggling off its visibility in the **Layers** palette. A checkerboard pattern signals that the background is now transparent. Choose **File > Save For Web** and click on the **Optimized** tab in the **Save For Web** dialog box. Set the format to **GIF**, and

When using a single-color background, hide the layer before using the Save for Web command.

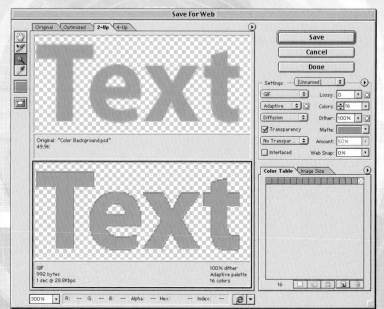

make sure that the **Transparency** option is selected (it is selected by default). Select a color in the **Matte** pop-up menu: Choose between **Eyedropper Color** (the color in the upper-left corner of the dialog box), Black, White, and Other. If you select **Other**, the Photoshop **Color Picker** will appear. You can select your color, and Photoshop will anti-alias the edges with this color.

3. Click OK. The File Selector dialog box appears, giving you the option of saving your image along with an HTML file (click on **Options** and choose the appropriate settings). You can use this file to check the result in a browser. Save in HTML, then open the file in Netscape Navigator or Microsoft Internet Explorer to see how your text looks in front of the background color you selected.

USING TRANSPARENCY WITH MULTICOLORED BACKGROUNDS

Creating transparency for a solid-colored background is easy, but this technique won't work if your element is later placed in front of a textured or multicolored background. In previous Photoshop versions this was a more complicated process, but Adobe has improved this greatly. The only limitation is that it only works if the color isn't also used in the element itself. Also important: If you want to export an element from your design, you might have to use the Slicing tool first to isolate the element.

1. Use the Save For Web command from the **File** menu. In this technique you don't have to make the background layer transparent; the transparency is assigned directly in the **Save For Web** dialog box.

2. Choose the Eyedropper tool and hold the Shift key while selecting all the colors in the background that you want to be transparent. In the **Color Table**, all the selected colors will have an outline, and when you click the **Transparency** button (it maps selected colors to transparent), the colors will become transparent.

When using a multicolored background just open the Save for Web command, then select the colors you want to be transparent and click on the Transparency button at the bottom of the Color Table.

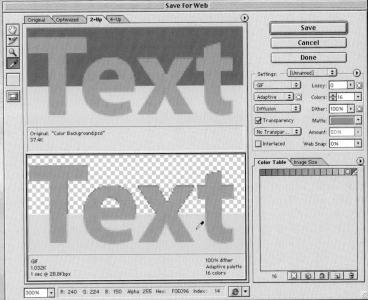

Tutorial: Developing a Web Site in Photoshop

I created this simple mock-up, trying to incorporate as many as possible of the elements that you find in real-world Web sites. This design will also show you how to work with the shape layers, which are still fairly new (they were introduced in Photoshop 6.0). This tutorial will lead you through every step of the development from the design and the optimization of the images up to the point of the final HTML page in GoLive.

1 Creating a sidebar: After creating a new file (**File > New**) 640 pixels in width by 600 pixels high, you need a second (temporary) document for the fill pattern, with the dimensions 4 pixels (width) by 1 pixel (height). Make the color of the first pixel a light gray (RGB: 204, 204, 204), the second pixel a dark gray (RGB: 102, 102, 102), and the third and fourth pixels a medium gray (RGB: 153, 153, 153). Use the maximum magnification to paint the pixels with the **Pencil** tool. (This tool may be hidden in the **Paintbrush** tool slot; a click on the Paintbrush tool will reveal it.) To define a color, click on the foreground color field in the toolbox. When the **Color Picker** dialog box appears, make sure that the **Only Web Color** option is selected.

Edit > Define Pattern will store this small document as a pattern. You won't need this document anymore, but you can save it for later in case you want to edit it. Switch back to your first document and display the rulers (**View > Show Rulers**).

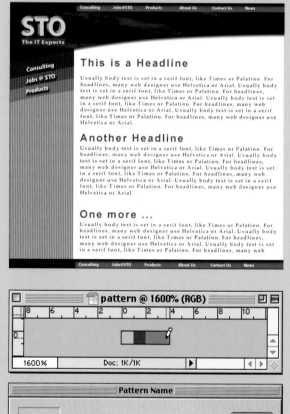

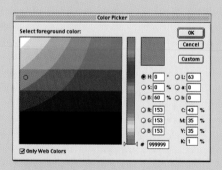

Use the Only Web Colors option when creating the pattern.

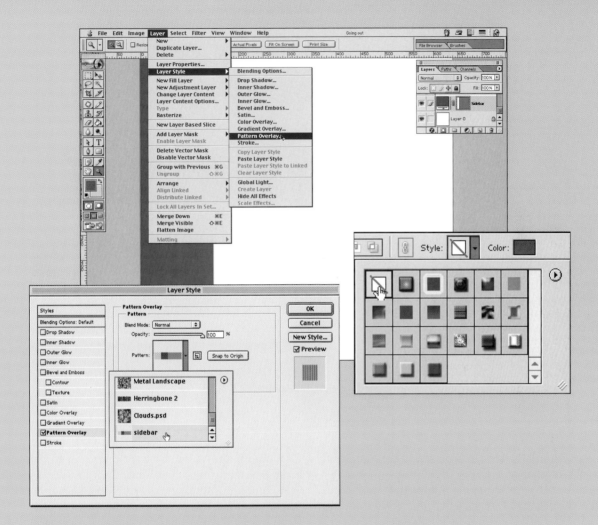

2 Before you start to create the actual sidebar, make sure that the **Create New Shape Layer** option is activated and that no style is selected (click on **Layer Style** in the options bar at the top of your working environment; in the pop-up menu select **No Style**). With the **Rectangle** tool from the toolbox, draw the sidebar with a width of 150 pixels. This sidebar is now filled with the foreground color. To actually fill it with the pattern, we create a pattern overlay in the Layer Style dialog box (**Layer > Layer Style > Pattern Overlay**). From the pop-up menu, select the pattern that you saved previously, and your sidebar is done.

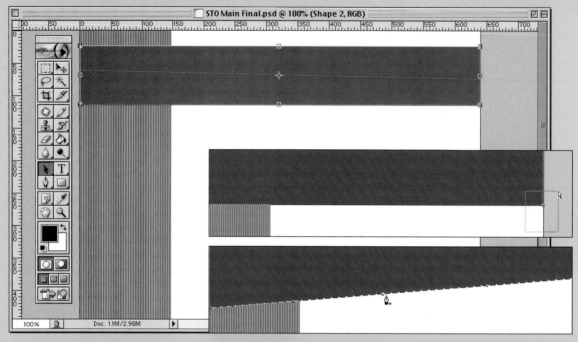

After the lower-right Anchor was moved up, an anchor point was added to the path and then moved to create the arch.

3 Creating the arch: When designing a Web site in Photoshop, you should decide early on whether you want to use frames or stick to HTML tables. This decision can have an impact on your design, but this particular design can be created with either.

With the **Rectangle** tool, draw a shape with a height of 95 pixels, and with an offset of 20 pixels from the top—you will have to zoom in to do this precisely. If you need to adjust the shape, use the **Free Transform Path** command (**Edit** menu). Double-click in the rectangle after you are finished resizing.

To change the shape to an arch, select with the **Direct Selection** tool (white mouse arrow) the lower-right corner of the rectangle, and then click on the anchor point and drag it up while holding the Shift key to restrict the movement to the vertical axis. Add an anchor point in the middle of the path with the **Add Anchor Point** tool, and move this anchor with the **Direct Selection** tool until you get a nice arch.

Fill this path with a pattern using the same technique as with the sidebar, above: Open a texture, define it as pattern, and then select **Pattern Overlay** in the **Layer Style** dialog box (**Layer > Layer Style > Pattern Overlay**). While you are there, also select **Drop Shadow**.

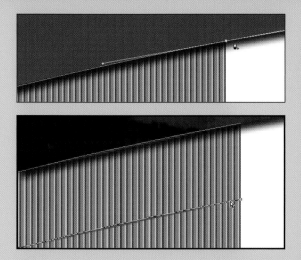

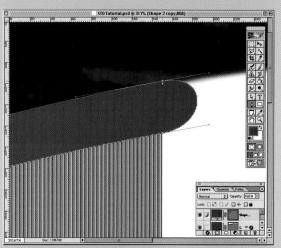

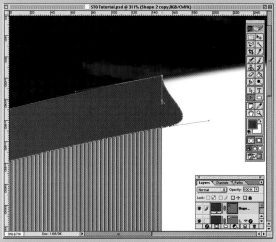

4 **Creating the sidebar navigation buttons:** If you are familiar with Adobe Illustrator and working with the **Path** tool, this should be no problem. Duplicate the arch layer using the **Duplicate Layer** command in the **Layers** palette menu. **Layer > Layer Style > Clear Layer Style** gets rid of the layer style in the copy. The intention is to cut out just the part of the arch that lies over the sidebar to use it as a basis for the buttons (this ensures that both arches will match later). With the **Direct Selection** tool, select all the anchor points—except the two that we need for the buttons—and hit the Delete key. Then drag the path parallel while holding the Shift key and then clicking the Alt key before releasing the mouse button (this creates a copy automatically). Connect the two ends of the paths with the **Pen** tool and use the **Convert Point** tool to adjust the handles of the anchor point. Change the color of the shape to black with **Layer > Change Layer Content > Solid Color**. Finally, use the **Opacity** slider in the **Layers** palette. The other two buttons are simply created by duplicating this layer and then moving and adjusting the paths and transparency.

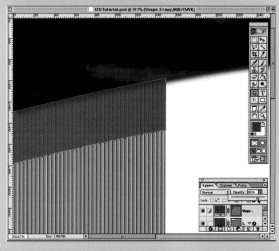

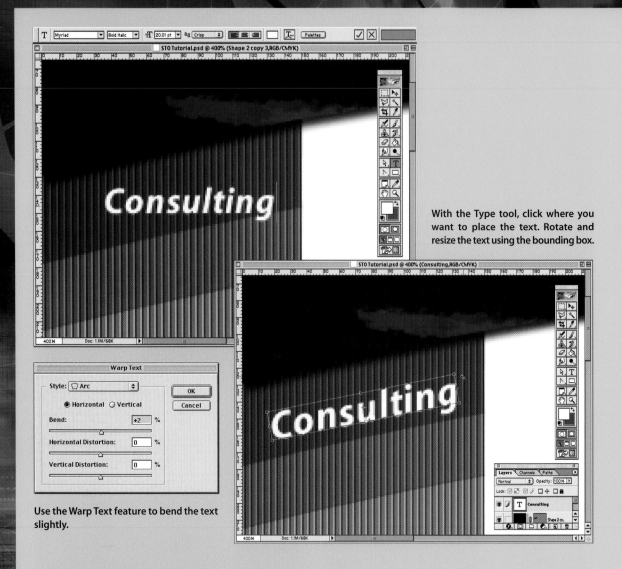

With the Type tool, click where you want to place the text. Rotate and resize the text using the bounding box.

Use the Warp Text feature to bend the text slightly.

5 With the **Type** tool, click at the location where you want to place the buttons' labels and then type the text. Make sure that the foreground color is set to white before you do this (otherwise, you have to change the color later by highlighting the text with the **Type** tool and changing the color in the **Color Picker**). To rotate the text layer use **Edit > Free Transform** (if this is grayed out in the menu, try selecting the **Move** tool first). You see the same bounding box as before, which

you can use to scale and rotate the text by moving the **Free Transform** tool along the left or right side of the bounding box (consult the Photoshop manual on how to work with the **Free Transform** tool). Once the text is in position, use the **Warp Text** feature to bend the text slightly. Duplicate the layer twice and change the text as necessary.

6 Creating the top and bottom navigation bars:
For the buttons' background, create the shape with the **Rectangle** tool. Instead of using beveled buttons, we'll use the **Inner Shadow** effect and disable the effect for the onMouseOver rollover state in ImageReady, which will make it look like the gray background is moving up when the mouse is over the button. Once you've placed the text for the buttons (and the black rectangle on the left side), create a new folder (Layer Set) in the **Layers** palette and drag all the elements of the top navigation into it. Being able to organize the contents of the **Layers** palette in folders is a true blessing of Photoshop; not only does it help you to keep an overview, but it makes it easy to duplicate several layers at once. Select the top navigation bar layer set in the **Layers** palette and use the **Duplicate Layer Set** command in the **Layers** palette's menu. With the **Move** tool, drag the new set to the bottom of the document.

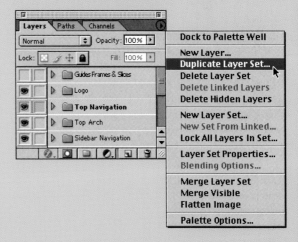

ImageReady

ImageReady is a fully functional image-editing program that comes as part of the Photoshop package. It is optimized for Web graphics, but works almost identically to Photoshop. I prefer working in Photoshop and then transferring the design only at the end, which is why most of the techniques in this book are explained for Photoshop. However, if you prefer working in ImageReady, you can easily adapt every technique in this book to ImageReady. In this chapter I'll focus entirely on ImageReady and walk you through some of the Web features it has that Photoshop lacks, such as the creation of rollover buttons, animations, and image maps.

PHOTOSHOP VS. IMAGEREADY

Photoshop's **Save For Web** dialog box offers virtually all of the same file-optimization capabilities of ImageReady, but I would argue that the Photoshop interface is more familiar to most designers, and Photoshop also has many more color-correcting and image-manipulation features than ImageReady does. Compare Photoshop's **Image > Adjustments** commands to ImageReady's: Photoshop offers **Curves, Color Balance, Replace Color, Selective Color, Channel Mixer, Equalize,** and many other important commands for working with images and creating photocompositions that ImageReady lacks.

Another benefit of designing images and photo illustrations in Photoshop is that it now offers the **Pen** and **Custom Shape** vector tools. But that's not all! Photoshop also lets you draw multiple paths on one layer, and like the Pathfinder palette in Illustrator, it lets you combine those paths into a more complex shape by adding or subtracting them. ImageReady

doesn't have a **Pen** or **Custom Shape** tool, and it allows only one shape in a layer. While it is possible to move and transform those shapes in ImageReady, only in Photoshop can you edit them to add or delete anchor points.

But after you've designed the images for your Web site—adjusted the colors, composed and colorized images, and received client approval—then you can turn to ImageReady to take your content to the next level of Web design. In ImageReady, you can create rollover buttons and image maps, slice images and animate GIFs, and export the final elements to an HMTL authoring program such as GoLive. These are tasks that you just can't perform in Photoshop and that are important in the second phase of Web site design. If you don't intend to use any of these features, you might as well finalize your images using Photoshop's **Save For Web** command, since ImageReady offers no actual advantage over Photoshop for optimizing images. And remember, Adobe makes it easy to switch between Photoshop and ImageReady with the **Jump to ImageReady/Photoshop** button in each application's toolbox. Personally, however, I find it cumbersome to deal with two software interfaces, even if the differences between them are only marginal.

One of the most common misunderstandings about ImageReady is that you can use it as an HTML authoring tool. Here's my advice: Don't expect to be able to create slices, click some buttons in ImageReady, and produce an almost-finished Web page that you can use right away in GoLive. Even though ImageReady can generate some HTML code, you should use it only in rare cases. Most of the time it is better to export the images and create the page in

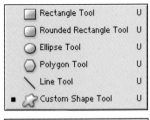

Photoshop has more path and shape tools than ImageReady does, but most importantly, you can edit paths in Photoshop.

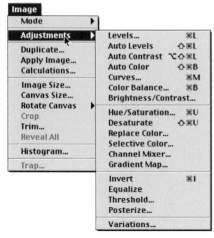

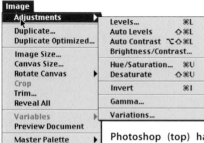

Photoshop (top) has more color-manipulation commands than Image-Ready (bottom), so Photoshop is therefore better suited for photo composition and manipulation.

Switching between Photoshop and ImageReady is simple: click on the Jump To button in the toolbox to save the current document and open it in the other application.

animation with unnecessary frames, because both design elements are based on image layers. Chances are that you will unwittingly record a layer change for a rollover button or in an animation, or vice versa.

So what is the best way to proceed? Ideally, you should open your Photoshop design in ImageReady, crop the individual elements, and save them as separate files. In the scenario just described, this would mean that you crop the banner ad and save it as one file before you start animating it. That way, when you're opening and creating the banner ad animation, you can focus on the animation alone and even delete the redundant layers, which makes the Layers palette more manageable.

One last piece of advice: Don't start working on the rollover buttons if you still need to make some changes in your design. It's far too easy to accidentally record one of the changes in the Layers palette as one state of a rollover button. Creating rollover buttons should be the very last step in the process.

GoLive, which reduces mistakes and offers more control over the code.

For example, imagine that you want to design a Web page with a background image, a navigation bar containing rollover button states, and an animated banner ad. If you attempt to create the rollovers and animation in one document in ImageReady, you will most likely end up with rollovers that act strange or an

To create rollover buttons, select the slice with the Slice Select tool and define the rollover effect in the Rollovers palette.

CREATING ROLLOVER BUTTONS

After opening the design in ImageReady, you must use the **Slice** tool to create the rollover buttons. Every time you place a new marquee with the **Slice** tool, ImageReady optimizes the slices and even creates adjacent slices if necessary (e.g., if you place your first slice in the middle of your document, ImageReady will create five slices in total: the one that you created and one for each side of the marquee). When you export your images together with some HTML code, each slice represents a cell of an HTML table. But ImageReady (and Photoshop) also allow you to export only selected slices.

Use the **Slice** tool to draw a marquee around each button and name the slices in the Slice palette, using an intuitive system: for example "bttn_" along with the button's text.

To create a rollover state (an action that occurs when a mouse cursor is rolled over the slice), select a slice with the **Slice Select** tool and then click the **Create New Rollover State** button in the **Rollovers** palette. By default the rollover state is "Over," but the state can be changed by double-clicking the entry in the **Rollovers** palette.

In this example, I want to change the color of the button text for my rollover effect. The easiest way to do this is to use a color overlay. So I select the text layer in the **Layers** palette, choose **Layer Style > Color Overlay** from the Layer menu, and select a different color.

After I create the rollovers, each slice is individually optimized. Use the **Slice Select** tool to select one slice and then open the **Optimize** palette (**Window > Show Optimize**). In this example from the tutorial, 16 colors are plenty, and I chose an **Adaptive** palette. It is important to not dither here; otherwise, the background of the buttons dithers and will make the buttons noticeable when they are later placed on top of the sidebar. Another important feature is the **Use Unified Color Table** option at the bottom of the **Optimize** palette. This option is only visible when double-clicking on the **Optimize** tab (ImageReady extends or collapses the palette). Using this option will ensure that there is no color shift when the mouse is brought over the rollover. This is mainly necessary if you are expecting that many visitors to your Web site have only 256-color monitors. To preview the rollover buttons, click on the **Preview Document** button at the bottom of the toolbox.

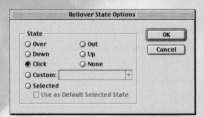

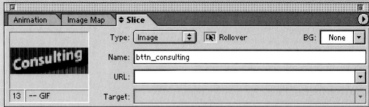

Double click on a rollover state to pick one. Later on, the name of the slice will be used as the basis for the image's name.

Before saving the slices you may want to customize the output settings that you find in the **File > Output Settings** dialog box. ImageReady has a vast number of options for naming slices automatically. I prefer to use the slice name combined with the abbreviated rollover state (over becomes "o") and the image format extension (which is required). In the **Saving Files** section of the **Output Settings** dialog box, you also can specify a subfolder in which to place the images.

When you then use **File > Save Optimized As** command, give the HTML document a name (something like "navigation.html" for our example), then select **HTML and Images** in the **Format** pop-up menu to save the images along with their HTML code. Since the document is not cropped, choose **Selected Slices** from the pop-up menu at the bottom of the dialog box. Otherwise you'll end up with one large HTML table containing all the slices of the entire image.

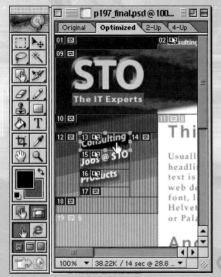

A nice little feature: if you click on Rollover Preview, the buttons in your design will behave as they will later in the browser. Below: use the Unified Color Table option for rollover buttons.

Rollovers Palette Options can be accessed from the Rollovers palette's pop-up menu.

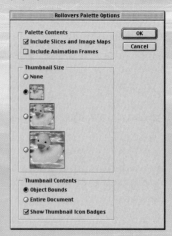

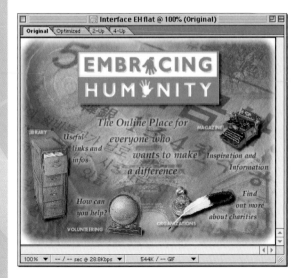

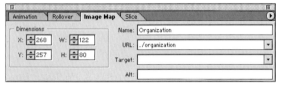

When you click the Image Map tool in the toolbox, ImageReady reveals a list of shapes. With these shapes, mark the hot spots on your image and set the URL in the Image Map palette.

The image map needs to be saved using the Save Optimized As command. In Output Settings, select the type of image map (usually Client-Side).

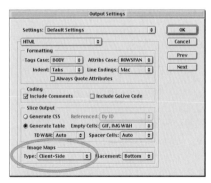

CREATING IMAGE MAPS

For basic image maps—or image maps that use basic geometrical shapes—you can actually use GoLive: Just place an image in an HTML file and check **Use Map** in the Inspector. Then, with the Shape tools (**Rectangle**, **Circle**, and **Polygon**), create your hot spots and establish their links in the **Links** tab of the Inspector.

If you need to create a more precise or more complex image map, however, GoLive isn't the best choice. Let's say that you've created rollover buttons as we just did. In that case, re-creating the shapes of the different states on a map can be tedious. GoLive can't zoom in, and working at the edge of an image map is almost impossible. The mouse pointer changes when it's five pixels from the border, because GoLive assumes that you want to move the image.

So ImageReady is your solution. Just use any of the **Image Map** tools to draw your hot spot shapes, then enter the name and URL of that hot spot in the **Image Map** palette. Choose **File > Save Optimized As**, and select **HTML and Images** from the **Format** menu. In **Output Settings**, choose **Client-Side** as the type of image map you're creating, and save the image map into your GoLive site folder. (Alternatively, you can simply define your hot spots in ImageReady, save the file, and then open it in GoLive, where you can use the **Point and Shoot** tool to define the URLs in a snap.)

Now start GoLive and choose **Site > Rescan**. Two new files will be listed: your image and the HTML document that defines the image map areas. Move the image to your "Images" folder, open the HTML document, and copy and paste the image map into the target HTML document. Finished! Dispose of the redundant image map HTML document by putting it in the trash in the **Site** window.

Layer-Based Image Maps

ImageReady offers another particularly helpful feature for creating polygonal image map areas: You can have ImageReady create an area automatically based on a layer. Just choose **Layer > New Layer Based Image Map Area** to create a rectangular image map area. To change the shape into a polygon, open the **Image Map** palette and select **Polygon** from the **Shape** pop-up menu. With the **Quality** pop-up you can specify the accuracy with which ImageReady matches the form of the layer. As you can see in the example with the metallic bird, even the layer effects are taken into account. By the way, Adobe Illustrator can also save polygonal image map areas, which is a great help if your image map consists of complex shapes.

OPTIMIZING IMAGES WITH IMAGEREADY

The only time you'll have to optimize images in ImageReady is when you're using rollover buttons, image maps, or GIF animations; otherwise, you can use Photoshop's **Save For Web** command, which is the method I describe most often in this book. ImageReady offers as much control over image optimization and exporting as the Save for Web command—as long as you know where to look. The tools on the left side of the **Save For Web** dialog box—**Hand, Slice Select, Zoom,** and **Eyedropper**—are in the regular ImageReady toolbox. The color values displayed at the bottom of the **Save For Web** dialog box are available in ImageReady's **Info** palette. The optimization settings and **Color Table** palette on the right side of the **Save For Web** dialog box are available in ImageReady as their own respective palettes, but there is no **Image Size** palette—you must choose **Image > Image Size** to access this information. Finally, the pop-up preview menu in the **Save For Web** dialog box is split in ImageReady: Color preview commands are available if you choose **Image > Preview,** and the download rates are available in the **Image** Information pop-up menu at the bottom of the image window.

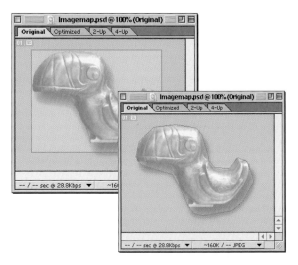

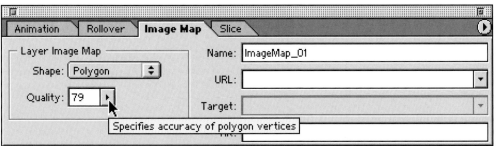

It is possible to create an image map area automatically based on a layer. In the Image Map palette you can specify the accuracy of the tracing.

TUTORIAL: CREATING SLICES AND ROLLOVERS

Here is the mock-up of the Web site for a consulting company done entirely in Photoshop, created in the tutorial on page 172. Now we'll slice and export the design and create the rollover buttons in ImageReady.

The red lines in the screen shot above delineate a frame layout (blue are the embedded tables). The red and blue lines in the image at right show how the design could be laid out with embedded tables. It's almost the same!

1 Thinking it through: As you design your Web site in Photoshop, you should be thinking about how you will ultimately re-create it in HTML. It isn't always possible to know this in advance, of course, especially if you want to try something new, but you should ask yourself early on whether your design is better suited to be laid out with frames or just with tables. For this example, we can go either way and create the same slices regardless.

Using Frames: It makes sense to divide this page into three horizontal frames, creating a top that contains the logo, the navigation buttons, and the dark and some of the white background; a middle section that contains the navigation buttons on the left and the body of the page; and a bottom that contains the lower navigation buttons. The middle section needs to

be split into two vertical frames to isolate the navigation bar so that it doesn't scroll out of view along with the body of the page. In the top frame, the navigation buttons and the arched background pattern and logo need to be sliced and put back together in a table, as do all the navigational buttons at the top, on the left, and at the bottom. Since the upper and lower navigational buttons are identical, we need to export them only once, but the backgrounds in the top and bottom frames do need to be sliced and exported separately.

Using Tables: In theory, you could place everything on this page in one large, complex table, but this is not advisable (doing so would be a beginner's mistake). For one, it is very hard to control and fix such a table, but above all, if the content—maybe because of some user preferences in the browser—expands beyond the cell of the container table, your entire design can break apart. A better HTML table for this design would split the page into one large table (shown with red lines in the screenshot at left) that contains smaller embedded tables for the navigational buttons and other page elements (in blue). You probably noticed that the container table has an extra column on the right side. The only purpose of that column is to display the backgrounds for the top and the bottom part of the design. It is possible to set the table up in such a way that this column will automatically adjust to the browser width (see the tutorial in the GoLive chapter).

2 **Creating slices and rollover buttons:** Create slices and rollovers as described earlier in this chapter, being sure to name each slice before you begin selecting them individually to create the rollover effects.

The rollovers for the top navigation buttons were created by deactivating the **Inner Shadow** effect and activating a **Color Overlay** for the text instead.

Note that the curved border of the upper background image needs special handling. To avoid an abrupt edge if you're using frames, the background for the top frame needs to continue the gray of the very top buttons and the black of the arch. You can accomplish this by slicing a piece out of the design at the very upper-right side and using it as a background image in the HTML document, which will later be loaded into the top frame. Do the same thing for the sidebar and the bottom navigation buttons: export a slice of the texture for later use as a background image.

This design requires 16 slices. A, B, and C represent the slices for the background image.

3 Optimizing: Once the page is sliced, open the Optimize palette (**Window > Show Optimize**), select one slice, and choose the appropriate settings. It helps to view the slice in the **Optimized** tab of the image window so that you can see the results as you experiment with settings. Note that you can select several slices at once and change their settings at the same time. Some slices for this tutorial were best as JPEGs, others were better suited to be GIFs. Here are the settings I used:

GIF

Slice No.	Colors	Palette
1	2	Web
2-7	16	Selective
10, 17, 18, 20, 22	8	Adaptive
12-16	16	Adaptive

JPEG

Slice No.	Quality
8	10
9	30

For the GIFs, I did not apply dithering or the **Lossy** option, but I did use a unified color table for slices 2 through 7, and for slices 12 through 16. The JPEG slices called for different quality settings, but neither needed blurring. Slice 10 was tricky. It had to be saved as GIF so that it matched the color of the slices beneath, but at the same time, it contained part of the arch, which was saved as JPEG. In this case, we had to go with a GIF and check it in a browser*.

---

* Browsers might dither the JPEG and the GIF differently when viewed with 256 colors. A few years ago this would have been a bigger concern because 256-color monitors were more common then. Today, however, most people have monitors that support at least thousands of colors. And even if they don't, this difference is probably negligible.

4 **Exporting:** Use the **Preview Document** button in the toolbox, and if everything seems to work as it's supposed to, select slices 1 through 7 with the **Slice Select** tool and export them via **File > Save Optimized As**. Since this is going to be a component (top_navigation.html), use the **Save Images** and **Save Selected Slices Only** options. Then select slice 10 and slices 12 to 17 and save them as another component (sidebar.html). Finally, select slices 8, 18, 20 and 22 and export them to the Images folder in your Web site.

After the HTML page is imported into GoLive, it can be broken up into stationery and components (here is the navigation component).

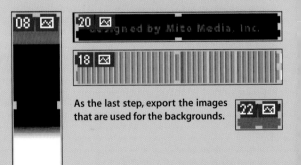

As the last step, export the images that are used for the backgrounds.

GIF Animation

GIF animations are still popular because they are small, they don't require any special plug-ins, and they are easy to create. With ImageReady, you have an excellent Web design tool that provides great support for GIF animation.

GIF animation works exactly like cel animation: Several frames are displayed in rapid succession, which creates the illusion of movement. For each frame in the GIF animation you can define attributes such as position, transparency color, disposal method (whether or not the current frame should be discarded before the next frame is displayed), and how long it will be displayed.

To see the **Animation** palette in ImageReady, choose **Window > Show Animation**. By default, the **Animation** palette is grouped with the **Image Map** and **Slice** tabs. If one of those is already open, just select the **Animation** tab.

Let's create a tiny animation to get a feel for the process. To do this, create a new image in ImageReady and type a word into it, such as "Animation." In our example, we've used the **Type** tool for this. Your image is now the first frame in your animation, as you can see

in the **Animation** palette. Click the **Duplicate** frame button at the bottom of the palette, and then use the **Move** tool to reposition the text in the image window. Now when you click on the **Play** button, you can watch your two-frame animation.

This hardly qualifies as state-of-the-art animation. You could, of course, add additional frames and move your text layer around some more, but your animation probably won't be very smooth because it's very difficult to manually position your text with the accuracy required for professional-looking animation. Fortunately, ImageReady offers a great command called **Tween** that makes it easy to create and control a sequence of frames based on layers. To see how this works, select the first frame in your animation and add some layer effects, such as an outer glow or a bevel and emboss. Then choose **Tween** from the **Animation** palette pop-up menu. The **Tween** dialog box lets you decide how to apply your effects to subsequent

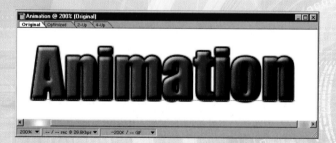

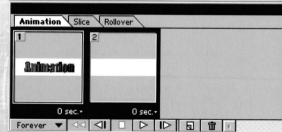

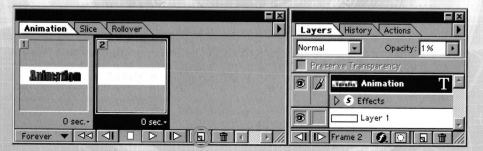

Click on the Create New Frame button to create a new frame in the animation. Every change in the Layers palette will now be recorded.

frames, and it also lets you specify how many frames you want in the final animation. You can choose to apply effects you have created to all layers or just to the selected layer, and whether to vary position, opacity, and/or effects. Then you can add intermediate frames and specify whether to add them in between the next, previous, or a selected frame.

After clicking OK, you will see your text slowly fade away, move across the screen, or even gain or lose an effect, depending on what you've specified in the **Tween** dialog box. If you want to preview the animation, click the **Optimized** tab, although viewing it in the browser will give you a far more accurate idea of the animation speed. Use **File > Preview in > Internet Explorer** (or Netscape Navigator) to have ImageReady place your GIF animation in a temporary HTML file. In ImageReady, even though frames' delay value might be set to the default of No delay (0.0 seconds), the animation will still play rather slowly, because ImageReady has to process all the layers. Only after all the layers have been flattened and the GIF has been optimized will you get a true sense of the speed of your animation—after which you might want to change the timing on certain frames.

Changing the speed, or delay, of the animation is very simple. The display time (in seconds) is shown beneath each frame; click on it to reveal some preset options. If you don't see a time value that suits your needs, choose **Other**. You can set the delay time within 1/100th of a second.

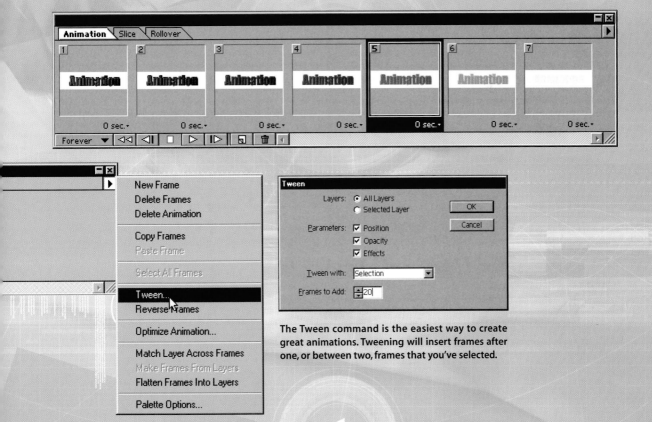

The Tween command is the easiest way to create great animations. Tweening will insert frames after one, or between two, frames that you've selected.

LOOPING AN ANIMATION

Do you want your animation to play more than once? No problem. The Loop options are set in the lower-left corner of the Animation palette. Choose **Once** to play the animation one time from beginning to end, **Forever** to play it endlessly, and **Other** to specify a particular number of repetitions.

Unfortunately, there is no option for backward and forward—if you need that kind of animation, you must create it manually. However, that's very simple: After you have created your animation with the Tween command, just Shift-click to select the inter-mediate frames (not the first and last frame), and then press Option (Mac) or Alt (Windows) while dragging the frames to the right side of the last frame, then choose **Reverse Frames** from the Animation palette pop-up menu.

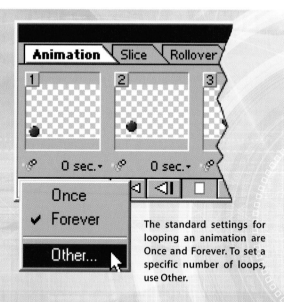

The standard settings for looping an animation are Once and Forever. To set a specific number of loops, use Other.

SAVING ON BANDWIDTH BY SCALING ANIMATIONS

Since an animation consists of a series of images, its file size is necessarily larger than that of a single image—and as you know, file size is always an issue on the Web. If color reduction and other compression tricks don't shrink the file enough, consider using a little HTML trick that can save as much as 75 percent on file size. In HTML, you set the dimension of an image with the IMG tag's two attributes, WIDTH and HEIGHT. The browser usually uses these attributes to determine the size of the image before it has downlo-aded, but you can also use them to scale an image. So to gain savings in file size, consider shrinking the ani-mation to 50 percent via **Image > Image Size** and then doubling its dimensions in the HTML code. Because it's an animation, the decrease in image qua-lity is in most cases not as obvious as with a regular image. (For those of you wondering how we end up with a 75-percent saving when we reduced the image size by only 50 percent, remember that the 50-percent reduction applies to both the width and height of the image, and therefore the final image is only a quarter the size of the original.)

DISPOSAL METHODS

Since GIFs support transparency, you can create ani-mated GIFs that use transparency. When that's the case, you can select what's called a disposal method to specify what, if anything, is visible through the trans-parent areas of your frames. Think for a minute about cel animation, where the background of a scene and all the characters are painted on separate sheets of transparent celluloid. This lets the animator reuse the background and animate the characters indepen-dently. The same idea lies behind disposal methods. They let you hold a previous frame as a background image, while subsequent frames add the animated character.

You can see the disposal method of a frame by right-clicking (PC) or Control-clicking (Mac) on it. A pop-up menu will appear, offering the options **Auto-matic**, **Do not dispose**, and **Restore to background**.

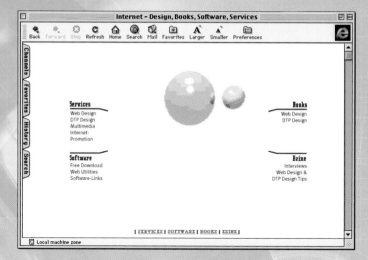

This animation of two rotating balls was scaled to 200 percent in GoLive, which kept the file size under 10 K.

Automatic discards the current frame if the next frame contains layer transparency. According to Adobe, this is the best option for most animations, so it is the default setting.

Alternatively, you can choose **Do not dispose**, which keeps the current frame onscreen while the next frame is displayed. If the second frame contains transparent areas, the first frame will show through. If you start with a full frame (an image that uses the entire frame), define it as **Do not dispose**, and follow it with several partially transparent frames. All the frames with partial transparency will be combined with the frame that was specified as **Do not dispose**.

Finally, **Restore to background** is like **Automatic** in that it discards the current frame when the next one comes up, but it's different in that you can set a background color or pattern that shows through transparent areas. Use this method if you want to use transparency to have a moving object blend in with the background in the browser.

Important: ImageReady does not simulate the disposal method when watched in the **Optimized** view, so you always have to check your result in the browser by using **File > Preview in > Internet Explorer/Netscape Navigator.**

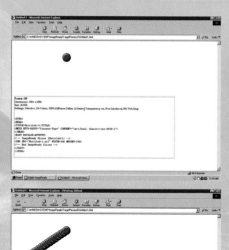

You can have ImageReady import the animation into a browser to check if everything works. This is particularly important if you work with transparency and disposal methods, since those aren't displayed in ImageReady. In this example, you see an animation of a bouncing ball, but the bottom one has the disposal method set to "Do not dispose."

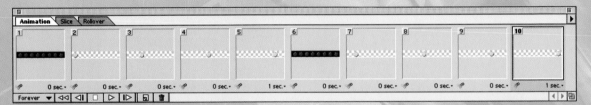

To create an animation of a string of blinking lights, I set the delay to zero and the disposal method to "Do Not Dispose," as indicated by the circled icon. This way the background string of "darkened" lights will remain visible while individual lights flash.

THE ZERO-SECOND TRICK

Another great way to optimize animations is to use the zero-second trick. Theoretically, you can set a delay time of zero seconds (No delay) for each frame in your animation, but in reality, browsers need some time to display each frame. However, this minimal display time is brief enough to make a frame appear almost simultaneously with the previous frame. You can use this to optimize GIF animations by splitting up a frame into two frames and putting them together by setting the first frame to a zero-second delay.

For example, I created the effect of a string of blinking lights composed of a background image with all lights off (red) and one single image with a light on (yellow). I placed the image of the yellow light on the background image in several positions and set all the frames to a zero-second delay. Then I selected **Do not dispose** as my disposal method to keep the background with the darkened lights visible when the yellow lights displayed in sequence, making them appear to blink. (The delay will be more visible on slower computers.) Obviously, it takes a lot of work to create an animation this way, but you can substantially reduce the amount of data because you eliminate redundant pixels.

This technique is also ideal if you have two animations that you want to run asynchronously. For instance, if you want to animate a clock, you need an hour hand and a minute hand that move at different speeds. You'll need 12 positions for the hour hand, and let's assume that you'll use 8 positions for the minute hand (to make life easier). With the zero-second trick,

In this particular animation, the glow of the lights needed to fade into the background, so the Matte option was used.

As you can see in the Layers palette, the entire animation is based on the background layer with all the lights off and one layer with one light on. This layer is moved and the effects settings are changed. It's important that for all the frames with the light on, the background must be hidden.

your animation requires only 21 individual images (20 images for all the hand positions, plus the background image) instead of 96. So you can see that certain animations benefit tremendously from this technique, but there are limitations on how far you can push it; after all, even a frame that contains a preloaded image requires some memory—and all the information on position, disposal method, and transparency color can add up.

OPTIMIZING ANIMATIONS

As you may have realized by now, you don't have to use full frames in your animation, which means you can reduce your final file size by cropping frames to only the parts that are important. ImageReady has a special feature that does exactly this for you. It actually goes through your animation frame by frame and figures out if there are identical parts in two sequential frames. If there are, it crops the frame to only the part that changes. Static areas are eliminated, so they don't use up precious memory. To activate this feature, select **Optimize Animation** from the **Animation** palette pop-up menu, and then check **Optimize By: Bounding Box**. Because this technique is so effective, you should try as often as possible to create animations in which subsequent frames build on the previous one.

This feature can be particularly helpful if you are converting QuickTime movies to GIF animations, something that ImageReady can do easily. Just choose

File > Open and select the QuickTime file. An Import dialog box appears and prompts you to specify the number of frames and other parameters. Optimizing the converted file with the **Bounding Box** option will reduce the file size tremendously. Just make sure that you select **Automatic** as your disposal method.

Another great feature is the **Redundant Pixel Removal** option in the **Optimize Animation** dialog box. It improves the animation by replacing every static pixel with transparency. Since this allows for a better compression (remember, GIF uses a pattern-recognition algorithm that makes same-color areas compress well), the file-size savings can be amazing—particularly in cases where the **Bounding Box** option doesn't work so well. Such a case might be an animation that has changing elements in the upper-right and lower-left corners. Since the **Bounding Box** can't crop very much, you still end up with large frames even though all the pixels in between might be static. **Redundant Pixel Removal** fixes the problem.

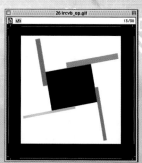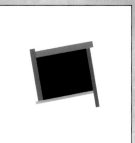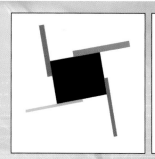

On the top you can see some screen shots of the animation on the Little Rock Web site. On the bottom, the individual frames are displayed. You can see clearly how the Frame Optimization cropped each frame to just the parts that change.

ROTATING A LOGO

Probably one of the most common animations is the rotating logo. To prepare such an animation in ImageReady, you first need to create the 3D logo in an animation application and export the animation as either an image sequence or a QuickTime movie.

1 **Importing frames:** To import a QuickTime movie, use the **File > Open** command; to import an image sequence, choose **File > Import > Folder as Frames**, which will import all images in a selected folder. To avoid having to rearrange the order of the frames manually later on, make sure the files are named sequentially.

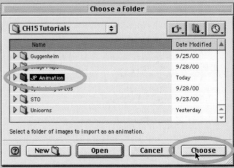

Select File > Import > Folder as Frames and navigate to select the folder that contains the frames of your animation. For this tutorial you can use your own images or download this example from www.mitomediabooks.com.

2 **Setting the delay:** Since this animation requires that each frame have the same delay, first select the frames with the **Select All Frames** command on the **Animation** palette pop-up menu. Alternatively, you can select the first frame, hold down Shift, and then select the last frame. Click at the bottom of the frame to change the delay time.

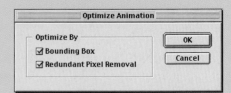

Make sure these two options are selected—they help to keep the file size small.

3 **Optimizing and testing:** From the **Animation** palette pop-up menu, choose **Optimize Animation** and check the **Bounding Box** and **Redundant Pixel Removal** options as desired. Also note another trick: the animation only shows a 180-degree rotation, which saves 50 percent of the file size. Click on the **Preview in Default Browser** button in the toolbox to open the animation in a browser, where you will get a true sense of the animation speed. (The animation preview in ImageReady is much slower.)

4 **Scaling the animation:** When you import the animation into your HTML authoring tool, try scaling it to twice the size. This makes for an eye-catching splash screen (you can see an example of this at www.plenk-josef.de).

Always preview the animation in a browser after you specify the delay time. The preview in ImageReady is not accurate.

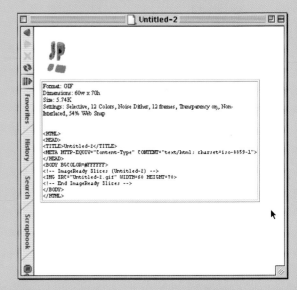

SWIPING EFFECTS

One way to make text in a banner ad interesting is to have the text appear in steps. You can do this by using a layer mask and animating it. The technique described in these steps is basically a swiping effect and can be used in different ways.

1 **First place the text on a text layer.** Then, with the text layer active, click the **Add a mask** button in the **Layers** palette. An icon for the layer mask appears next to the layer icon. (The layer mask should automatically be activated; if not, be sure to click the layer mask icon before the next step.)

2 **With the Rectangular Selection tool**, make a selection over the areas of the text that you want to cover, then, using the **Paint Bucket** tool, fill this selection with a black foreground color. Deselect the selection, open the **Animation** window, and click on the **Duplicate Frame** button.

3 **Before you can move the layer mask,** you have to unlink it from the layer; otherwise, you will move both at the same time. With the **Move** tool, move the layer mask to the right until it does not cover the text anymore.

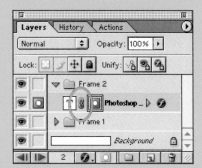

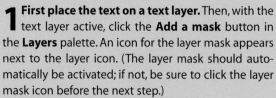

4 **You now have the beginning** and end states of your animation. To create the intermediate steps, use the **Tween** command. Select both frames, and from the menu in the **Animation** palette, choose **Tween** and pick the number of frames that you want to insert.

Illustration: **Jens Karlson/Vinh Kha** from the CD **Outjection**

OPTIMIZATION

Optimization is a major part of Web design. Even if you work in a large agency where you have a specialist doing the optimization, it is still important to know the problems and challenges. Only this way you can come up with a design that later works. Despite the fact that more and more people surf the Internet with DSL or Cable modems, many users still access the Web with 56 K modems, particularly people who travel and use their laptops. The importance of image optimization is probably going to become even more important in the coming years, due to the many handheld devices that can access the Web. These devices have speeds of less than 14 KB, which imposes even more restrictions on Web designers. However, it is fair to assume that this field will become huge. Given the increase in cell phones with Internet connection, I wouldn't be surprised if one day most people access the Web from a portable device. But even if that is never the case, what is safe to predict is that optimization is going to be the field with the most growth. Adobe already supports this area by offering the WBMP image format in the Save for Web dialog box. GoLive even has a special preview mode that simulates the display of a cell phone. Any Web designer who wants to stay ahead of the game should look into this. Ironically, issues that seemed to have disappeared, like optimizing images for 256-color displays, are coming back. So welcome back to the future.

GIF–Graphical Interchange Format

GIF is the most flexible of all the image formats for the Web. It can display photos with a decent level of quality, does an excellent job of compressing graphics, and even offers animation. So it should come as no surprise that our coverage of GIF is so extensive.

How Does GIF Compress?

GIF applies two compression techniques to images. One is called **CLUT**, which stands for **Color Look-Up Table**. The other is the **LZW** compression algorithm. Let's take a closer look at each of them to understand why GIF yields much better results with certain images than with others.

CLUT—Color Look-Up Table

To understand why a CLUT is so useful for data compression, it is helpful to understand how image formats work without it. For each pixel that your scanner creates when it digitizes a photo, 24 bits of color information are saved. For an image of 100 by 100 pixels, this requires 240,000 bits of color information. Since very few photos require a full spectrum of 16 million colors (which is what 24-bit color gives you), someone had the clever idea of limiting the total number of colors to 256 and saving those values (each of them still with a color depth of 24 bits) in a table. Then, instead of saving a full 24 bits of information for each pixel, you only need a reference to the location in the table. Eight bits are enough to address 256 locations in the CLUT, a two-thirds reduction in the amount of data. So instead of 240,000 bits, the same 100-by-100-pixel image can be stored in 86,144 bits.

You probably already realized that this is a little less than a two-thirds reduction. The reason is that the CLUT itself requires some data. In fact, a CLUT with 256 colors

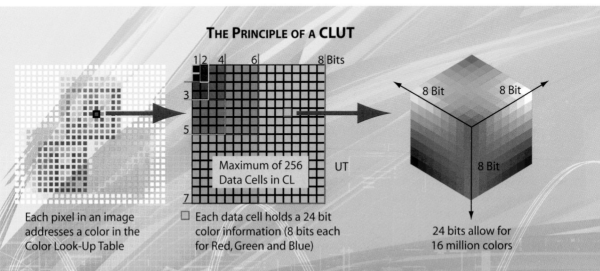

The Principle of a CLUT

Each pixel in an image addresses a color in the Color Look-Up Table

Each data cell holds a 24 bit color information (8 bits each for Red, Green and Blue)

24 bits allow for 16 million colors

Every pixel in a GIF contains a CLUT value. The size of the CLUT depends upon the number of bits used: one bit can only address two values (0 and 1), two bits can hold four values, and eight bits can store 256 values. Regardless of how many colors a CLUT holds, each color always has 24 bits, which means that GIF has a color range of more than 16 million colors.

needs 256 x 24 bits, which equals 6,144 bits. Our 100-by-100-pixel image therefore will be down to 10,768 bytes. The Save For Web command in Photoshop is intelligent enough to reduce the CLUT to the absolute minimum requirement. For example, if you have only two colors in your image but you choose to save it in 256 colors, the Save For Web command realizes that the CLUT is much bigger than it has to be and reduces it accordingly. And the smaller your CLUT, the less memory your file requires.

So let's have a pop quiz: How large would a 100-by-100-pixel image be if it had a CLUT with only two colors (black and white)? Since the image has to refer to only two color values, it needs only 1 bit per pixel to reference the CLUT. The CLUT itself has two colors, each with 24 bits of color information. The total then is 10,024 bits, or 1,253 bytes. If you save the same image with a 256-color CLUT, you'll end up with 16,114 bits instead—an increase of almost 60 percent. In fact, if you save this image with Photoshop's Save For Web command, you will actually get an even smaller file:

266 bytes instead of 1,253 bytes. That additional 80 percent savings comes from GIF's second compression technique: the LZW algorithm.

The LZW Algorithm

CLUT is only part of the reason for GIF's great compression capabilities. The other part is the LZW compression scheme, developed by and named after the researchers Lempel, Ziv, and Welch. The LZW algorithm is based on pattern recognition: Basically, it goes through an image file row by row, from top left to bottom right, looking for adjacent pixels of the same color. Let's say, for example, that five pixels in a row are the same shade of red. Here, the LZW algorithm would write down "Five x Red" instead of "Red, Red, Red, Red, Red." Although I've over-simplified a bit, you can see why graphics with large areas of identical colors are well suited for GIF.

THE FILE SIZE OF A CLUT

	Colors	Bits	Bytes	KB
1 bit	2	48	6	0.006
2 bits	4	96	12	0.012
3 bits	8	192	24	0.024
4 bits	16	384	48	0.048
5 bits	32	768	96	0.096
6 bits	64	1536	192	0.192
7 bits	128	3072	384	0.384
8 bits	256	6144	768	0.768

This 100-by-100-pixel image was indexed with 256 colors and saved as a GIF with a file size of 6,664 bytes, although it should require 10,768 bytes. The difference is due to the LZW compression algorithm.

BALANCING COMPRESSION WITH QUALITY

When you save an image in GIF, your goal is usually to get the smallest possible file size along with the best quality. To achieve this, you may have to adjust the color depth of the CLUT relative to the LZW compression; the fewer colors the CLUT uses, the better the LZW gets. However, if the image loses too much of its quality and detail, you may want to try dithering to get a better-looking image—even though dithering is counterproductive to the LZW compression.

Luckily, the complex process of adjusting these factors is a breeze with ImageReady and Photoshop. Both programs let you view as many as four versions of your image side by side, so you can compare the quality at different settings and optimize an image more easily.

To get an idea of how different bit depths, palettes, and dithering settings affect various types of images, check out the GIF comparison table on page 206. The chart shows the results for a photographic image (Image A), a graphic illustration (Image B), a photo-illustration (Image C), and a color spectrum (Image D), which serves as more of a reference than a real-life example. A spectrum makes a poor GIF since the LZW algorithm can't find many patterns, but it still gives you a good idea how the CLUT affects the image.

I saved each of the files with four different levels of color—with 8, 16, 24, and 32 colors. For the photograph (Image A), I used the Adaptive palette, which displays a much better image to site visitors with a monitor card that supports thousands or millions of colors. You should also make the effort to test images

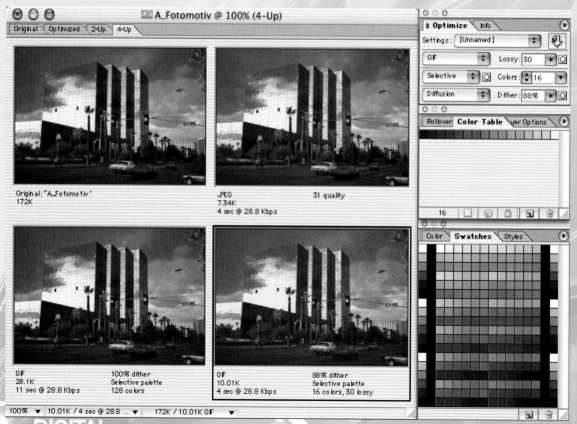

All the same commands and parameters in Photoshop's Save For Web dialog box are available in ImageReady's palettes and menus. So whenever I explain how to do something in the Save For Web dialog box, remember that you can perform the same tasks in ImageReady.

that use the Adaptive palette in a browser with a 256-color monitor. For Images B, C, and D, I used the Web-safe color palette.

At each color depth, I experimented with dithering. Many people avoid dithering a GIF because it limits the effectiveness of LZW compression, but it is an important tool for simulating intermediate colors, and the increase in file size isn't as bad as you might think. The drawback of the larger file is often offset by the improved image quality, particularly if you choose Noise dithering in the Save For Web dialog box. If you want the best of both worlds, you can consider partially dithering an image through the use of an Alpha channel, as explained later in this chapter.

In a printed book it is difficult to see the subtle color differences in the various GIF settings because of the conversion of the indexed RGB color space to CMYK. Some colors that can be displayed in RGB just aren't available in print; also, dot gain and rasterizing cover up a lot of fine artifacts. So to give you a better idea of the quality differences, I included a quality value—a number between 1 and 10, 10 being the best—next to each image in the chart. While this is definitely a subjective evaluation, I hope it's a useful point of reference.

LZW PATTERN RECOGNITION

Are you hopelessly curious about why things are the way they are? Then this section is for you: an in-depth look at LZW compression. The fact is, the LZW algorithm works quite a bit like the Color Look-Up Table. The only difference is that LZW stores patterns it finds in the image and indexes them. One funny thing is that once the algorithm builds the look-up table, it then throws it away—it is not stored along with the compressed data. But since there is a logic behind the indexing, the decoder can re-create the look-up table when needed.

Let's look at an example. Say we wanted to compress this chain of characters: ABACABA (imagine that they represent colors). We know that we have four possible values (A, B, C, and D in a 2-bit Color Look-Up Table), so we could start by putting those four values in a table and calling them 0, 1, 2 and 3. As we check to see through the chains of pixels that make up the image, we will always be checking to see if two adjacent pixels match one entry in the index table. If they do, we include the next adjacent pixel and look if this pattern is also already indexed. We keep on checking and including the next pixel until we find one pattern that doesn't match. Then we note the last match in the index, give the new pattern an index number, and go to the next pixel until we're at the end of the image.

In our case the first two characters are AB. Since this pattern is not in our table, we put it down and write 0 for the A that we found. The second character is a B, so we check to see if this character and the previous one are already recorded in our table as a pattern. Since they are not, we give this pattern a new index (4) and write down 1 for the B. The character after that is the A again, so we check if the pattern BA is in the table. That is not the case, so it is indexed as 5 and we note 0 for the third character (A). Since neither the next letter, C, nor the pattern AC is in the table, we put it down as 6 and write 2 for the C. The next character is A and the combination CA gets indexed since it is not in the table, but (!) we realize now that the A and the following character already exist as a pattern, so we write down 4. For the last character, A, we can only write down 0 since there is nothing following, but not before we register the combination ABA as 8.

This example hasn't produced much of a saving—instead of seven characters we now have six numbers, but you can imagine that with larger images the LZW algorithm finds more and more patterns it has already indexed. Once the image is saved, the LZW doesn't require the index table any more (it also helps saving data). To decompress the image, the browser regenerates the index table for each GIF, which takes some time and processor power.

ENCODING EXAMPLE	
ABACABA	010240
A	= 0
B	= 1
C	= 2
D	= 3
AB	= 4
BA	= 5
AC	= 6
CA	= 7
ABA	= 8

This is an example of how the LZW-algorithm would index seven pixels (each letter in ABACABA represents a pixel with a color; same letter equals same color.) Each line in this table represents a position in the index table: in the first four position of the index are the basic colors (ABCD), followed by the various patterns that the algorithm finds. At the end the result is 010240, which is only a saving of one (instead of seven letters you have six numbers), but if the image was larger, the savings would be more substantial.

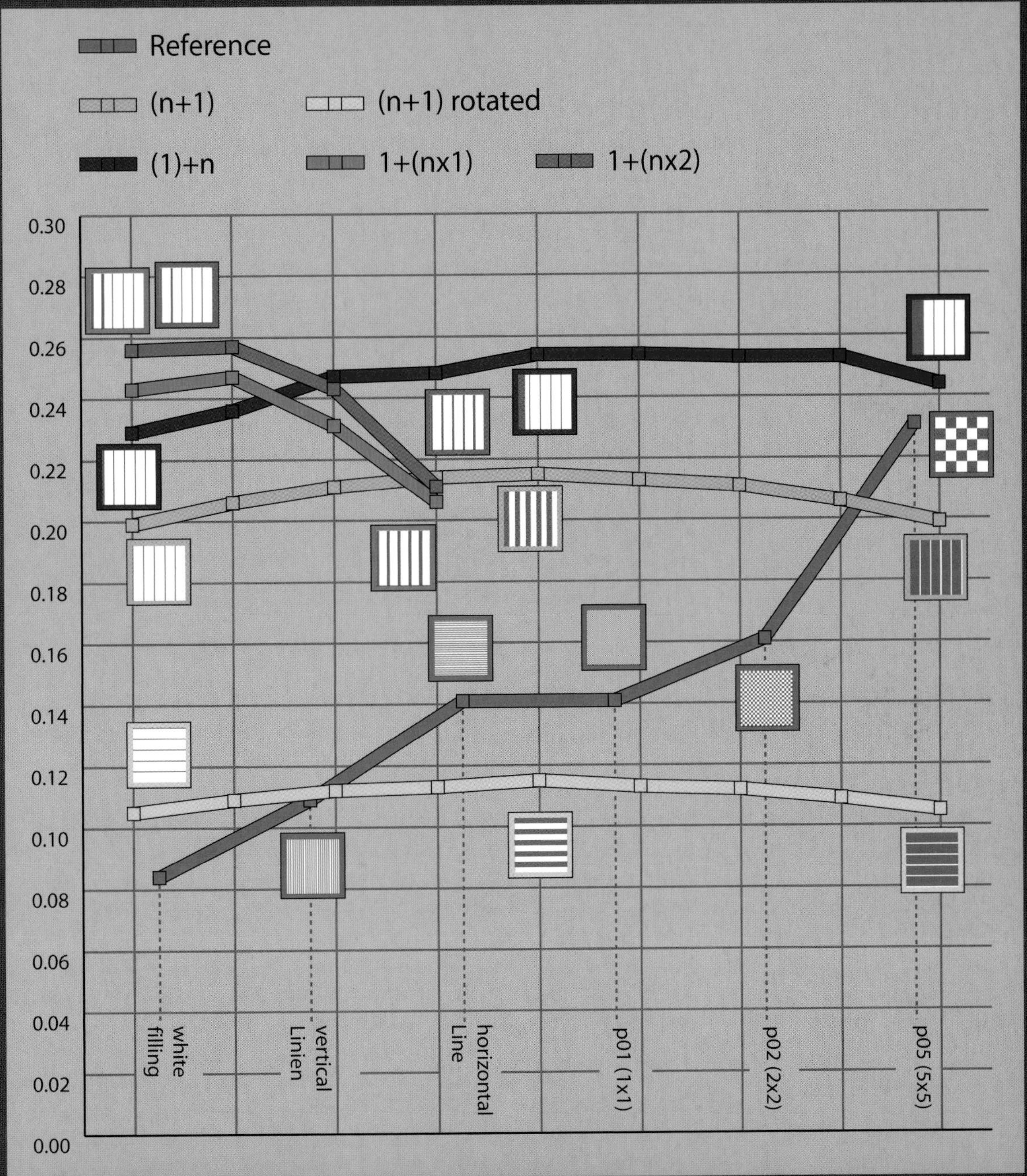
Reference
(n+1)
(n+1) rotated
(1)+n
1+(nx1)
1+(nx2)
0.30
0.28
0.26
0.24
0.22
0.20
0.18
0.16
0.14
0.12
0.10
0.08
0.06
0.04
0.02
0.00
white filling
vertical Linien
horizontal Line
p01 (1x1)
p02 (2x2)
p05 (5x5)

To get a better feeling for the LZW algorithm, look at this comparison of a group of one-bit GIFs that all are variations on patterns. See the next two pages for the individual graphs.

1+(nx1)	KB
01+2x1	0.243
01+3x1	0.247
01+4x1	0.231
01+5x1	0.206

1+(nx2)	KB
01+2x2	0.256
01+3x2	0.257
01+4x2	0.243
01+5x2	0.211

The width of the five vertical lines was continuously increased by one pixel.

(1)+n	KB
01+1	0.229
01+2	0.236
01+3	0.247
01+4	0.248
01+5	0.254
01+6	0.254
01+7	0.253
01+8	0.253
01+9	0.244

For reference, only the first red line was widened by one pixel until it measured 10 pixels in width.

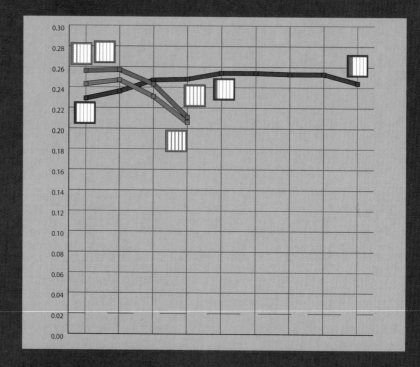

Now that we have gone through this explanation of LZW compression, can you see why an image with horizontal lines compresses better than one with vertical lines? Look at the comparison chart on page 203: the image with vertical lines requires more memory than its rotated version. This makes sense, since same-color runs create fewer patterns than if pixel colors alternate.

But there are exceptions to this rule. If you look at the chart on the top of page 203, you will see that a pattern with one-pixel vertical lines requires less memory than its rotated counterpart with horizontal lines. It's a bit confusing, but the reason is that after LZW has indexed the patterns and written all the index numbers, it compresses the resulting byte patterns. To simplify this, just imagine that while earlier we looked for horizontal patterns, now we are looking for vertical patterns. The image with the horizontal lines is much more complex in that respect, and it therefore carries more data.

What does all this mean to our work? Not much, really, since you don't want to design an image on the basis of how well it compresses. But it will help you to make a more educated choice when you need to decide which format will yield the best results and what compression settings to use.

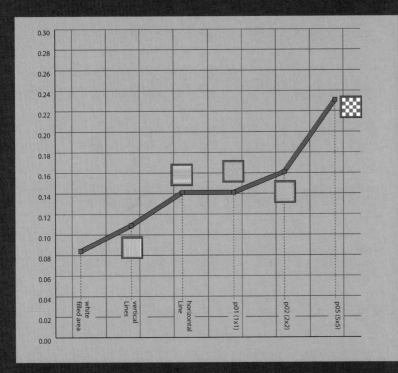

Reference	KB
white	0.084
vertical lines	0.109
p01 (1x1)	0.141
horizontal lines	0.141
p02 (2x2)	0.161
p05 (5x5)	0.231
Noise**	2.900*

*(-0.76 kByte for the CLUT)
** not shown in graph

I created several files as references. As expected, the white file is the smallest, and the Noise file, created with the Add Noise filter, is the largest (not shown on the graph). Strangely enough, the file with vertical lines is smaller than the one with horizontal lines—this has to do with final byte compression (see the previous page for details).

	vert.	horiz.
01	0.199	0.105
02	0.206	0.109
03	0.211	0.112
04	0.214	0.113
05	0.215	0.115
06	0.213	0.113
07	0.211	0.112
08	0.206	0.109
09	0.199	0.105

A red vertical line with a width of 1 pixel is repeated every 10 pixels. With every instance, the line is widened by one pixel. As expected, the file size decreases as soon as the line width surpasses five pixels. Rotating the files to make the lines horizontal decreases the file size.

GIF COMPARISON TABLE

This table focuses on color depths of 3 bits to 5 bits (8 to 32 colors), which is the range commonly used for saving GIF images. Images that require more than 32 colors should be saved as JPEG. I applied the Adaptive palette to Image A and the Web-safe palette to Images B, C, and D. Compare the file sizes of the images and my own subjective quality scale, a Q value of 0 to 10, with 10 being highest quality.

8 COLORS

Dithered	Non-Dithered

IMAGE A

9451 bytes   Q=5.0   6689 bytes   Q=4.0

IMAGE B

11,643 bytes   Q=4.0   7411 bytes   Q=2.0

IMAGE C

7739 bytes   Q=4.0   6424 bytes   Q=7.0

IMAGE D

8695 bytes   Q=6.0   1579 bytes   Q=1.0

16 COLORS

Dithered	Non-Dithered

13,311 bytes Q=7.0	

9736 bytes   Q=5.0

13,488 bytes   Q=6.0

8189 bytes   Q=2.0

13,450 bytes   Q=9.0

9769 bytes   Q=6.0

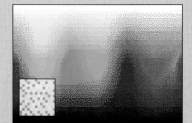

11,524 bytes   Q=6.5

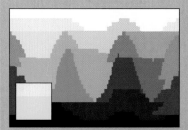

2412 bytes   Q=1.5

The JPEG comparison chart on page 248 features this image, labeled Image C, as an example of when GIF would produce the smallest file with the best quality.

If you're interested, here are the GIF results for the image above:

WITHOUT DITHERING	
Colors	Size
8	4,465
16	5,277
24	5,733
32	6,092

WITH DITHERING	
Colors	Size
8	6,127
16	6,463
24	6,875
32	6,875

All images measure 264 pixels (width) x 180 pixels (height). Uncompressed file size is 140KB.

32 COLORS

Dithered	Non-Dithered

17,182 bytes Q=9.0 | **13,752 bytes** Q=6.0

16,609 bytes Q=8.0 | **9754 bytes** Q=3.0

16,975 bytes Q=9.0 | **10,005 bytes** Q=6.0

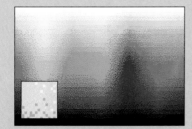

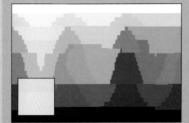

13,679 bytes Q=7.0 | **3311 bytes** Q=2.0

DITHERING COMPARISON CHART

The graph to the right shows the file size of the four images A, B, C, and D, saved with dithering (line graph). For reference, the quality values are displayed as well (column graph).

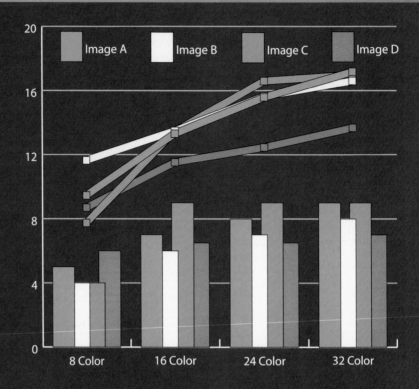

These graphs show how much the dithering affects the file size of each image.

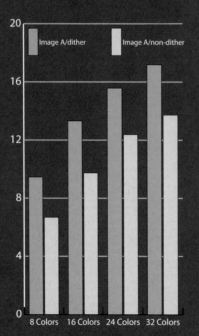

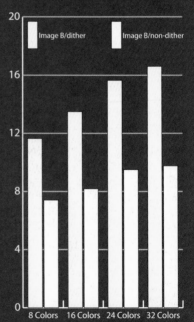

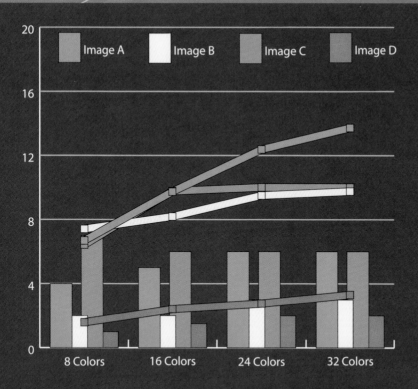

This diagram shows the file sizes of the four images from the GIF comparison chart (beginning on page 206) saved *without* dithering. They are significantly smaller than the dithered files on the previous page. For reference, the quality values are displayed as well (column graph).

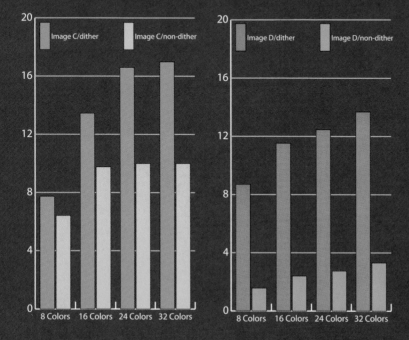

THE LOSSY OPTION

To interpret the graphs, look for dots that represent the same number of colors in each of the three files (they're connected with narrow yellow lines). The vertical axis in each chart is the file size, and the horizontal axis represents the quality; dots in the lower-right corner of the charts indicate the best images.

Both the Save for Web command and the Optimize palette in ImageReady o the Lossy option. This option reduces file size by replacing pixels with alrea indexed patterns (as explained on page 202). The result can look either lik pixel storm, in the worst case, or like a dithered image, in the best case.

To get a better idea of the effects of Lossy on file size and image quali compressed a photo (Image A), a photo with graphics (Image B), and a sp trum (Image D), with a Lossy setting of 30%, which is pretty much the up limit if you want to obtain good results. I also used a regular GIF with an ad tive palette as a reference image. Each image was compressed with vari CLUT sizes between 2 and 256 colors. First I looked at the quality of images compressed with the 30% Lossy setting, then I looked at each of th again with a Dithering setting of 100% and a Lossy setting of zero and g them a (subjective) quality value (between 1–10 with 10 being the best).

I left out the graphic image used in the GIF comparison chart (Image because it consists mostly of areas of flat color; the Lossy option has no ef on the quality, and its file size stays pretty constant no matter what the Lo setting is.

The chart shows that with Image A, the photograph, Lossy achieves the best results between 16 and 64 colors. With 64 colors, the Lossy GIF is 45 percent smaller than the regular GIF while maintaining the same image quality. The 16 color version shows 30 percent less quality with Lossy, but it's also 1KB smaller than the regular GIF. These results suggest that a photographic image saved as a GIF can greatly benefit from the Lossy option.

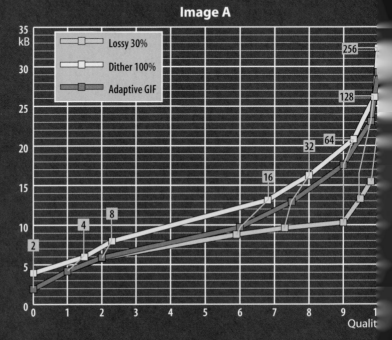

Image A

Image B

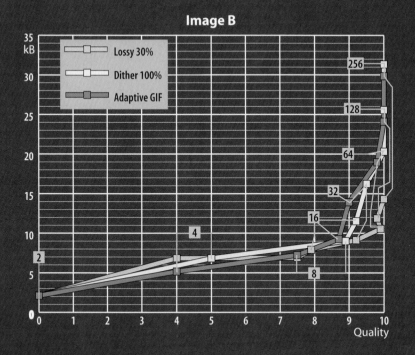

Legend:
- Lossy 30%
- Dither 100%
- Adaptive GIF

Image B is a photo-illustration, which is easier for LZW to compress. The results in the chart are similar to those of Image A; the difference is that the three GIFs are much closer to each other in file size and quality. The best ratio of file size reduction/image quality occurs between 32 and 64 colors.

Image D

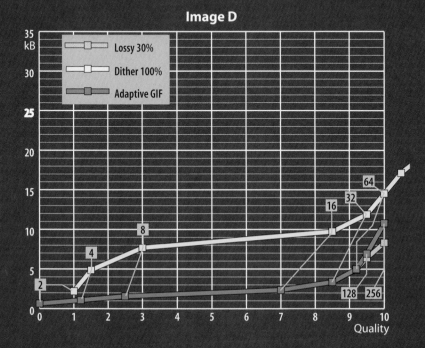

Legend:
- Lossy 30%
- Dither 100%
- Adaptive GIF

Image D is the color spectrum, just about the worst kind of image for a GIF. Although the graph shows quite high marks for quality, keep in mind that these are just relative assessments; they're not meant to be compared with the quality of the other two images. You really need at least 64 colors to get a decent result with this image. Dithering improved the results quite a bit, which is why a couple of the results are actually better than 10.

CREATING GIFS

As I've said, the most effective way to create a GIF in Photoshop is to use the Save For Web command. On certain occasions, you may want to prepare a GIF by converting an RGB file to indexed color in the **Image > Mode** submenu. The options presented in the **Indexed Color** dialog box are similar to those in the **Save For Web** dialog box, but the latter offers more features for maximizing quality and minimizing file size. Here is an overview of the options you have when saving GIF images for the Web in Photoshop.

Color-Reduction Algorithms

First you must decide which colors to include in the CLUT. This is a difficult task because each image is unique and requires an individual setting. Photoshop offers the following choice of color-reduction algorithms, also called palettes, and CLUT templates accessible from both the Indexed Color and **Save For Web** dialog boxes (I've listed them in order of their importance for your work):

Perceptual & Selective: Adobe suggests **Selective** as the best choice for Web design and uses it as the default setting. The **Selective** color table is similar to the **Perceptual** color table, but it favors broad areas of color and the preservation of Web colors. **Perceptual** gives priority to colors for which the human eye has greater sensitivity. You can see the effect best if you set the **Web Snap** slider to 25% and then switch among the **Selective, Perceptual,** and **Adaptive** palettes. The **Selective** reduction algorithm usually generates more **Web-safe** colors than **Adaptive** or **Perceptual**.

The best way to learn how the different color algorithms work is to create a full-spectrum gradient test blend and save it as **Perceptual, Selective,** and **Adaptive**, as I've done here. In the screenshot below, each version of the file has 16 colors, but each color-reduction algorithm renders a different range of hues. That's why it's important not to use the **Selective** color algorithm just because it's the default setting. For best results, you should consider the colors in your image and choose the palette accordingly: For more detail in dark areas, use **Selective**; for more detail in lighter colors, use **Perceptual** or **Selective**; for more detail in the red spectrum, use **Adaptive**.

Adaptive: I favor the Adaptive color palette and believe that it is perhaps the most important palette for GIF images. It lets you reduce the size of the CLUT to 32 colors or fewer and still achieve excellent results. As

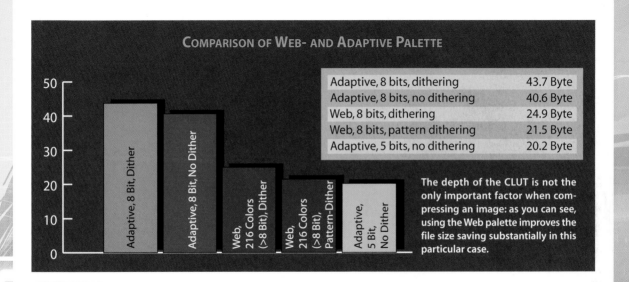

COMPARISON OF WEB- AND ADAPTIVE PALETTE

Adaptive, 8 bits, dithering	43.7 Byte
Adaptive, 8 bits, no dithering	40.6 Byte
Web, 8 bits, dithering	24.9 Byte
Web, 8 bits, pattern dithering	21.5 Byte
Adaptive, 5 bits, no dithering	20.2 Byte

(Bar chart labels, left to right: Adaptive, 8 Bit, Dither; Adaptive, 8 Bit, No Dither; Web, 216 Colors (>8 Bit), Dither; Web, 216 Colors (>8 Bit), Pattern-Dither; Adaptive, 5 Bit, No Dither. Y-axis: 0 to 50.)

The depth of the CLUT is not the only important factor when compressing an image: as you can see, using the Web palette improves the file size saving substantially in this particular case.

This image, the reference image in our comparative example, was saved with the Adaptive palette setting, 8 bits, and no dithering.

Photo: Paul Ehrenreich

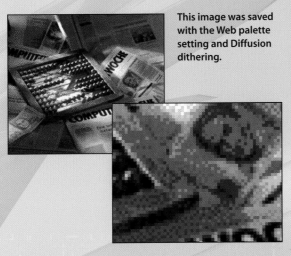

This image was saved with the Web palette setting and Diffusion dithering.

This image was saved with the Web palette setting and Pattern dithering.

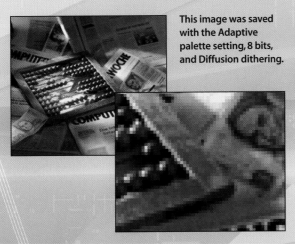

This image was saved with the Adaptive palette setting, 8 bits, and Diffusion dithering.

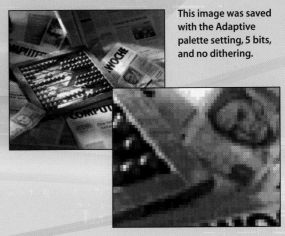

This image was saved with the Adaptive palette setting, 5 bits, and no dithering.

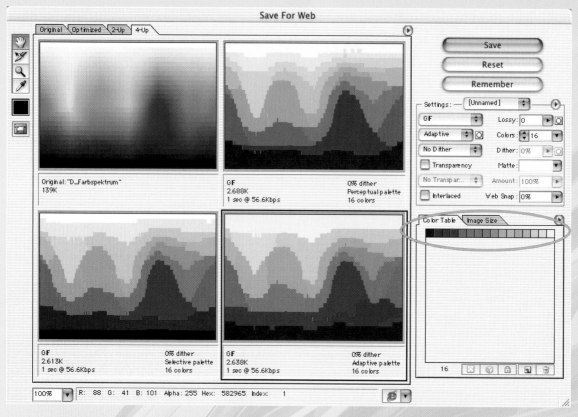

To get a better feel for the three color-reduction algorithms, optimize an image with each one and then use the 4-Up option to display the results and compare their color tables.

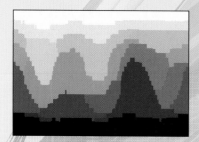

PERCEPTUAL
The Perceptual palette is more detailed in the brighter parts of the image, so bright colors are differentiated more than in the Adaptive color palette. Both the Perceptual and Selective palettes emphasize the yellow part of the spectrum.

SELECTIVE
The Selective palette shows more detail than the Perceptual palette in dark areas, and it favors the preservation of Web-safe colors.

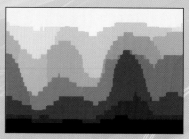

ADAPTIVE
The Adaptive palette's spectrum offers less differentiation between the bright and dark parts of the image, but it yields more detail overall throughout the spectrum (for instance, look at the magenta).

its name suggests, this palette adapts to the colors in the image, meaning that it picks the most frequently occurring colors for the CLUT. Since those colors are rarely in the Web-safe color palette, you will always have some additional dithering or color shifting when Adaptive images are viewed on systems with 256 or fewer colors. Luckily, the **Web Snap** option in the **Save For Web** dialog box gives you some control by letting you shift individual colors to their closest Web-safe alternative (Web-safe colors are marked with a diamond dot in the Color Table).

Web: The advantage of the Web palette is that all 216 colors display almost identically on all platforms. The different Gamma on each platform will still create slight shifts, but using this color table ensures that for the most part, what you see really is what you get, with no additional dithering or color changes. In real life, however, this color table is not used very often because it means saving your image in the worst possible color mode just to be sure it will look good on 256-color displays.

Custom: Custom allows you to create or import your own CLUT, which can be helpful if you want to use a common palette for all your images. There are two situations in which you might create and use your own palette. The first situation occurs if you save every image on your page with its own Adaptive palette; if you do this, you might run out of video memory on

The Save for Web dialog box lets you display the image in the browser. This is important when you don't use the Web-safe Color palette because Netscape and Explorer adjust the CLUT quite differently on monitors with 256 colors.

  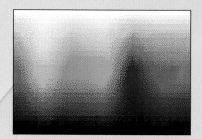

The reference image best demonstrates what dithering does: Without dithering, the spectrum gets reduced to flat color areas; with dithering, the colors blend gradually.

256-color displays. For example, if you had 10 images with 32 colors each, then the total number of colors would be 320—which means that 64 colors on your page would shift. To prevent unpredictable color shifts or dithering, you might consider using one Custom palette for all your images.

The second situation in which you might want to use a custom color table is if your page contains many images with different shades of a single color, such as yellow. If you were to optimize each image individually, you would end up with many different CLUTs, because the frequency of certain yellows would vary in each individual image. This might mean that the same color would shift differently in the individual images. This could be a problem if the images are adjacent (for example, in an image table).

Black & White: This reduces the colors to just black and white.

Grayscale: Converts all colors to grayscale.

Mac OS and Windows Systems: These choices let you save the image with a platform-specific color table. These two modes are most important for multimedia designers who might want to optimize the images for specific computers. For Web design, neither palette has much significance unless you really need to optimize your images for one specific platform.

Using the Adaptive color palette and a reduced CLUT (maximum of five bits) is a better, albeit more labor-intensive, way to get predictable colors and better results on high-end monitors. As I explained previously, because the color table is adaptive, it picks the colors that occur most frequently in the image, giving you the best possible display. The only drawback is that you have to view the image in each browser and on each platform with a monitor display setting of 256 colors, to be sure that your image looks decent under those viewing conditions. Using ImageReady, you can get an idea of how the image will look by choosing **Browser Dither** in the **View > Preview** submenu, but that is just an approximation.

Dithering

In addition to selecting the CLUT, you can also define the dithering in the Indexed Colors and Save For Web dialog boxes. Dithering improves the visual quality of an image by taking two colors from the color table and calculating a missing intermediate color. In general, dithering makes GIF compress less efficiently (it creates bigger files), but you can usually reduce the overall number of colors in the image by increasing the dithering percentage. Most of the time, reducing the number of colors is the key to producing smaller files. Therefore, you should reduce the number of colors to a point just before you can see a substantial drop in quality, then use the Dithering slider to improve the display, all the while keeping an eye on the file size. The example on page 215 shows that there is virtually no visual quality difference between an 8-bit image with an Adaptive palette and the 5-bit version, but the chart on page 214 reveals that the

text layer.psd @ 100% (Text Layer, RGB)

Text Layer

100%   Doc:131K/159K

To use the Transparency option in the Save For Web command, the background layer needs to be transparent. A transparent layer is displayed as a gray-checkered pattern.

5-bit image is half the size of the 8-bit image. Dithering the 8-bit version didn't add much to the image's file size; this image contains so many colors that it is hard for the LZW algorithm to find any patterns. (In fact, this image should really be saved in JPEG format.) Finally, indexing this particular image with the Web-safe color palette (page 214) produced great results because the palette disregards all the subtle color changes and many adjacent pixels get flattened to the same color, which improves the pattern recognition.

Photoshop and ImageReady let you choose from three dithering options: Diffusion, Pattern, and Noise. Pattern dithering mixes the two adjacent colors in a regular pattern that's easy for the eye to detect, so you should avoid it. Diffusion and Noise dithering, which use similar algorithms, yield much better visual results. In my experience, **Noise** dithering does a better job, but Diffusion dithering has the advantage of letting you set the amount of dithering using a slider. Remember that although dithering increases file size, the increase is usually offset by the improved image quality. You can always counteract the file-size increase using the Lossy slider.

Lossy

The Lossy option works miracles with many GIF files. It uses the patterns found by the LZW algorithm and stores them in a compression table. Then you can use the Lossy slider to specify how much you want to reuse those patterns in the image, thereby improving compression further.

Transparency and Matte

Photoshop's Save For Web dialog box and ImageReady's Optimize palette both offer a Transparency option. This allows you to make parts of your image transparent so that the background color of your Web page shows through and has the GIF image blend with the browser background. There is only one problem: If the edges of your object are anti-aliased (which they are in most cases), you might easily end up with a "halo." That's where the Matte option comes in. Matte lets you select a color—the background color of your Web page—which Photoshop then blends with the anti-aliased pixels in your image.

To get a better idea of how this works, choose the Type tool in Photoshop and write some text on its own layer, then hide the background layer by toggling off visibility in the Layers palette. Choose Save For Web, check the Transparency box, and select a Matte color that matches the color of your HTML page background; it will look like a halo in the Optimized preview, but it will blend seamlessly with the background in a browser.

With Photoshop 7.0, there is a second way to create transparency. Instead of putting the element on a separate layer and hiding the background layer, you just choose the **Save For Web** command. Here you select one of the colors in the Color Table, then click the little Transparency button at the lower left of the Color Table (maps selected colors to transparent). The benefit of this feature is that you can select more than one color to be transparent. This is an important feature if, for

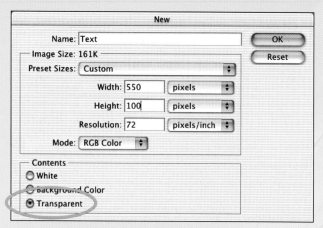

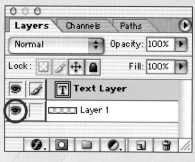

You can either create a new document with a transparent layer or hide the background layer before you call up the Save For Web dialog box. Activate the Transparency option in the Save For Web dialog box and select a Matte color.

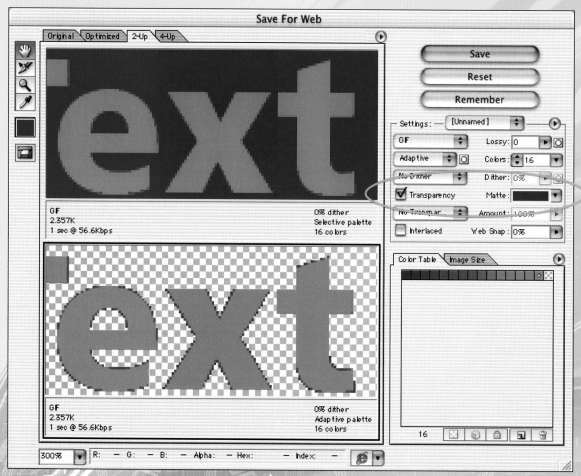

As you can see, the blue Matte gives the edges of the text a halo effect against a transparent background. But if you place it in an HTML document with a blue background, the text blends seamlessly. If the background color changes, just change the Matte color.

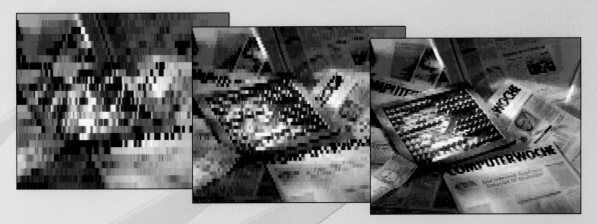

The Interlace option will encode an image in multiple passes. GIF always uses four passes—you can see how the first three passes are displayed in a browser. Some browsers, such as Internet Explorer, will display it line by line instead.

example, you have an element that will placed in front of a two-colored background. With the Matte feature you can only anti-alias to one background color, meaning that part of your object will show a halo. The ability to assign several colors as transparency colors means that you don't need to hide the background layer anymore; all you do is pick the background colors that need to be transparent and click the button. Ironically, this is a feature that was lost when Adobe abandoned the Gif89a Export filter and I'm really glad Adobe picked it up again.

Interlaced

The Interlaced option is important when you have many images on your Web site. Browsers can display a low-resolution "preview" of the images while downloading the remaining data. (Some browsers, such as Internet Explorer, actually display interlaced GIFs line by line.) Gradually, the resolution gets sharper and clearer until the image is finished downloading. Because visitors can see the image take shape as it's being downloaded, they get the impression that the process is faster than waiting for a whole image to appear. In fact, an interlaced image actually takes slightly longer to download than noninterlaced images, because to perform its trick, interlacing has to rearrange the pixel rows when you're saving a GIF or JPEG.

GIF interlacing works by transmitting every eighth row of the image (1, 9, 17, and so on) on the first pass. The second pass sends every fourth row (5, 13, 21, and so on), the third pass sends the remaining odd row numbers (3, 7, 11, 15, and so on), and the final pass sends the remaining even-numbered rows (2, 4, 6, 8, and so on).

While GIF interlacing always uses these four passes, JPEG interlacing lets you choose three to five passes. Interlacing also affects the file size of the two formats differently: A GIF will increase slightly in size because the scrambled rows reduce the number of patterns that the LZW algorithm can use, but an interlaced JPEG is generally smaller than a noninterlaced JPEG.

Using interlacing and transparency in the same image can sometimes cause "ghost" pixels to appear. This happens because some browsers use the first data pass to display a low-resolution preview that stretches the rows to the full size of the image, which may cause colors to appear in areas that will later become transparent. And since not all browsers refresh, those pixels may remain visible. You might never encounter this problem, and I would not be too concerned about it, but double-check it in the browser (older browsers in particular) to be on the safe side.

Web Snap

Not many designers use the Web-safe Color palette for their images because it subjects visitors to the worst display quality even if they have a monitor with millions of colors. The Adaptive and Perceptual palettes produce much better results on monitors that display millions of colors. This comes with the risk that the images will have some color shifts on monitors with 256-color displays, but this risk is currently not very high simply because there are very few 256-color monitors left (surveys show that the majority of users have monitors with at least thousands of colors). So if you choose to work with a non-Web-safe color palette, just check the result by switching your monitor to 256 colors.

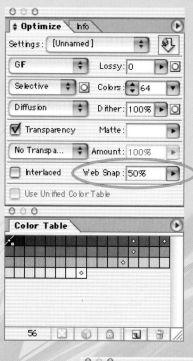

The **Web Snap** option in Photoshop's Save For Web dialog box (and ImageReady's **Optimize** palette) is handy if you're using a non-Web-safe color-reduction algorithm and you are suffering from too many color shifts in your image. Use the **Web Snap** option to increase the number of Web-safe colors in your image, making its appearance on different color monitors more predictable. Adjusting the slider sets the tolerance for shifting colors to the closest Web-safe equivalents.

If you need only one or a few colors brought into the Web-safe spectrum, use this technique instead: Click the color in the image with the **Eyedropper** tool (Shift-click to select additional colors), which selects the hue or hues in the Color Table, or select the colors directly in the Color Table. Then click the cube icon at the bottom of the Color Table palette to shift the selected colors to their closest Web-safe match; a diamond in the color swatch indicates that it's Web-safe.

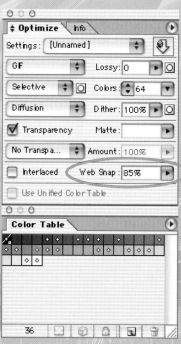

After you specify the colors that you've snapped to the Web palette, you can preview how the image will look on a 256-color display by choosing **Browser Dither** from the Preview pop-up menu (the right-pointing arrow at the top-right corner of the image window) in the **Save For Web** dialog box. In ImageReady, click on the Optimized tab and choose **View > Preview > Browser Dither**.

Web Snap, shown here in the Image-Ready Optimize palette.

OPTIMIZING A CLUT

Since the goal of creating GIF images is to minimize the number of colors used while maximizing final image quality, it's important to make good use of the Color Table palette. Here are some techniques for optimizing a CLUT using the Color Table.

First, select **Sort by Popularity** from the palette's pop-up menu, which places the most frequently used color at the top left of the table and works down to the least-used color at the lower-right corner. Look for adjacent colors that are similar, and chances are that you can delete one of them without a significant detrimental effect on overall image quality. It's a good idea to start with less-popular colors—those at the bottom of the table. To delete a color, click it in the table and then click the trash icon. Keep in mind that you can't undo this command: If you make a mistake, you'll have to start over again by pressing the **Reset** button—hold Option (Mac) or Alt (Windows) and the **Reset** button appears instead of the **Cancel** button).

If you choose to reduce the number of colors in an image by increasing the **Web Snap** factor, and you want to keep certain colors from shifting, you can lock them first. To do this, click the color in the table and then click the lock icon to prevent it from being dropped when the number of colors is reduced and to prevent the color from dithering in the browser. A small white square in the corner of the color swatch indicates that the color is locked.

Unfortunately, sometimes color-reduction algorithms drop colors that are important to an image; they analyze the histogram and select the most common colors in an image, but since they can't actually see the image, sometimes a color in an important detail is lost. In the image on page 228, for example, the yellow traffic light and the car's red brake lights were dropped when the Selective palette was applied.

There are two ways to approach this: One way is to determine which colors are important in your image and then lock them before reducing the colors. You do

this by setting the number of colors in the **Save For Web** command to 256, choosing the color-reduction algorithm, and then using the **Eyedropper** tool to pick up the colors in the image. Do this while holding the Shift key until you have a little more than 32 colors activated (they appear with an outline in the Color Table). To prevent them from shifting, click the lock icon at the bottom of the **Color Table** and then decrease the number of colors until you get the best result with the least number of colors. Some of the colors you picked up will obviously disappear, but the advantage of this technique is that you have total control over what colors were used as a basis for the color reduction. Which of the locked colors disappears first is then dependent on the color-reduction algorithm, so you might want to try this technique with different algorithms. Photoshop remembers which of the colors were locked, so you can switch between the algorithms.

If you already did your optimization, but one of the colors got lost, here's the second way of forcing a color into the **Color Table**: Click to select the original image in the **Save For Web** dialog and use the **Eyedropper** tool to select the color you want reinstated in the CLUT, then click on the **Optimized** version of the image, and click the **New Color** icon at the bottom of the palette. Voilá, the color is added to the palette and locked in. Since you already have set a size for your **Color Table**, there is a good chance that by forcing one color in the CLUT, another important color gets dropped. To avoid this, I recommend that you first increase the number of colors in your CLUT by the number of colors that you want to pick up. If you don't do this, you might have to reset your image and start from scratch.

STEP BY STEP: OPTIMIZING A GIF

Welcome to the art of optimizing a GIF. Art probably makes it sound more complicated than it is, but compared with optimizing a JPEG, it is way more complex. There are far more choices and possibilities, and it requires much more experience and expertise to get a great result. Before you start optimizing, you may want to consider making a selection of the areas of the image that are most important. With Photoshop you can control the application of the color-reduction algorithm, Diffusion dithering, and the Lossy option by making selections that are saved as Alpha channels. The way you create your selections is key to getting the best result.

1 If you want to create a channel for the color-reduction algorithm, use the **Lasso** tool and circle areas in the image that are more significant in terms of color but might not necessarily be the dominant colors in the picture. Take, for example, the red shirt below. While it's only a small part of the photo, it might be crucial to help this image look natural. While pressing the Shift key, select all the important areas with the **Lasso** tool and save them as a channel (**Select > Save Selection**).

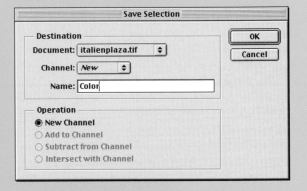

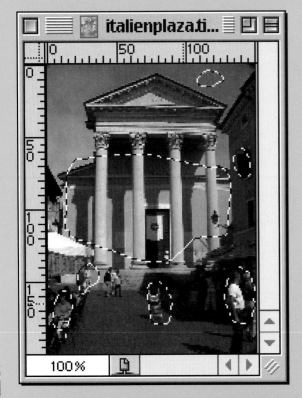

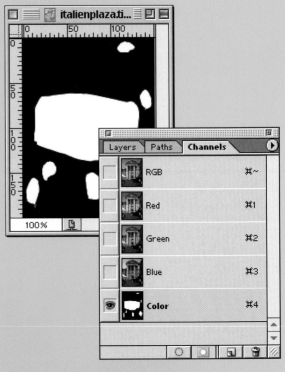

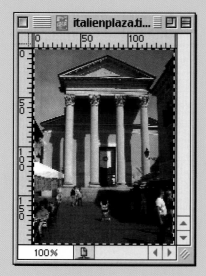

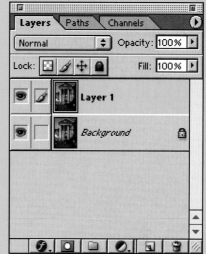

2 If you would like to control the dithering in your image, select all the areas that should get the maximum amount of dithering. Later, when you use a channel to modify the dithering, the selected pixels represent the areas for the **Maximum** slider, while the unselected pixels represent the areas for the **Minimum** slider.

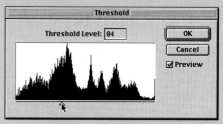

If you want to create an Alpha channel for the Lossy command, select the part of the image that should get the least amount of **Lossy**. So, when creating your selection for the **Lossy** command, pick the most important parts of the image and then save the selection.

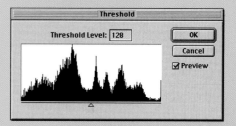

I recommend that you create one channel that can be used for both dithering and Lossy. This is possible because the black areas of an Alpha channel will affect the Maximum slider in the Modify Lossy Settings dialog box, and the Minimum slider in the Modify Dithering Settings dialog box.

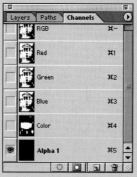

Select your entire image and choose **Layer > New > Layer via Copy**. Then choose **Image > Adjustments > Threshold** and move the Threshold slider so that only the dark areas of the image are visible. Select everything and copy it to the clipboard. Now switch to the Channels palette and create a new channel and paste the clipboard contents into it.

3 In the **Save For Web** dialog box, you can view both the original image and one or more optimized views, which show you how your image will look after it is compressed. After you click on the **Optimized** tab in the upper-left corner, it will take Photoshop a moment to produce the result; you'll see a progress bar at the bottom of the window. Since it's easier to make a decision if you can see the original and the compressed image simultaneously, you can also choose between **2-Up** and **4-Up**. These tabs will present either two or four views together and thus allow you to select compression settings independently for each view.

If you work with the **2-Up** or **4-Up** views, you may not be able to see the entire image at once, so use the **Hand** tool to move to the part of the image that you want to see. You will also find the **Zoom** tool and the **Eyedropper** tool in this window. The **Zoom** tool allows you to magnify the view; you can see the exact percentage in the lower-left corner.

4 Set the number of colors to 32 and the color reduction algorithm to Adaptive and then choose the Color Alpha channel in the Modify Color Reduction dialog. As you can instantly see, the image quality improves significantly. Now hold the Command key (on Macs; the Ctrl key in Windows) and select all the colors in the color table that are important. Lock these by clicking on the lock icon at the bottom of the palette. Then reduce the colors further to the point where the quality drops (in this example it is around 20 colors).

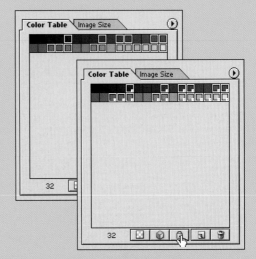

5 Make sure that **Dithering** is set to **None** and then set **Lossy** to 0 and click on the **Modify Lossy** button. In the dialog box, choose the Alpha channel that you created by using the **Threshold** command. The maximum for **Lossy** should be (in general) between 20 and 40. After closing the dialog, set **Dithering** to **Diffusion** and click the **Modify Dither** button. Now pick the same Alpha channel that was used for the **Lossy** command. As you can see, now the white areas represent the **Maximum** slider. This makes sense because dithering is most important in the light areas of your image. In this example a value of 40 improves the image without too much of a file size gain. After closing the dialog, the image is ready to be saved, or you could use the **4-Up** view to create variations and try to improve the result. I recommend that you use the same settings and experiment with different color reduction algorithms.

The before and after images. Despite a compression of 10:1, the final image looks decent on the monitor.

When you choose a color-reduction algorithm, many of the colors in your image get dropped, such as the yellow traffic light here.

CREATING CUSTOM (MASTER) PALETTES

Custom, or "master," palettes are useful when preparing multiple banner ads, especially when all of the ads include a company or product logo whose colors cannot shift. If you convert each banner ad with a Perceptual or Adaptive 16-color palette, you might run into problems if the logo isn't dominant in the color scheme of some of the ads. In such instances, it's quite possible that the logo color might be dropped, and the logos would look different in various banners.

This is undesirable (to put it mildly), and the only way to avoid it is to create a Custom palette that includes the logo color. This is a rather laborious process in Photoshop: First you have to pick a couple of the most important ads, index them, and save their color tables. Then you combine those color tables into one, delete duplicated or unwanted colors, and save it. When you've done this, however, you can apply the Custom palette via batch processing for a consistent look for all your images. Here's how:

Open one of your banner ads and optimize its CLUT in the **Save For Web** dialog box. You have two choices: either use the CLUT of one banner ad as the Master and

add a few colors from the other banner ads, or index several banner ads and combine them. If you do the latter, don't bloat the table with excess colors. If you would typically use 16 colors, try going with only 8. There is no one right way; what you do depends on the situation. To save a color table, use the Color Table palette's pop-up menu.

After you have saved several CLUTs, you need to combine them—and since the **Color Table** palette menu doesn't offer this option, you have to do it via the **Swatches** palette. Choose **Window > Show Swatches**, and choose **Load Swatches** from the **Swatches** palette's pop-up menu. Load the saved CLUTs one by one. (Note: The **Load Color Table** command in the **Color Table** palette's pop-up menu replaces the current table, but **Load Swatches** in the **Swatches** palette's pop-up menu actually appends the new colors to the existing palette.) Now you probably have more colors than you need, so delete extras by pressing Command (Mac) or Ctrl (Windows) to bring up the Scissors cursor and then click on the swatch that you want to delete. To add a color, select it from the image with the **Eyedropper** tool. Move the mouse cursor over a free spot in the **Swatches** palette and the **Paint Bucket** tool will appear. Click to add the color to the palette.

To force the yellow color of the traffic light back into the Color Table, select the color with the Eyedropper tool in the Original view, then click on the Optimized view and the Add Foreground Color icon at the bottom of the Color Table palette. The color will be inserted and locked (marked with a dot in the lower-right corner).

When you've refined your swatches to include the colors for your Master palette, choose Save Swatches from the palette's pop-up menu, and append the file with a .act extension. Then load the palette in the **Save For Web** dialog box via the **Color Table** palette's pop-up menu; the color-reduction algorithm automatically switches to **Custom**.

Now it's a snap to optimize a whole slew of banner ads so that the logo colors are consistent. Just record an action that optimizes one of the ads using the **Custom** palette, and choose **File > Automate > Batch** to process the rest of the ads automatically.

Creating Custom palettes is much easier in Image-Ready, which has a handy little command called **Build Master Palette**.

Open an image and switch to **Optimized** view. **Choose Image > Master Palette > Clear Master Palette** (the command will be grayed out if it's already been cleared; if this is the case, just skip to the next step). Select the color-reduction algorithm and specify the size of your color table (for example, a 16-color Selective palette) in the **Optimize** palette. Then choose **Image > Master Palette > Add to Master Palette**.

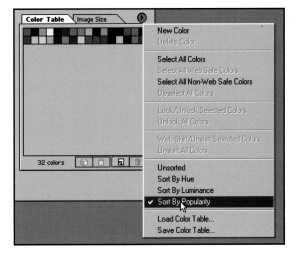

The Color Table has its own menu that you can access by clicking on the triangle in the upper-right corner.

If you want to batch process a series of banner ads in which it is important that certain colors are always included (such as the red of the logo), you have to create a Master palette.

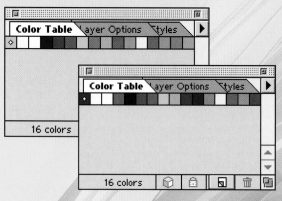

Here are the color palettes of the banner ads above.

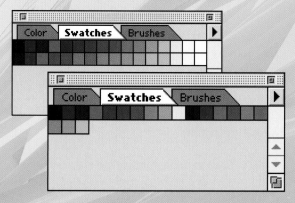

Use the Swatches palette to combine the color palettes from the top two images. Click on the colors while pressing the Command (Mac) or Ctrl (Windows) key to delete redundant colors.

Repeat this process for the most important and representative images. Choose **Image > Master Palette > Build Master Palette**, and then choose **Save Master Palette**. ImageReady prompts you for a name and saves the palette in the **Presets > Optimized Colors** folder in the Photoshop 7.0 folder. Now this palette can be accessed by ImageReady and Photoshop.

To edit your new color table, open an image and select it from the color-reduction algorithm pop-up menu; you can then see it in the **Color Table** palette. Colors that seem very close are probably redundant and can be deleted by selecting them and clicking the trash icon at the bottom of the palette.

Finally, create an action in which you index an image with your Master palette, and then select **Batch Options** from the **Actions** palette's pop-up menu to automate the process for other files.

WEIGHTED OPTIMIZATION

Before you choose **File > Save For Web**, you can use Alpha channels to tell Photoshop to favor colors in certain parts of an image. This is called weighted optimization.

Use the **Lasso** tool to draw a marquee around the part of the image that contains the important colors. The selection doesn't have to be precise; it's sufficient to roughly circle the main area or areas. (In most cases you need to include multiple areas; hold the Shift key to add to the selection.) Then save the selection as an Alpha channel in the **Save Selection** dialog box (choose **Select > Save Selection**).

When you go to the **Save For Web** dialog box and specify GIF, the **Channel** button appears next to the color reduction algorithm pop-up menu—it's a small vertical rectangle with a white circle in the center. Click it to choose the Alpha channel that you created previously, and the color table instantly weights the optimization accordingly. Try experimenting with the color-reduction algorithms to find the best one for the image.

APPLYING LOSSY TO PART OF AN IMAGE

Photoshop also lets you use Alpha channels to control the application of **Lossy** compression. This is particularly useful because the **Lossy** option has a very negative effect on image quality. So the best way to use **Lossy** is to apply it only to areas in your image where image quality won't be as noticeable, such as in areas that are already dithery (think beaches with grainy sand) or very dark (think shadows). Dark areas hide the **Lossy** effect particularly well because the human eye is less capable of distinguishing hues in the darker range.

To select the dark parts of an image, you could use the **Magic Wand** or **Lasso** tool, but Photoshop offers an even better way: the **Threshold** command, which provides a histogram of the luminance levels in the image and allows you to you adjust that threshold with a slider. First copy the image into the clipboard using **Edit > Copy**, then open the Channels palette (Windows > Channels). Create a new Alpha channel by clicking the **Create New Channel** icon at the bottom of the palette. Your document window will fill with black, because Photoshop automatically switches to the newly created channel. Now paste the content from the clipboard into the channel to get a grayscale version of your image. You could

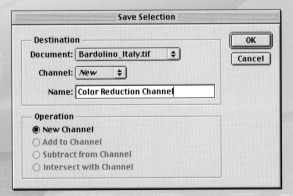

To force certain colors into the Color Table in the Save For Web command, select all the important areas in your image, and then save the selections into an Alpha channel.

use this grayscale version as your Alpha channel, but I find that you get a better result when you create a black-and-white version of the Alpha channel. Now apply the **Threshold** command: With the Alpha channel active in the Channels palette, choose **Image > Adjustments > Threshold**. You can accept the default level or adjust it; I prefer to reduce the grayscale Alpha channel to only the parts that are very dark, since those areas will hide the lossy effect most effectively. When you're satisfied with the results of the **Threshold**, click OK and switch back to the RGB view in your **Channels** palette.

Now open the Save For Web dialog box and click the Channel button to the right of the Lossy text box. In the Modify Lossiness Setting dialog box, choose your Alpha channel and adjust the sliders. Usually if it's applied to the entire image, the maximum lossy value lies around 30, but you can use a maximum value of up to 60 for your Alpha channel without much visual deterioration (if the dark areas in your image take up half the image). This means that you can greatly reduce file size without compromising bright portions of an image.

On the left you see the image with a 16-color Adaptive palette, on the right the same image with Lossy set to 50%. Used moderately (10–20%), the effect looks a little bit like dithering, but when it's increased, the visual quality drops drastically.

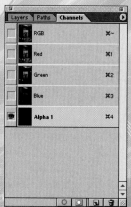
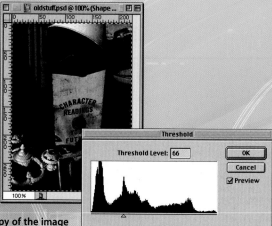

The best way to create an Alpha channel for Lossy is to use a copy of the image and paste it into a channel. Using the Threshold command will allow you to specify precisely where Lossy should be applied.

DITHERING PART OF AN IMAGE

As I've explained previously, dithering increases file size, but it can also substantially improve the quality of an image. An excellent way to minimize file size is to use dithering only on areas that really need it and keep the rest of the image dither-free. As with weighted optimization and the application of partial lossy compression, you do this through an Alpha channel.

Use the **Lasso** tool or any other selection tool to marquee all of the areas in the image that you want dithered. Then save the selection by choosing **Select > Save Selection** and choose **New** from the **Channel** palette's pop-up menu. Name this channel (for example, Dither1), then deselect the selection. When you go to the **Save For Web** dialog box and select **Diffusion**

dithering for your GIF, you can limit dithering to the areas inside the white areas of your Alpha channels. Click the **Channel** button next to the **Dither** box, select the Alpha channel that you saved before, and adjust the sliders.

If, however, you are already using an Alpha channel to weight the color-reduction algorithm, you need to make a different type of selection with regard to partial dithering: Use the **Magic Wand** tool or the **Color Range** command (**Select > Color Range**) to select the most important colors in the image. The logic behind this is that these colors need less dithering because they are already favored in the CLUT. Then go through the regular steps of saving the selection as a new channel and specifying that channel in the **Modify Dither Setting** dialog box, which appears when you click the

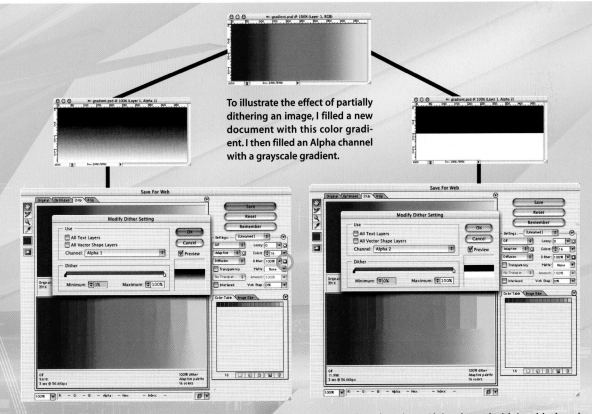

To illustrate the effect of partially dithering an image, I filled a new document with this color gradient. I then filled an Alpha channel with a grayscale gradient.

You can see how the Alpha channel gradually modifies the amount of dithering in the view at the bottom.

In comparison, here is an Alpha channel with just black and white areas.

Channel button next to the **Dither** box in the **Save For Web** dialog box. Use the right (white) slider to set the amount of dithering for the areas that need it the most.

Sometimes you are already using an Alpha channel to apply lossy compression to part of an image. If that is the case, you can also use that channel for partial dithering, because the black and white sliders in the **Modify Dither Setting** and the **Modify Lossy Setting** dialog boxes are switched, meaning they work inversely. I am not sure if this was intentional or accidental on Adobe's part, but it doesn't really matter. It saves you the trouble of creating an extra Alpha channel.

Finally, if you are using Alpha channels for both the color-reduction algorithm and the lossy compression, the selection for your dithering channel should be a combination of the areas for these two commands: For the color-reduction algorithm, you've selected the areas of the image that are important in terms of color; for the lossy Alpha channel, you've probably selected areas with a busy texture, which makes the lossy effect less noticeable. The selection for your dithering Alpha channel should be a combination of the areas that are less important in terms of color (and are not featured in the Alpha channel for color reduction) and the areas that are in the lossy Alpha channel.

The image with 0%, 50% and 100% dithering (from top down). It is clear that the shadow looks best with 100% dithering, but the rocket itself requires only 50% dithering.

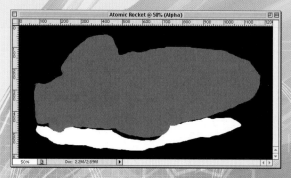

This is how the Alpha channel looks before going into the Save for Web dialog box.

The final result was worth the work: It looks the best and it saves 1.5 KB, which makes about a 20 percent file-size saving.

CREATING EFFECTIVE ALPHA CHANNELS

The best part of being able to modify the color-reduction algorithm, dithering, and lossy compression with an Alpha channel is that the Alpha channel is based on a grayscale mask. That means you can apply not only minimum and maximum values, but also in-between values. This is most helpful for dithering and lossy compression, in particular if you have a very colorful image like the toy rocket in our example.

Before creating any Alpha channels, you'll need to determine which settings you would like to apply. Since everything depends on the color-reduction algorithm, first optimize your image with regard to color. Open the **Save For Web** dialog box and choose **No Dither** and set **Lossy** to 0. Choose a color-reduction algorithm and perhaps use the **Eyedropper** tool to add colors that were dropped. After you've optimized the color table, press Option (Mac) or Alt (Windows) and click Remember, which appears in place of the OK

button. Now experiment with different dithering and lossy-compression settings. Take note which areas look best with a particular setting and then click **Cancel** to close the **Save For Web** dialog box.

In this example, I determined that I wanted to have 100% dithering for the shadow, 50% dithering for the toy rocket and 0% dithering for the white background. First I clicked the **Create New Channel** icon in the **Channels** palette to create a channel. Then I switched to the RGB channel and selected the areas of the image that required 100% lossy compression (the shadow). With the selection still active, I switched back to Alpha 1 and clicked on the background color field in the toolbox. In the **Color Picker**, I deselected the **Only Web Colors** option and then did some math: x * 2.55. If x = 100 (the desired amount of dithering), the result of the equation is 0; then I entered this value in the R, G, and B fields in the Color Picker, and clicked OK. After I pressed the Delete key, the selection was filled with the background color (white).

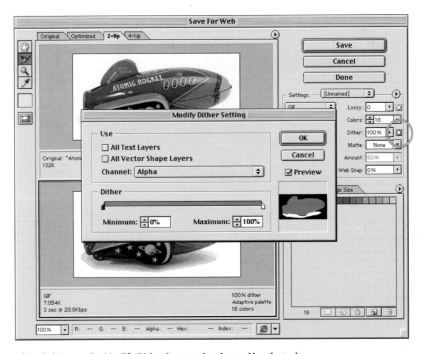

After clicking on the Modify Dither button the channel is selected.

For the toy rocket I wanted to have 50% dithering, so I made my selection and set the background color to 127 (50 x 2.55), switched to the Alpha channel and hit Delete. In the Save for Web dialog box I clicked on the Modify Dithering button and selected the Alpha channel in the pop-up. Then I set the Maximum slider to 100 and closed the dialog. The result: a perfect looking image and a file size saving of 1.5 KB.

By the way: for the creation of an optimized Lossy Alpha channel, the value of the formula must be deducted from the value 255.

Is it overkill to use multiple Alpha channels to optimize lossy, dithering, and color-reduction commands, and then use grayscale values to differentiate these even more? Certainly it is for a personal home page that hosts just a few visitors a day, but consider that an additional 5 KB on a Web site that gets 1000 visitors every day is 5 MB more data per day that your server has to transfer. That is 150 MB per month, 1.8 GB per year. So it is very important for designers of professional Web sites to optimize images to the greatest extent possible.

SIMULATING MULTIPLE LEVELS OF TRANSPARENCY

The GIF format has only one level of transparency, which is nothing like the 256-level Alpha channel transparency available in PNG format. However, it is possible to simulate a multilevel transparency with GIF. The trick is to use a transparent pattern, which is a technique that I invented in 1998 for the first edition of this book (for Photoshop 5.0). It is great that Adobe picked up this trick—it makes it so much easier to create multiple levels of transparency.

Create a new document, make the background transparent by clicking on the eye icon in the **Layers** palette and then, on a new layer, place all the elements for which you want to create drop shadows (in our case, a text layer). In the **Layers** palette, click the Add a **Layer Style** icon and pick **Drop Shadow**. Adjust the **Opacity** of the drop shadow to around 50%, so that you'll see the effect better. If you also want the text (or the layer) to be transparent, use the **Fill** slider in the Layers palette.

Now call up the **Save For Web** command and select the **Transparency** option. You can select a Matte color, which will adjust the colors of your layer and the shadow, but I would also make a version without it (**Matte: None**) and compare the results in the browser. Save the GIF and import it into GoLive. If you have a background image, you will see how the drop shadow seems to blend with the background.

The 50-percent transparency trick is used to simulate the plastic of the CD and to create a drop shadow of the blimp

In order to use Transparency dithering, you need to create a transparent element in your image (like the drop shadow here) and then hide the background layer before opening the Save for Web dialog box.

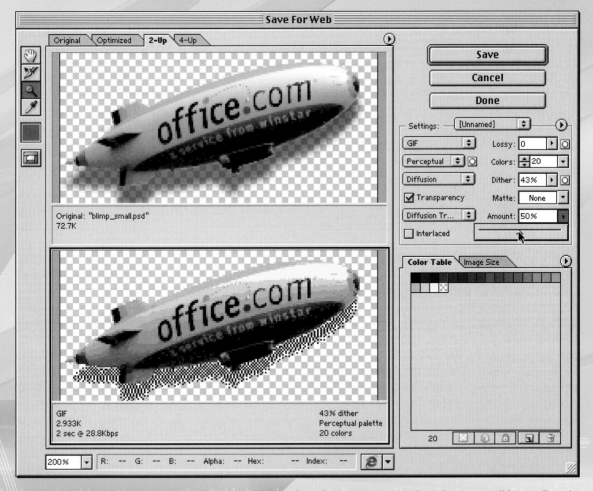

In the Save for Web dialog box, select Diffusion Transparency from the pop-up menu and use the Amount slider to adjust the dithering. If Transparency dithering is too obvious after placing the element on your Web page, try using a shadow whose color is similar to that of your background.

JPEG—Joint Photographic Experts Group

JPEG is currently the single most important format for photos and images requiring more than 256 colors. In the future, we may see JPEG losing ground to PNG, which offers some advantages, such as lossless compression and Alpha channel transparency, but for now, and certainly for the next few years, JPEG will remain an extremely popular and important format.

DCT Compression

JPEG uses a compression algorithm called the Discrete Cosine Transform, or DCT. DCT compression is based on the fact that the human eye is less sensitive to changes in color than to variations in brightness. While most image formats for the Web save the RGB color value for every pixel, JPEG actually splits color and brightness information and compresses each individually. The JPEG algorithm works on a block of 8 by 8 pixels at a time: First it calculates the DCT, which is then quantified, and finally, a variable-length code compression scheme is used on it.

Fortunately, you don't have to understand this to work with JPEG images, but it does explain why JPEG works so badly for images with extreme color changes: DCT tries to interpret the image as the sum of frequencies, and while this works pretty well for smooth color changes, such as gradients, if an image includes abrupt changes and high contrast, it can be a serious stumbling block for the algorithm. The DCT technique is also the reason why blurring a photo improves the ratio of the compression: Blurring smoothes color changes in the image.

Transparency

Unlike the GIF image format, there is no transparency feature in JPEG—which makes sense, since JPEG is a lossy compression technique. Every time you save a JPEG image it actually changes the image and shifts colors. This makes it impossible to assign a specific color as the transparency color as with GIF, and therefore transparency was left out.

JPEG Is Not Lossless

When I said JPEG changes the image and shifts colors every time you save it, I meant it. So if you open a JPEG image, make no changes whatsoever, and save it again, it will lose quality because the Discrete Cosine Transformation is applied every time. You can limit this effect by using the same settings under which the image was initially saved, but you will still have a loss in quality. The loss might not be as dramatic as it sounds, but saving a file over and over as JPEG will have some negative effect on the image.

At one point there was an initiative to create a lossless version of JPEG called JPEG-LS, but it never succeeded because its compression rate was only 2:1. And by now, PNG is the preferred solution.

Progressive JPEG

The JPEG standard has seen one important improvement over the years: Because of the growing popularity of the Web, JPEG can be saved as progressive, which works pretty much the same way as GIF's interlaced format. With a progressive JPEG, the image starts to appear in the browser while it is still downloading. At first it's a blurry preview of the image, then it gets more detailed as the stream of data comes in. While GIF is limited to four passes, you can choose between three and five passes for a progressive JPEG image.

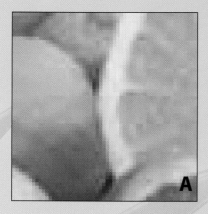 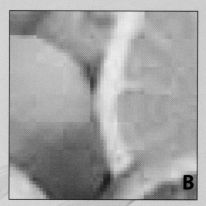 

To demonstrate the cumulative negative effect that the JPEG algorithm has on images, I saved the above image multiple times with different Quality settings and compared the results. I saved Image A 10 times with a rather low Quality (20) setting each time, and the image degradation is quite visible. I saved Image B 10 times, changing the compression settings each time (four times with a Quality of 20, three times with a Quality of 30, and three times with a Quality of 40). You would think that Image B would have the better visual quality because it was saved with higher Quality settings most of the time, but that is not the case. As a matter of fact, Image B is even slightly worse in quality than Image A.

HOW WELL DOES JPEG COMPRESS IMAGES?

You're probably wondering how much space you can save with JPEG compression. Compared with other methods, it is quite impressive. The best lossless compression methods can reduce the amount of data for a 24-bit image by about half, or 2:1. By comparison, JPEG can compress the same image between 10:1 and 20:1 (high quality) without visible loss, which is why most stock photos on CDs are saved as JPEG images. After all, this means that you can store a 20 MB high-resolution image in only 2 MB of disk space.

At a compression rate of 30:1 to 50:1 (medium quality), you will start seeing some visible shifts, which are generally quite tolerable. Only with the maximum (low quality) setting will you end up with a serious loss in visual quality, but the benefit is a whopping 100:1 compression ratio.

For color photos, there's no question that JPEG is the way to go. With grayscale images, however, GIF may yield better results. That's because JPEG does most of its compression on colors, not on luminance (brightness) information.

The question remains, how noticeable are the differences in quality between different compression settings? To answer this, I saved three images (a regular photo, a photo with text, and a graphic) in nine different compression settings in Photoshop, and then I viewed all the JPEGs and compared the quality. Unfortunately, it wouldn't help much to show the images here, as a lot of the subtle shifts in quality are lost in print, so you'll have to trust my subjective assessments I've made, based on my experiment.

JPEG is really excellent for use on the Web. It produces astonishingly small files, and while you will see slight degradations in quality, they are really quite acceptable. In the worst case, quality might decrease by 20 percent. In the graph on page 248, you can see that the compression rate is most effective with a setting of zero to four with Photoshop's **Save a Copy** command, and with zero to 40 with the **Save For Web** command.

I always use a setting between 20 and 30 with the **Save For Web** command because it seems to offer the best compromise between quality and file size. Images look great, without major distortion, and the file sizes are usually small enough for my needs.

The Correlation of Compression and 8-By-8-Pixel Blocks

As already mentioned, JPEG's compression algorithm divides the image into blocks of 8 by 8 pixels. But what if the dimensions of the image are not exactly divisible by eight? Does this have an impact on the file size? And does the algorithm create additional overhead? To answer these questions, I cropped a 240-by-240-pixel image gradually, by one pixel at a time. I then saved the image as JPEG and as TIFF (without LZW compression). The TIFF was my reference to ensure that potential variations in the file size weren't caused by the motif itself.

As you can see from the graph at the bottom of the page, there is indeed a correlation between the 8-by-8 blocks and compression. In the graph, you can clearly see a notch at every eighth pixel in the JPEG curve (yellow line), while the TIFF curve (red line) is linear. (Note: The file size of the TIFF was divided by 10 in order to display the lines closer together).

The notches also appear in the coefficient that was derived from both values (blue line). As you can see, the possible savings in file size are between 2 and 4 percent—not very much. Still this is useful to know, especially for images that you use as background in the browser. Keep their dimensions to a factor of eight to optimize the file size.

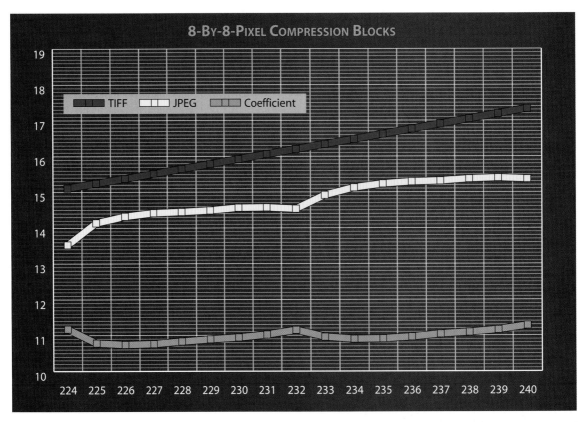

To determine the correlation between image size and JPEG's 8-by-8-pixel compression blocks, I gradually cropped a 240-by-240-pixel image by one pixel at a time in both directions and saved the files as TIFF and JPEG. The height and width of the images are recorded along the x-axis here, and the file size in kilobytes on the y-axis. (TIFF values were divided by 10 for easier viewing.) Compression blocks do appear to create some overhead, so whenever possible, image dimensions should be in multiples of eight.

Quality Differences Among JPEG Decoders

You may never have considered it, but the way a JPEG image looks will vary in quality from one program to another. A good JPEG decoder will try to adjust and smooth the edges of the 8-by-8 blocks to make them less visible. This is totally dependent on the program; it is not built into the JPEG standard.

Another trick that a JPEG decoder uses is to save processor power by doing a "fast" decompression, which basically involves rounding values. Similar tricks exist for color mode conversion. (This is not really applicable to Web design, but if, for example, you want to save your JPEG image in CMYK mode, the browser would have to convert it to RGB in order to display it. The accuracy of this conversion depends on the decoder.)

All this means that you should view your JPEG images in both browsers to get an idea of how they are really going to look. Don't rely on Photoshop or ImageReady, since their decoders differ from those in Internet Explorer and Netscape Navigator.

JPEG or GIF?

For larger photographic images, you will definitely get better compression with JPEG. But the question remains, where is the threshold when it becomes more efficient to use GIF? This question is particularly important when you're slicing an image or using small navigational elements like buttons. To answer this question, I cropped an image and saved it as GIF and JPEG with different Quality settings.

My results suggest that large photo images should always be saved as JPEGs. Even with low-compression/high-quality settings, you will get a smaller file size than with GIF, and the visual quality of the JPEG will be better. However, this doesn't hold true for images with an original file size of 10 K to 25 K (roughly 900 pixels in total, such as a 15-by-60-pixel image) that require a color depth of 8 to 32 colors. In such cases you'll get better results with a GIF than a JPEG, as you can see from the graph below.

Since this test is based on only one image and is therefore not conclusive, your results might vary, but that's OK. What's important to know is that the smaller the image, the smaller the benefit of the better format. This can be of significance when you slice an image to create an image table. All of a sudden, you might end up with a number of smaller files. Keep this in mind when exporting and optimizing: Always use the **4-Up** view in the **Save For Web** dialog box when you're optimizing small images and compare the results of JPEG versus GIF.

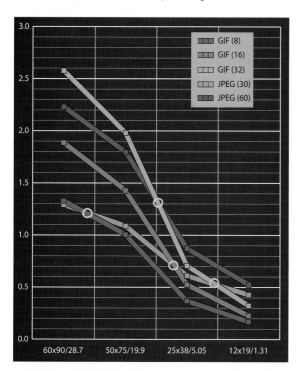

Wherever the red lines (GIF) cross one of the blue lines (JPEG), the file-size saving with GIF surpasses that of JPEG.

How a JPEG is Encoded

For those of you who would like to know how a JPEG encoder works, here's an overview that will give you some understanding of the complex process that goes on behind the scenes.

1. Separation of Brightness/Color

The JPEG baseline compression algorithm works in several steps. For the first step it is irrelevant whether the RGB or CMYK color model is used, although a CMYK JPEG is larger than its RGB counterpart (for use on the Internet, the image should, of course, be saved as RGB). You can make JPEGs from grayscale images, but since the algorithm mainly compresses the color information, the compression factor in grayscale images is significantly less.

2. Reduction of the Color Space

When saving, the encoder has the option of reducing the color space by a horizontal and vertical factor of 2:1. The encoder can also scale the color information on the horizontal axis only, leaving the vertical unchanged (1:1). Both options leave the brightness information, with its resolution and measurements, untouched. This compression step is used by only a few programs.

3. Compilation in 8-By-8 Blocks

The pixels in the image are divided into 8-by-8-pixel blocks and then analyzed with the Discrete Cosine Transform (DCT) algorithm, which is closely related to the Fourier analysis. In the process, the higher color frequencies are deleted, while lower frequencies, containing the significant color changes, are retained.

4. Quantization of Color Frequencies

In every block, each of the remaining 64 frequency components is divided by an individual quantization coefficient and then rounded to the next integer.

This is a JPEG as it is displayed in the browser or in Photoshop. If it were possible to see how a JPEG stores the information, the result would look like the image on the right: an image that includes only color information and one that contains only grayscale information. This separation makes sense, because to the human eye, the difference in luminance is more important than subtle changes in hue.

The image is divided into 8-by-8-pixel blocks. The color frequencies are rounded, which results in a loss of detail that you can see here. The left image is the original image, the middle image is an enlargement of the original image, and the right image is the enlargement after compression.

This step creates the biggest savings. The higher the quantization coefficient, the more data will be truncated. Even the lowest possible quantization coefficient—1, which equals Quality 100 in Photoshop's Save For Web command—will change the color information, because the DCT doesn't generate integers.

Because of the larger coefficient, higher frequencies are quantized less accurately than lower ones—it's OK, though, because the eye can't perceive those subtle differences anyway. Brightness information (luminosity), however, is quantized with a much higher level of accuracy (64 possible values) than the color information (chroma). The quantization table can be set by the JPEG encoder, but most encoders use only the simple, linear scaling that is set by the JPEG standard. The quality level that the user sets in the encoder defines the scaling factor of this table.

This quantization table is responsible for the different qualities among some of the JPEG encoders, because JPEG's standard table works well only with medium-quality settings, not so well for high or low levels. So you can get a smaller file size with an encoder optimized for low-quality settings, as is necessary for the Web (this explains the differences between the Save As and Save For Web commands).

5. Arithmetic or Huffman Encoding of Coefficients
This step is lossless. Although arithmetic encoding generates 10 percent better compression, its Q Encoding is patented. Therefore, Huffman encoding is usually used instead.

6. Inserting the Correct Header and Saving the File
All compression parameters are saved with the image, so the decoder can reverse the process accordingly. These parameters contain the quantization table and the Huffman encoding table, for example. The specification also allows you to omit this information, which saves several hundred bytes. However, the image can then be decoded only if the decoder itself contains the required tables.

IMPROVING COMPRESSION WITH BLURRING

One of the best-known tricks for reducing the file size of a compressed JPEG image is to apply a **Gaussian** blur to an image before saving it. With JPEG compression, drastic color changes cause artifacts—visual flaws—but a **Gaussian** blur addresses this problem by looking at each pixel and adjusting the colors of the pixels that surround it, thereby minimizing those abrupt shifts and increasing compression. Of course, you must be careful because this improved compression sometimes reduces image quality: Text in an image, for example, is particularly vulnerable to reduced quality when blurred and compressed.

But while you can learn this trick from pretty much any book on Web design, I'll bet you didn't know that there are alternatives to applying a **Gaussian** blur for maximizing JPEG compression. For example, you can

also use a **Smart Blur** filter or a **Despeckle** noise filter. What is the difference between these techniques?

A **Gaussian** blur filter blurs a selection by an adjustable amount, adding low-frequency detail and creating a hazy effect. The **Blur** option in the **Save For Web** dialog box actually applies a **Gaussian** blur.

Smart Blur offers a bit more control: First, it allows you to specify a radius. All the pixels within the radius will be adjusted, not just adjacent pixels. This sometimes creates a graphical effect because it makes the area within the radius look flat. The **Smart Blur** filter also offers a **Threshold** slider that lets you adjust what the filter should recognize as an edge. Set the **Threshold** to 100 (the maximum), and all subtle color changes will disappear. Finally, you can specify a blur quality (low, medium, or high) and a mode (normal, edge only, or edge overlay).

	Original	D1	GB 0.3	D2	GB 0.6	D3	GB 0.9	D4	GB 1.2	Smart Blur
Q 70	50.8 KB	41.7 KB	42.7 KB	38.3 KB	37.7 KB	36.0 KB	33.0 KB	34.5 KB	29.2 KB	42.1 KB
Q 30	19.3 KB	16.3 KB	16.6 KB	15.1 KB	15.0 KB	14.3 KB	13.3 KB	13.7 KB	11.9 KB	16.5 KB
Q 0	8.5 KB	7.8 KB	7.8 KB	7.5 KB	7.4 KB	7.2 KB	6.9 KB	7.2 KB	6.4 KB	8.0 KB

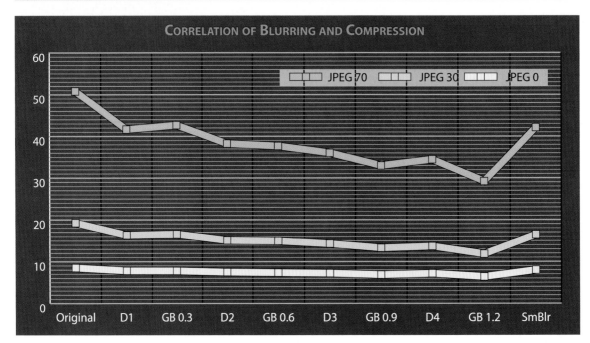

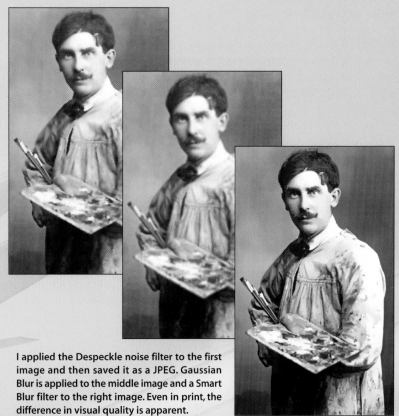

I treated this original image (290-x-470 pixels, 400 K) with various filters to see how they affected JPEG compression.

I applied the Despeckle noise filter to the first image and then saved it as a JPEG. Gaussian Blur is applied to the middle image and a Smart Blur filter to the right image. Even in print, the difference in visual quality is apparent.

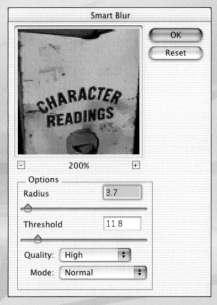

Smart Blur lets you define a radius within which it equalizes the colors of all pixels. With Threshold, you can set the level of detail. In the image on the left it is easy to see the effect: The rust on the vintage fortune teller has almost vanished.

Despeckle (**Filter > Noise > Despeckle**) attempts to preserve the edges when blurring. It does so by looking for any strong contrasts and exempting them from the blurring process. Since **Despeckle** always works with a fixed value, you sometimes have to apply it several times until you achieve the desired level of blurring.

So just how much savings do these filters actually buy? To find out, I applied a **Gaussian** blur (with values ranging from 0.3 to 1.2 pixels), a **Despeckle** filter (applied between one and four times), and a Smart Blur filter (Radius 3.7, Threshold 11.9, Quality: High) to the same image in various combinations and then compared the results.

As you can see from the results printed on the previous page and from the graph on page 244, applying these filters to an image before saving it as JPEG does make a difference, but more filtering is not necessarily better. A **Gaussian** blur of 0.3 or a **Despeckle** filter applied once rendered the best results. An increase in the **Gaussian** blur from 0.6 to 1.2 and multiple applications of **Despeckle** from two to four times don't result in proportional file size savings—and the visual quality drops substantially. For a **Gaussian** blur of 1.2, the decrease in quality is (subjectively) about 50 percent, and after four applications of **Despeckle**, it's about 30 percent.

What's nice is that you can apply the **Despeckle** and **Smart Blur** filters before going to **Save For Web**. Then, if you like, you can apply a **Gaussian** blur with the **Blur** option. When you do that, you get the greatest file savings (roughly 20 percent) for higher Quality settings. The lower the image quality, the less can be gained (10 percent). The bottom line: You can get smaller image files if you use a **Gaussian** blur, a **Smart Blur** filter, or a **Despeckle** noise filter before saving a JPEG image, but don't overdo it. You'll get the best compression-to-quality ratio if you blur as little as possible. Using **Despeckle** and **Smart Blur** in combination with **Blur** in the **Save For Web** dialog box is great, but if you do that you can use a smaller **Blur** setting because most of the work has already been done.

OPTIMIZING SAVINGS THROUGH AN ALPHA CHANNEL

The **Save For Web** command lets you set the **Quality** level of JPEG compression on a scale of zero to 100, where zero results in the best compression, but the lowest image quality. With Photoshop it's possible to modify the **Quality** level with an Alpha channel.

Before opening the **Save For Web** dialog box, select (for example with the Lasso tool) the area or areas to which you want to assign the maximum **Quality**. Remember that JPEG uses 8-by-8-pixel blocks in its compression algorithm, which means that you should not (!) make a tight selection; otherwise, the edges of the two different **Quality** settings will be more obvious. If you are unsure about where to put the edge of the selection, study your image first in the **Save For Web** dialog box. Use 0 as your **Quality** setting and zoom in. The 8-by-8-pixel blocks should be easy to distinguish and they'll give you an idea of how to draw your selection. Then cancel out of the **Save For Web** dialog box, make your selection, and save it by choosing **Select > Save Selection**.

Now open the **Save For Web** dialog box and click on the **Channel** button next to the **Quality** text field. In the **Modify Quality Setting** dialog box, choose the Alpha channel that contains your selection. The channel is visible in a thumbnail: The white areas represent the **Maximum** slider (marked in white) and the black areas represent the **Minimum** slider. When adjusting the **Maximum** value, don't go overboard: The **Maximum** value should be 30 (plus or minus 10) and the **Minimum** should be 10 (plus or minus 10); otherwise, the file will grow too much. The idea behind this feature is not to save the JPEG with a higher **Quality** value than you would usually do, but rather to squeeze out the last bit of savings where possible.

Since this Photoshop feature is most important when you have text or solid-colored areas in your image, Photoshop offers two options in the **Modify Quality Setting** dialog box: **All Text Layers** and **All Vector Shape Layers**. These use any text layers and vector shape layers and add them to the selected Alpha channel.

As with GIFs, you can use a grayscale Alpha channel to modify the **Quality** gradually, but this is rather redundant and offers little real-world gain. You're better off specifying a Blur value in the **Save For Web** dialog box (this reduces edge artifacts and color shifts and also improves the compression), or applying a **Gaussian** blur, a **Smart Blur** filter, or a **Despeckle** noise filter before saving for the Web.

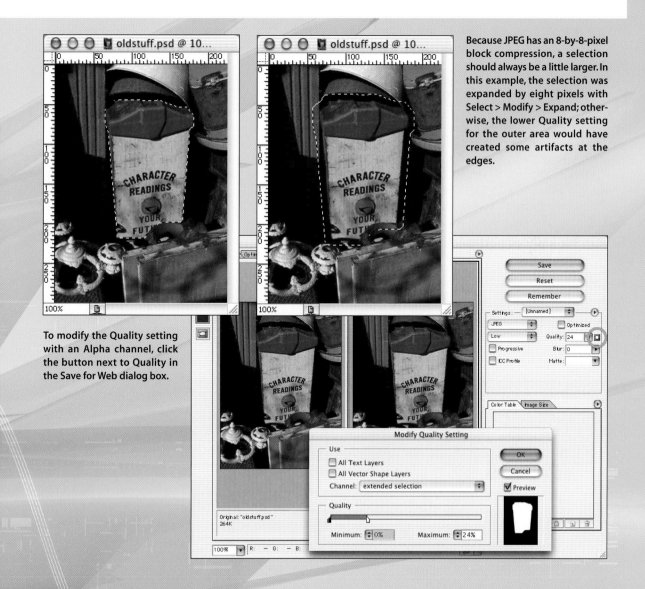

To modify the Quality setting with an Alpha channel, click the button next to Quality in the Save for Web dialog box.

Because JPEG has an 8-by-8-pixel block compression, a selection should always be a little larger. In this example, the selection was expanded by eight pixels with Select > Modify > Expand; otherwise, the lower Quality setting for the outer area would have created some artifacts at the edges.

JPEG Comparison Charts

These charts compare the file size of the test images that I used: a photograph (Image A), a photo illustration (Image B), a graphics file (Image C), and a color spectrum (Image D). Note that Image D is almost a best-case scenario for JPEG compression and is therefore an excellent reference. All images measure 256x180 pixels, require 140 K uncompressed, and were saved using both the **Save for Web** and **Save As** commands.

Although the **Save for Web** command offers quality values of 0 to 100 and the **Save As** command offers settings of 0 to 12, settings above 80 (or 8) are never used in Web design, so I excluded them here. In reality, only quality levels up to 40 are ever used with **Save for Web** (up to 5 with **Save As**), because the JPEG algorithm delivers excellent and sufficient results at these lower quality settings. Only quality levels of 0 to 10 introduce a deterioration in quality. (Because the nuances between these quality levels would be difficult to discern in print, and the differences aren't dramatic anyway—especially compared to GIF—there was no point in showing them here.)

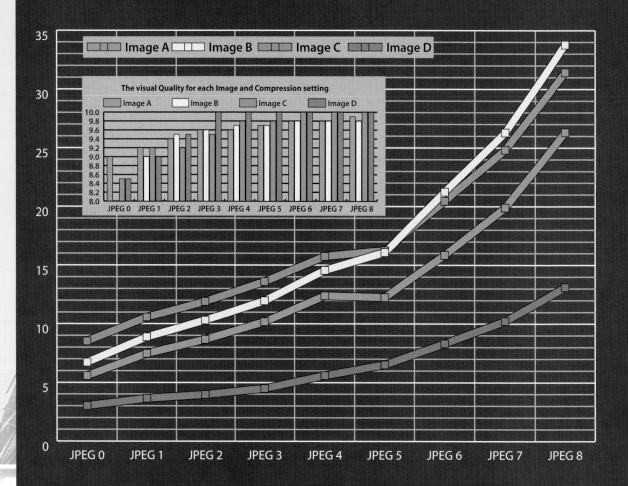

As you can see, **Save for Web** (right) achieves better compression than **Save As** (left). Also notice the flatter slope of the curve between quality values 4 and 5 in the **Save As** chart: This is because **Save As** uses the standard JPEG quantization table, while **Save for Web** uses a quantization table that better optimizes these low- to medium-quality JPEGs for the Web. That's why you should always use the **Save for Web** command to save your JPEGs for the Web; it also gives you the option of blurring the file and attaching an ICC profile.

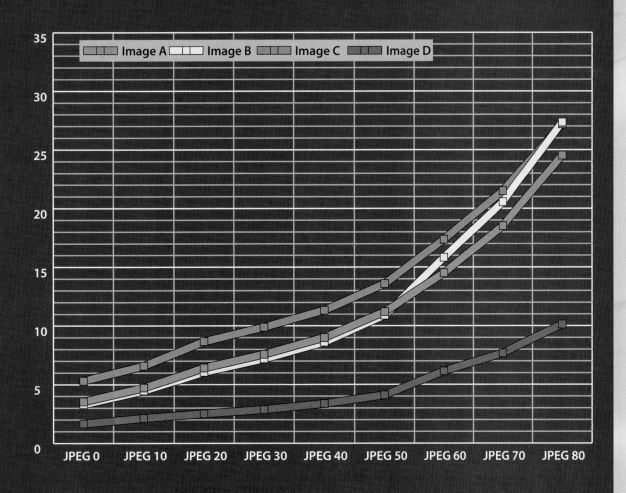

PNG—Portable Network Graphic Format

The PNG (Portable Network Graphic) format was supposed to be the next-generation image format for the Web. It was developed to bring the best of two worlds together: JPEG and GIF. In fact, it has many of the benefits of those formats, but it transcends some of their limitations.

PNG allows lossless compression with 24-bit color, which yields more than 16 million colors. It comes in two flavors: PNG-24, which you can use for photographic images in lieu of JPEG, and PNG-8, which is an alternative to GIF. Like JPEG, PNG supports interlacing; unlike GIF, it does not support Lossy. PNG stands apart from both formats in a couple of ways. First, PNG-24 provides 256 levels of transparency through a dedicated Alpha channel, which lets you create transparent drop shadows that blend seamlessly with the background; PNG-8 supports one level of transparency. JPEG doesn't support transparency at all, and transparency can be problematic with GIF, where you sometimes get a halo effect with anti-aliased images.

That's not all. PNG saves a Gamma curve along with the image. As you may recall, the Macintosh uses a different Gamma than Windows, so images that are optimized for a Mac will appear darker on Windows PCs, while images created on a Windows PC look too bright on Macs. PNG solves this problem by correcting the Gamma, so regardless of which computer you use to create the image, it will look the same on both platforms. ImageReady lets you see how your images will look under different Gamma settings by switching between Macintosh Gamma (called Standard Macintosh Color) and Windows Gamma (called Standard Windows Color) in **View > Preview**.

When PNG was created, it was hyped as the next big image format for the Web, but the truth is, it never became that and probably won't anytime soon. For one thing, PNG files are substantially bigger than their GIF or JPEG equivalents. And when I say substantially, I mean substantially. Take an image saved as PNG-24 and as JPEG with Quality 100: They'll be of comparable visual quality, but the PNG version will be twice as big. Likewise for an image saved as PNG-8 compared to a GIF. The size difference is not quite as drastic, but the PNG-8 file will be 20 to 30 percent bigger than a GIF version of comparable visual quality. So although PNG's lossless compression pays off in terms of visual quality, you pay for it in terms of file size.

Other factors holding back the PNG format's widespread acceptance are that it doesn't support animation and it isn't universally and seamlessly supported by browsers, in particular older browsers and Macintosh browsers. Because of these drawbacks, I wouldn't advise you to use PNG unless your Web site really requires 256 levels of transparency—the only real advantage of PNG. And if you use PNG, you should use a browser switch, which is some JavaScript code, to detect the browsers with no PNG support and redirect them to an alternate page. GoLive already comes with a browser switch (in the Objects palette under Smart) that allows you to specify for which browser a particular page is designed. Any of the browsers that are not specified in the browser switch are then redirected to an alternative page.

The Windows versions of Internet Explorer 4.0 and Netscape Navigator 4.04 both support limited features of PNG: Navigator 4.04 doesn't support the PNG Alpha channel. PNG support is even more limited on the Macintosh: Internet Explorer 4.5 and Netscape Navigator 4.08 *require* the QuickTime plug-in for basic PNG support, which doesn't include Alpha channel or Gamma support. PNG does work with the latest browsers, and since only a very small percentage of users still work with older browsers, the lack of support for these browsers is becoming less of an issue. However, if you decide to use PNG, you also want to check out how your page shows up in older browsers, or offer an alternative page for users with older browsers.

COMPARING PNG, GIF, AND JPEG FILE SIZES

The chart below compares the size differences of our four test images, each of which is saved in four formats: GIF, PNG-8, JPEG, and PNG-24. All four PNG-8 images are at least 20 percent bigger than their GIF equivalents (both are saved with an Adaptive palette, 100% dither, and 16 colors). The difference between the PNG-24 and JPEG images is even more dramatic: the PNG-24 images are as much as 400 percent bigger than their JPEG counterparts (saved with Quality 60). PNG-24 was particularly efficient for image C, where the PNG-24 file was only 11 percent larger than the JPEG version.

	Image A	Image B	Image C	Image D
GIF	13.450	11.930	6.104	9.616
PNG-8	16.290	14.850	6.100	10.100
JPEG	14.880	16.680	18.540	6.963
PNG-24	91.830	85.320	20.740	36.450

These are the Images A–D that were used to compare PNG with JPEG and GIF.

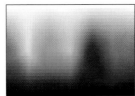

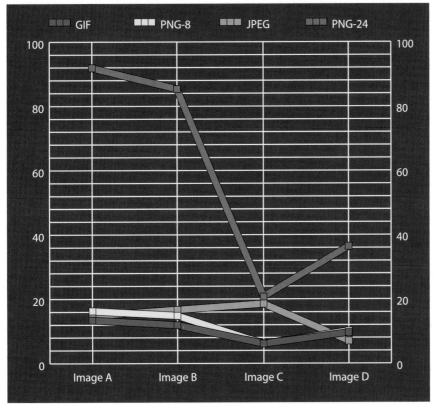

The results of this graph (above) should not be regarded as universal. After all, this is a test with just four images, so it is possible that different images would produce smaller file sizes with PNG. The folks at the PNG Web site, for example, claim that PNG-8 files are, on average, smaller than GIF files. They say that displaying an image in the 4-Up window to compare a GIF with a PNG-8 is not sufficient. True, the 4-Up display doesn't take the CLUT compression into account the way that PNG does when the image is saved. However, the maximal size of a CLUT is only 768 bytes, and when I compared file sizes via the desktop, the GIF still turned out smaller than the PNG. So, at least for this set of images, PNG-8 didn't work very well.

SAVING PNG IMAGES

To save an image as PNG you use the **Save For Web** command in Photoshop's **File** menu. In ImageReady you switch to the **Optimized** view and do all the settings in the **Optimize** Palette.

Saving an Image as PNG-24:

To experiment with PNG-24's 256 levels of transparency, create a new image in Photoshop, type in some text using the Type tool (which places the text on its own layer), and apply an effect, such as a drop shadow (**Layer > Layer Style > Drop Shadow**). Make sure that your text is large enough and that the drop shadow is very soft and blurry so that you will be able to see the effect clearly. Then hide the background layer in the **Layers** palette (**Windows > Show Layers**) by clicking on the eye icon; the checkerboard grid indicates that the background is transparent. Now choose **File > Save For Web**, and in the dialog, select PNG-24 as your file format. PNG-24 doesn't offer many options: You can only specify **Interlaced**, **Transparency**, and **Matte** color. Interlaced lets the browser display the image while it is still streaming from the server; for our experiment it's not important, so deselect it. Do check the Transparency option so that the transparent background doesn't get filled with a Matte color. Now click OK, and in the **Save Optimized As** dialog box, save the image with a ".png" extension. Since PNG is supported by GoLive, you might as well experiment with it and enjoy the 256 levels of transparency. Place this image on an HTML page in GoLive, set a background image for the page, and then see how the drop shadow will blend seamlessly with the background color or pattern.

Saving an Image as PNG-8:

Call up the **Save For Web** dialog box (in ImageReady the **Optimize** palette) and select PNG-8 from the **File Format** pop-up menu. You have the same options for optimizing PNG that you do for GIF, except for the **Lossy** command, as noted earlier. Select a color-reduction algorithm, pick the number of colors you want to use, and choose your dithering method, if any. Check the Transparency box again, but keep in mind that PNG-8 offers only one level of transparency, just like a GIF. The similarity between GIF and PNG-8 becomes very apparent here, especially if you use the **4-Up** view to compare the GIF and PNG-8 side by side. With identical color-reduction algorithms, color tables, and dithering, there is no difference between the two formats except for file size (PNG will be larger).

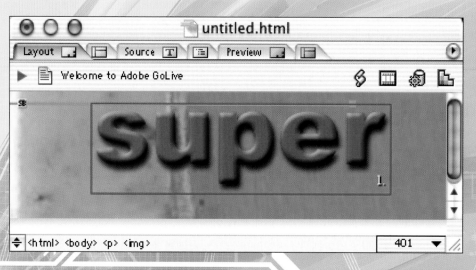

GoLive supports PNG; here you can see how the drop shadow of a PNG-24 image blends seamlessly with the background.

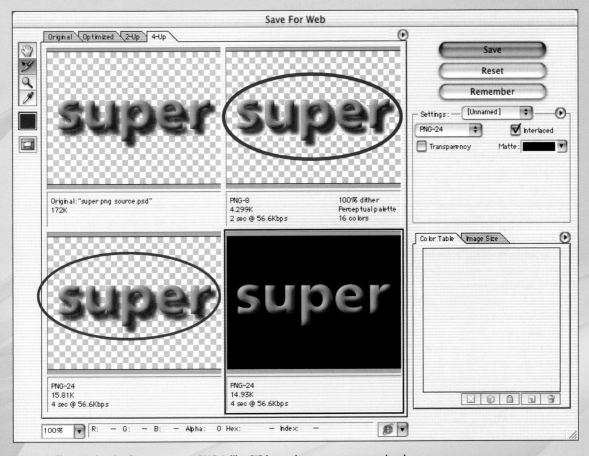

PNG-24 offers 256 levels of transparency; PNG-8, like GIF, has only one transparency level.

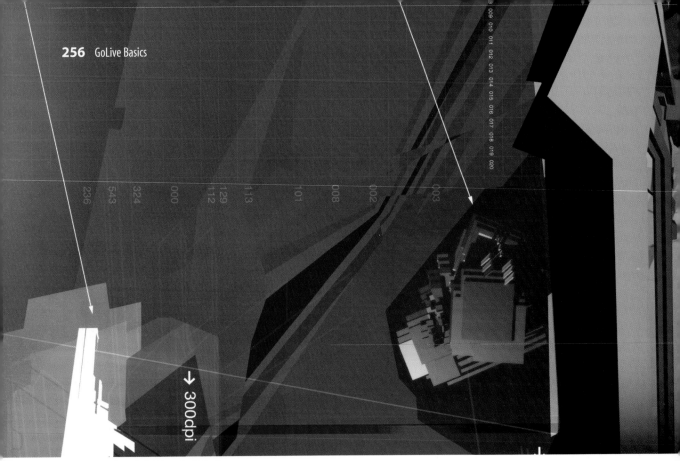

Illustration: **Anthony Kyriazis** from the CD **OnyFrax**

GoLive Basics

Once you and your client have finalized the main page and the design concept for all the body pages in Photoshop and/or ImageReady, it's time for you to move everything into GoLive and re-create the Web site as HTML documents.

Instead of designing the Web site page by page, you want to take advantage of GoLive's capability to automate and manage your assets. This requires the creation of a site, which is essentially a collection of folders and a database that keeps track of your files. The next step would then be to export all your images and rollover buttons from Photoshop/ImageReady to the Site folder and to start creating your stationeries. With these stationeries you then build the whole structure and architecture of the site, and after that, fill the pages with content.

The tutorial in this chapter walks you through such a scenario and illustrates the typical steps. But since the tutorial can't cover everything, I'll also explain some of the most common techniques and describe problems that you might encounter when creating your own Web site.

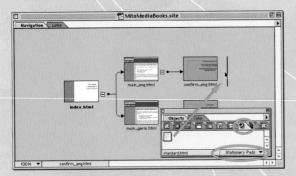 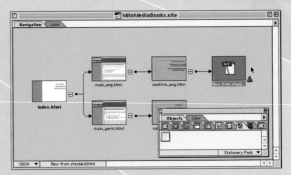

Stationery allows you to easily create the structure of your Web site. On the Site Extras tab of the Objects palette, choose Stationery Pads from the pop-up menu and then drag the page into the site (Design > Navigation View).

STATIONERY, COMPONENTS AND TEMPLATES

One of the most important features of GoLive is the capability to save HTML documents as stationery, components, and templates. This feature is the key to working efficiently, but it is often overlooked by designers who have just started working with GoLive. So let me explain how this concept can make your work easier.

Stationery refers to a predefined page that you can drag and drop into your site structure. If you have worked with layout programs such as Adobe Page-Maker or InDesign, you are probably already familiar with this concept; layout programs use the similar concept of Master Pages or templates. However, while Master Pages are linked to subsequent pages in a layout document, the pages that you create in GoLive's site structure are not linked to the stationery. Therefore, if you make changes on a stationery page, they won't show up on the pages in your site that use this stationery. GoLive stationery is, in fact, nothing more than a copy of a page; the only way to change something globally is if, for example, you overwrite an image that is used by every page. If you need to create elements that are dynamically updated, you have to create a component or a template.

A *component* is an element on a page that will be updated if the original component is changed. It's usually a good idea to save a navigation bar as a component. If one of the links changes, all you have to do is open the component, change the link, and save it. GoLive will then replace every occurrence of the component on the site with the new version.

Components can be placed on stationery, so you can, for example, create a component for navigation and place it on your stationery page. You could do the same thing with a company logo, a banner ad, or the navigation text link that usually comes at the bottom of every page. These items make ideal components. But that's as far as you can go with stationery: It is not possible to change a background color or link color globally.

Components also have limitations. For example, what do you do if you want a navigation bar that always displays the current section, such as an inverted Home button when the user is on the home page and an inverted Products button when the user is on the products page? This requires you to create multiple copies of the component, and if the links change, you have to go through all the copies of the component.

In GoLive 6.0, Web designers also get a new item called a *template*. The template is the equivalent of a Master Page in a desktop publishing program. A template has editable regions, so when another designer works with a template, only those editable regions can be changed; the others are locked. Only the original

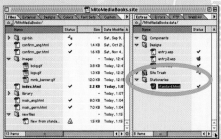

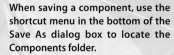

When saving a component, use the shortcut menu in the bottom of the Save As dialog box to locate the Components folder.

The Site window lets you manage the mirror site as well as other aspects of your Web site. On the Extras tab, you'll find a folder for stationery and components.

When saving the modified component, GoLive lists the documents in which the component is used.

designer of the template can make edits to the template. Any pages that are based on this template will then change accordingly.

Creating stationery, templates, or a component is simple: Create a new page with **File > New**. Place your elements and then save the page in either the Components, Templates or Stationery folder of the Web site. GoLive offers a shortcut in the Save As dialog box that lets you locate these folders by clicking on the button in the lower-right corner. Be sure not to strip the document of the ".html" extension; otherwise, it won't show up on the Site Extras tab of the Objects palette (**Window > Objects**). To switch among stationery, templates, and components (and Library, which is just snippets of HTML code or other elements), use the pop-up menu in the lower-right corner of the Site Extras tab.

A component is dragged from the Objects palette onto the document. In this example, the navigation component has only two buttons. To extend it, double-click the placed component.

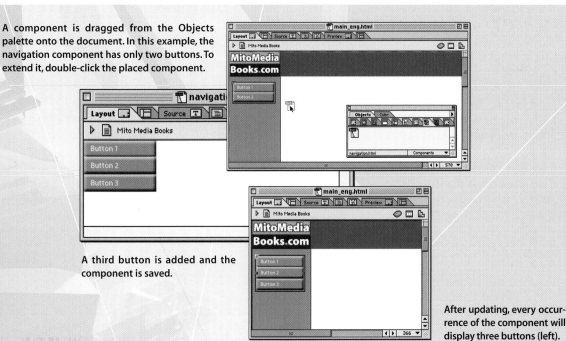

A third button is added and the component is saved.

After updating, every occurrence of the component will display three buttons (left).

CREATING HTML TABLES

Even though most browsers today support HTML layers, tables remain the most reliable way of laying out Web pages. To create a table in GoLive, just drag a table icon from the **Basic** tab of the **Objects** palette onto a document. By default, GoLive creates a table with three rows and three columns; the **Table Inspector** appears automatically, showing the table's dimensions and other attributes. The biggest problem you'll have when working with tables is making sure that they work with different browsers. Here are some guidelines for creating effective HTML tables:

● **Make the table invisible.** For a table to be invisible, the Border, Cell Pad, and Cell Space attributes must be set to 0. If the Table Inspector isn't visible, access these attributes by clicking on the border of the table in the GoLive document.

● **Vertically align to "Top."** The default vertical alignment for content in each table cell is centered, but it's better to align content to the top of the cell; otherwise, you might end up with a gap between the content and the edge of the cell (for example, if you're creating an image table). You can't change this universally, but you can do it by row. Click with the cursor to select a table cell and then switch to the **Row** tab of the **Table Inspector**. Set **Vertical Alignment** to **Top**, and then use the arrow keys on your keyboard to move to the next row, and repeat.

● **Set the proper height and width.** If you're placing an image in a table cell, make sure the height and width of the cell equal the image's dimensions. The best way to ensure that the cell fits the image it contains is to first set the width and height of the entire table and then go through each cell that contains an image and set its height and width individually.

● **Use the Spacer tag for empty cells.** It is not enough to set the dimensions of empty table cells and leave it at that. Internet Explorer will obey the Width attribute and maintain the cell's width with integrity, but Navigator might "collapse" the cell. To fix this, drag the **Horizontal Spacer** tag, which is a Netscape tag used exclusively by Navigator, into the cell from the **Basic** tab of the **Objects** palette. Then set the width to that of the cell itself.

● **Use Cell Pad instead of Cell Space.** If you have defined a background color or you're using a background image for your table and you want the table cells to appear continuously, without gaps between them, don't use Cell Space (it creates space between cells).

● **Check backgrounds.** It is possible to load an image into a table as a background, but Navigator handles backgrounds very poorly (see the example later in this chapter). If you intend to use images as backgrounds in tables, be sure to set your monitor to 256 colors and check them in older versions of Navigator. Before Netscape redesigned its rendering engine for Navigator 6.0, the Navigator browser would treat background images differently than regular images.

Netscape Navigtor (left) and Internet Explorer (right) render the table differently when the table color is set in the Inspector. Use the Cell Pad Attribute instead of the Cell Space Attribute to get a solid-colored background.

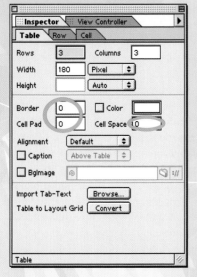 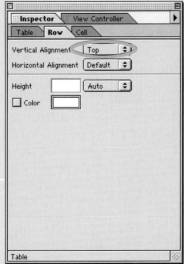 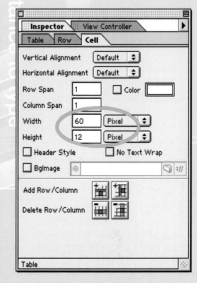

To set up a table so that it appears invisible, you must set Border, Cell Pad, and Cell Space to 0 (left). By default, the vertical alignment of the table cells is set to centered. You can change this row by row (middle). If the table cells contain images, then the Width and Height of the cell must be set to values that correspond to those of the image to prevent any gaps.

FIXING IMAGE TABLES IN HTML

Stitching the pieces of a sliced image together in a table doesn't seem particularly tricky, especially if you tell ImageReady to create the HTML code for you, but if for some reason you're doing this task manually in GoLive, you can end up with unwanted space between cells. It might also happen that the image table will look fine in one browser and not in another. In any case, you'll have to do some troubleshooting to find the HTML tag that's causing the problem. As there are several possible causes, here is a little checklist:

1. Check for spaces in the cells. Many authoring programs (not GoLive) automatically place a space in a cell because without it, the cell will not display the cell border. Delete those spaces. If you are not completely sure that your image is the only thing in the cell, look at the HTML code. It should read as follows: <td><img= ...></td>.

2. Check justification. You can justify the contents of a cell vertically and horizontally using the VALIGN and ALIGN attributes of the TD tag. Make sure all the cells use the same justification and that there are no conflicting attributes (such as VALIGN="Top" in the TR tag and VALIGN="Bottom" in the TD tag).

3. Adjust the height and width of the cells to fit the image. You can find the exact measurements of the image in the IMG tag. After you enter those values for the table cell, the table should fit the image tightly.

4. The TABLE tag may contain CELL SPACE or BORDER attributes. Remove all unnecessary attributes or set them to zero.

5. If an image is defined as a LINK, make sure it isn't defined with a border by entering the attribute BORDER=0 in the IMG tag. In GoLive, click on the image, and in the **Image Inspector**, select the Basics tab. Select the **Border** option with a value of 0 (in GoLive 6.0, the border is 0 by default).

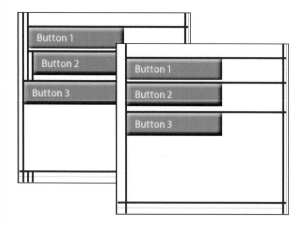

This is the underlying table architecture of the layout grid. As you can see, the table on the left is much more complex because the elements are not aligned. When working with a layout grid, always use the Align commands in the Options palette to get the best results.

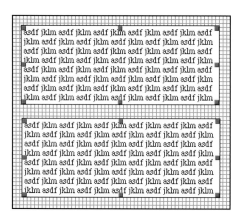

On the left you see a layout grid with two text boxes; next to it are the results in Explorer (middle) and Navigator (right). As you can see, they differ because of the fonts they are using. If you have a layout like this, use a table instead.

Using the Layout Grid

An alternative to HTML tables is the layout grid, which is an invisible table that uses a "control" row and column (with spacer tags) to optimize the table's display in Navigator. Each time an object is placed on the layout grid (or moved within it), GoLive automatically generates a new table to position the objects. This table contains the fewest cells that your grid's layout will allow, but when objects are not perfectly aligned vertically and horizontally, the table can become complex. And complex tables not only bloat HTML files but also may not display as expected in Web browsers. Internet Explorer, for example, may not correctly display tables produced with GoLive's layout grid if they contain unaligned objects; it may overestimate the table's width and display a horizontal scroll bar when it isn't needed.

You may want to use a plain table instead of a layout grid for some objects, such as those that won't be the same size in all browsers or operating systems. In particular, this applies to HTML forms—Internet Explorer and Netscape Navigator display form elements such as text boxes and pop-up menus in different sizes. When your document's design requires that paragraphs of text stay aligned with an image, you should put the text and image in a table. That way, they'll always line up.

In fact, you should opt for a table instead of a layout grid any time you're working with a lot of text, since you don't really know how the length of the text will vary between the browsers. Tables are always better than text boxes and layout grids (see the example below) because they adjust their height according to the text flow, whereas layout grids are static.

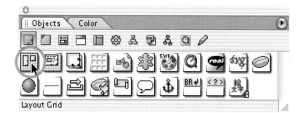

Drag a layout grid from the Basics tab of the Objects palette and adjust its size in the Layout Grid Inspector.

USING BACKGROUNDS IN TABLES AND GRIDS

Since the release of Internet Explorer 3.0 and Netscape Navigator 4.0, designers have been able to use images as backgrounds for tables. This allows for some nice tricks, such as the mock-up at right that simulates computer paper. The great thing about using background images in tables is that you can place your content inside a table cell, and if the text flows differently in one browser, the background will always adjust to the length of the table. Since layout grids are also tables, they also allow you to set a background color or image.

Table Limitations of Netscape Navigator

Older versions of Navigator, and by that I mean everything before version 6.0, do a terrible job when it comes to background images in tables. If you need your site to be compatible with those browsers, this fault automatically limits what you can do. For example, you can't use nested tables (tables within tables) with Netscape Communicator/Navigator, because the nested table inherits the background of the table in which it's embedded (even though there is no background set for the nested table). Since the embedded table tries to synchronize the background with its own zero origin point, this generally creates an offset and therefore becomes visible.

Another table restriction is that you can't use patterns with transparency. Although Explorer (and Navigator 6.x) renders them correctly, older Navigator versions display transparency in background images as white.

The last problem may not be so much Netscape's fault, but it is clearly an inconsistency between Navigator and Explorer: If you set a Cell Pad for your table, Navigator will display the background color of the browser in between the gaps (!) and will, in the next cell, start the background again at the zero origin. Explorer displays an image background simply over the entire length and width of a table; even Cell Pad will not interrupt the pattern. This inconsistency means that you can't just define one large background pattern for a

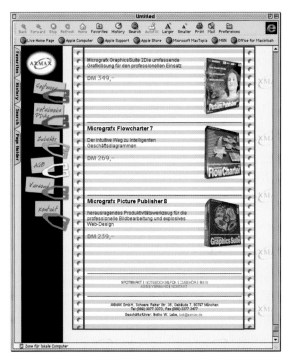

You can create elements like this computer paper by applying an image background to tables. This table contains three columns (marked in blue) and each one contains its own background image, which is necessary because Navigator handles background images differently than Explorer.

table. Instead, you have to split the pattern into individual pieces and define each cell with its own piece of the pattern. To illustrate this, I created a sample Web site that consists of a three-column table where each column uses a different background. The left column uses the left-hand guide holes, the middle column uses lines, and the right column shows the outer set of holes.

An invisible table (containing the computer images) was nested inside another table with an image background. Although Explorer displays it correctly (above), Navigator 4.x repeats the background pattern inside the invisible table, making it visible (see arrows at right).

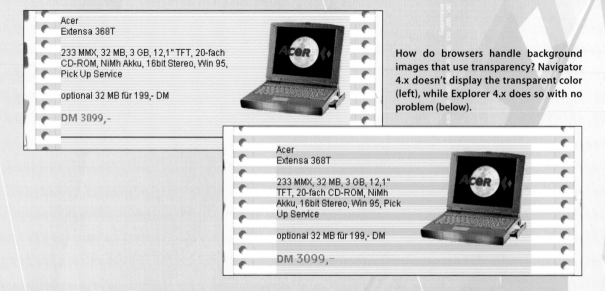

How do browsers handle background images that use transparency? Navigator 4.x doesn't display the transparent color (left), while Explorer 4.x does so with no problem (below).

IMAGE INFLATION

Although a background saved as a JPEG or GIF may be only 10 K, it will be decompressed to full size in the browser. This can amount to 1MB, 2MB, or more. This was an issue in the dawn of Web design because some designers wanted to use large (and dimmed) background images. Since a background image is repeated on the horizontal and vertical axis, the designer had to extend the background image down and to the left and fill it with a background color so that users with large screens wouldn't see the background pattern repeat. Luckily, there is a better solution that uses Cascading Style Sheets.

● **In Photoshop, create a background** with a maximum width of 600 pixels and select a color from the Web color table (to avoid dithering) to fill the rest of the image on the right side. Use the Airbrush tool to blend the image with the background color if necessary (in this example I just used a gradient fill to illustrate the principle). Save the finished background as a GIF or JPEG.

● **To create a Cascading Style Sheet,** in the **Layout Editor**, click the **Open CSS Editor** button in the upper-right corner of a document (the icon looks like a staircase) to access the CSS window.

● **In the CSS toolbar,** click the **New Element Style**(<>) button. In the **Basic** tab of the **Inspector**, type BODY in the name field. (What we are basically doing is overwriting the HTML BODY tag.)

● **Switch to the Background tab,** check the **Image** box, and then browse for the background image. Choose "Repeat x" from the Repeat pop-up menu to repeat the background horizontally or "Repeat y" to repeat it vertically. It's even possible to have the background repeated only once or to have the background stay at a fixed position by selecting Fixed from the Attach pop-up menu (however, this causes the background to be rendered black in older versions of Navigator, so I don't recommend using it). After you have saved this document, open it in Navigator or Explorer to see the effect.

On the first tab of the CSS Inspector, the element is named BODY (like the HTML tag). To change the background, use the Background tab and browse for the image. It is important to use "Repeat y" to have the background repeat only vertically.

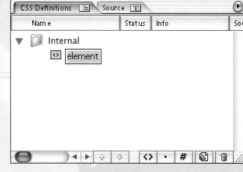

One click on New Element Style in the Options palette will insert a new element in the Cascading Style Sheet. In the Inspector, this style must have the same name as the HTML tag that it is supposed to overwrite.

ALIGNING FOREGROUND WITH BACKGROUND

When you use backgrounds in a design, you may discover that it's difficult to align objects in the HTML page with the background. This problem is caused by the browser offset, which unfortunately is not only different for Navigator and Explorer but also varies for different computer platforms. Browser offset is the distance that content is placed from the upper-left corner of the browser window. In the early days of HTML and the Web, it made sense for the browser to display the content with an offset so that it wouldn't crash into the upper-right corner of the window. But when the background image function was introduced to HTML, this browser offset became problematic: Since the background is positioned without an offset, you can't be exactly sure how a foreground graphic element will align with the background. Back in the "old" days (with

the 3.0 browsers) Web designers had to use JavaScript to detect which browser the visitor was using and then compensate for the offset by loading different background images. Luckily this isn't necessary anymore. Netscape and Microsoft fixed this problem, and all 4.x or later browsers let you set the offset by including some additional attributes in the BODY tag. However, since this was an extension to the official HTML specification, each company used different attributes, so to set the offset to zero for both browsers, you have to use a combination of these attributes in the BODY tag: <BODY leftmargin="0" marginwidth="0" topmargin="0" marginheight="0">.

In GoLive you don't have to manually type in these attributes. All you need to do is to click on the Page icon in the upper-left corner of your document and set Margin Width and Height to 0 in the Page Inspector.

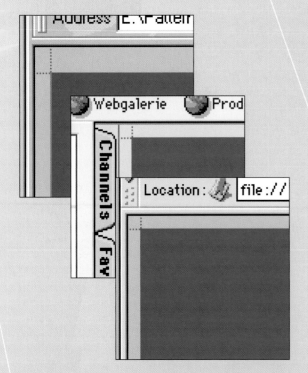

From top to bottom: the browser offset in Internet Explorer 3.0 for Windows, Internet Explorer 4.0 for Macintosh, and Netscape Navigator 4.0 for Macintosh.

Use the Page Inspector to set the browser offset.

The old Viagra Web site (designed by Andreas Lindström, Nicholson NY) uses a background image (see above) that needs to be aligned with an image in the foreground, which can be done by setting the browser offset to zero.

WORKING WITH TEXT

In Web design, the possibilities for formatting text are limited. You can use either the FONT tag or Cascading Style Sheets, but both require viewers to have the font you're using installed on their computers. This limits you to the serif combination Palatino/Times or sans serif Helvetica/Arial, because these fonts come with both the Macintosh and Windows operating systems. One of the solutions to this was a technology called Dynamic Fonts, which allowed you to save fonts in a special format that would then be attached to an HTML document. Unfortunately, this technology is not supported by Microsoft (what a surprise) in its latest browser. And Bitstream, which was the only company left that offered a font-conversion tool for Dynamic Fonts (called WebFont Wizard), has stopped selling and maintaining this product. The only way (to my knowledge) of embedding a font with an HTML page is using SVG (Standard Vector Graphic), which requires

the visitor to have a plug-in installed. So for the time being, there is not much you can do. Here are the options that you have:

Using the FONT tag

The FONT tag predates Cascading Style Sheets and is therefore understood by every browser. To format text with the FONT tag, you first need to create a font set (**Type > Font > Edit Font Sets**). In the **Font Set Editor**, click the New button underneath the Font Sets list to create a new set, and then specify the fonts that you want to be part of the set using the pop-up menu under the Font Names list. Specify more than one font in case your first choice is not installed on the visitor's computer. I recommend that you create two font sets, one for serifs (including Times and Palatino, in that order) and one for sans serifs (Arial and Helvetica, also in that order). After you have defined your font sets,

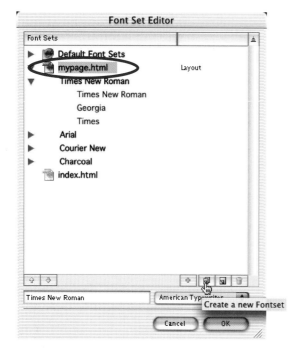

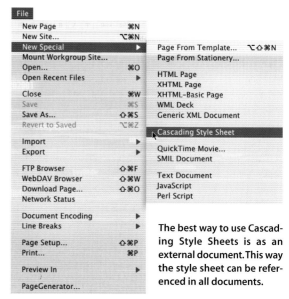

The best way to use Cascading Style Sheets is as an external document. This way the style sheet can be referenced in all documents.

You can create font sets in GoLive—even font sets that are specific to a page—by clicking on the page title in the list. Then create new font sets by clicking on the New Fontset button and use the pop-up menu to add fonts in the Font Names column.

they are available in the Type > Font submenu and you can apply them to selected text in HTML documents.

As you probably noticed, GoLive already has predefined font sets (similar to the one we just defined), but they include too many alternatives, and every time you apply a FONT tag to text, the entire tag gets placed into the HTML code:

<font face="Arial,Helvetica,Geneva,Swiss,Sun-Sans-Regular">This is an example</font>.

As you can see, this FONT tag uses more characters than the actual text in this example, and the HTML code gets quite bloated. Even though this doesn't cause much of a problem for browsers, it is extra data that needs to be transmitted and it makes editing HTML source code all the more tedious.

Using Cascading Style Sheets

Nowadays, most browsers are capable of reading Cascading Style Sheets, which are a better choice than the FONT tag. The CSS extension was included in the HTML specification to give designers more formatting capabilities than the FONT tag offers, including setting the font, color, or white space; background images; or borders of your text. Cascading Style Sheets seem to fulfill all the designer's needs—at least in theory. Unfortunately, the incompatibilities among the browsers are a disaster, and if you use anything beyond the basics (such as font, size, and color), you will have to check your page in all browsers. In particular, it is difficult to predict how CSS-formatted text will behave in tables. Some older versions of Navigator will not expand a table cell when a line height has been set, so the text will actually extend beyond the border of the cell.

But otherwise, Cascading Style Sheets have a lot of advantages. You can, for example, use one external CSS document for all your HTML pages, which lets you change the appearance of an entire Web site by editing just one document. Another great feature of Cascading Style Sheets is that you can overwrite the browser formatting of standard HTML tags. If you wanted all your headlines to be in a bold Arial font, for example, you could just name a style <H1>. Even if the browser doesn't understand Cascading Style Sheets, it will interpret the structural tags as usual. (The creators of Cascading Style Sheets didn't want to simply create additional HTML text-formatting tags; they wanted to ensure that HTML would remain a structural language.)

There are three ways to implement style sheets: Besides linking pages to an external CSS document as I just described, you can also use embedded styles or inline styles. Embedded styles define a document structure in the same way as a linked, external docu-

ment, but they are placed at the beginning of a document and apply to that specific document only. Inline styles, meanwhile, are for local formatting of single words or lines of text in a document. There is a hierarchy to these style sheets: Embedded styles overwrite any definitions of a linked style, and inline styles overwrite embedded styles. So if, for example, you are using an external style sheet in which the paragraph tag is defined as Helvetica, but in the embedded paragraph style in a linked document is Palatino, the paragraphs will appear in Palatino. If you've applied an inline style to one sentence to make it Arial, then that sentence will appear in Arial.

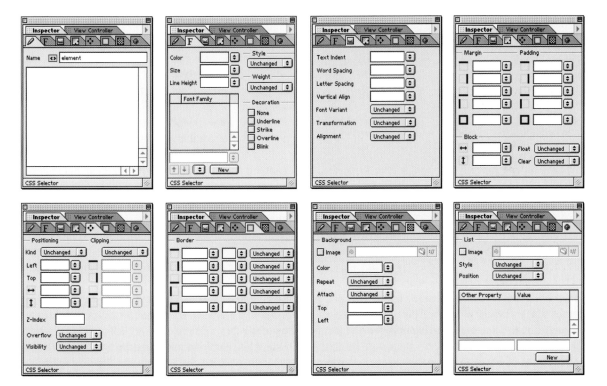

The Cascading Style Sheet specification is very complex. The CSS Selector Inspector palette has many tabs to set all the attributes. After typing in the HTML tag, you can set the font size and style in the first two tabs. On the third tab, you can set paragraph formatting characteristics such as alignment or text indent. The fourth and fifth tabs allow you to define the appearance and position of the box that surrounds each element. The sixth lets you set border attributes. On the seventh tab, you can determine the background, including how often it should be repeated. Because the background can be set for every tag, it is even possible to give a headline a textured background. On the last tab, you'll find the properties for lists and all unsupported properties.

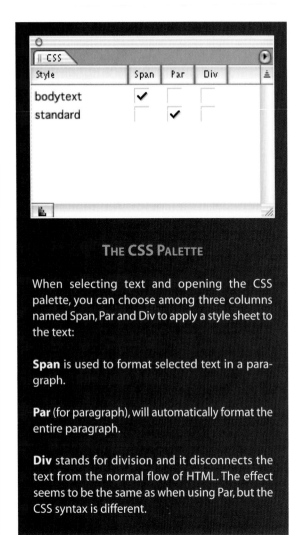

THE CSS PALETTE

When selecting text and opening the CSS palette, you can choose among three columns named Span, Par and Div to apply a style sheet to the text:

Span is used to format selected text in a paragraph.

Par (for paragraph), will automatically format the entire paragraph.

Div stands for division and it disconnects the text from the normal flow of HTML. The effect seems to be the same as when using Par, but the CSS syntax is different.

The three types of style sheets are often used together so that child styles modify the display of the parent style as described above. This is similar to style-tagging text in page-layout software, where you can format a paragraph but give individual words a different appearance. For example, in the linked style sheet, the paragraph tag might be defined as Arial. If the font color in the embedded style sheet is red, then the text in the document will be displayed in a red Arial font. You might then use an inline style to make text bold or give it a background color. Marking a paragraph <P STYLE="background: #660033">Top Ten</P> would

highlight the words "Top Ten" without affecting any of the other formatting. You can find more on Cascading Style Sheets in the GoLive manual or at www.w3c.org.

Cascading Style Sheets and browser incompatibilities could fill an entire book; I'd rather show you how to use them to format text as a replacement for the FONT tag. The most effective way to do this is to create a linked external style sheet in which you define all the standard text tags that occur in your document, such as <P>, <A>, and <H1> through <H7>. Unfortunately, there are always cases where the style sheet will not have any effect. For example, if the first paragraph in a table cell is not marked with a paragraph tag, this text will not be formatted. Since almost all the text on your page will be placed in a table cell, this is a problem, but luckily not a major one. You can fix it by inserting the paragraph tag manually in the HTML source code or including a CSS definition for the table data cell tag (<TD>). Neither way is optimal; it is easier to create a class definition and apply it to the text or to the whole page by checking the Area column on the Style tab of the Inspector. Classes work reliably in all the CSS-capable browsers, and you can apply them using the Inspector, with the benefit that you don't have to edit the HTML code.

Creating and linking external style sheets

1. Choose File > New Special > Cascading Style Sheet. Save this file in your Site folder.

2. Click on the New Element Style button in the toolbar on the bottom of the new style sheet window (marked with carets) or use one of the three predefined style elements. This lets you change the browser formatting of the HTML tags. To change the formatting of paragraphs, for example, click on the **p** element in the style sheet window and edit its attributes in the Inspector. Click on the Font tab of the Inspector and change the font family, size, and maybe the color as desired. The Style, Weight, and Decoration attributes will also be interpreted by most browsers, but the attributes that you can specify on the other tabs in the Inspector need to be checked in all browsers and on all platforms. To see what you've specified for the

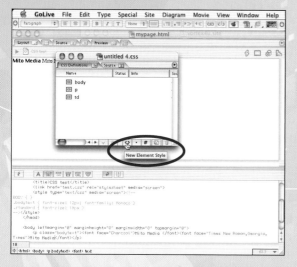

After clicking the New Element Style button, you can name the new entry and change its settings.

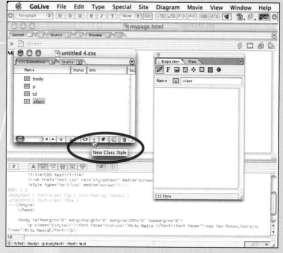

After clicking the New Class Style button, you can name the new entry and change its settings.

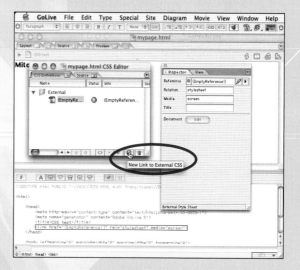

A click on the New Link to External CSS button inserts a new external style sheet reference.

paragraph tag, click back on the **Basics** tab of the **Inspector**. Then define attributes for heading (<H>), unnumbered list (<UL>), and ordered list (<OL>) tags.

3. Click on the New Class Style button in the toolbar of the style sheet window (marked with a dot). This will let you format all of the first paragraphs in table cells, which you'll do in the next step. It is important that the name of the class be preceded by a dot—in GoLive 6 this is done automatically. For example, call the class ".paragraph" and apply some of the same attributes that you used for the paragraph tag. When you're done, save your .CSS document.

4. Now open an HTML document that you previously created for your site and click the **Open CSS Editor** button in the upper-right corner of the document window; a new document appears. Click the **New Link to External CSS** button at the bottom of the CSS Editor document and an **External** folder with an empty reference appears. In the **Inspector**, link the

external style sheet that you just created to this document by browsing and selecting it in the **Reference** field. Now all the text in your document should adjust according to your external style sheet—except the first paragraphs in tables. To format those, select the text and open the **CSS palette** from the **Window** menu. The .paragraph CSS class that you previously created should be listed; now just check the Span, Par, or Div box to apply it to the text.

Troubleshooting CSS designs

As I mentioned before, it is important to apply Cascading Style Sheets to all the text on your page; otherwise, the visitor's browser preferences might cause some text to appear differently. It's a good practice to test your page in a browser after you've set the default font size to an extreme value, such as 36 points. If you have applied CSS to all the text on your page, nothing should happen, but if you missed some text, your design will probably break apart.

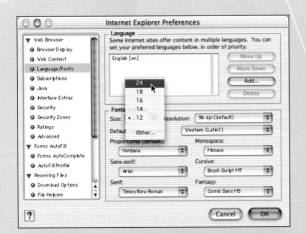

To test your Web site, try some extreme font settings (like 24 points for the size) in your browser's Preferences (here I've used Internet Explorer). If nothing changes, then you'll know that you formatted everything correctly.

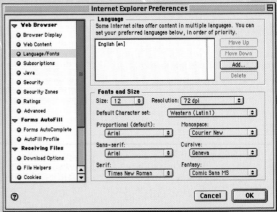

Visitors can set font preferences in Netscape Navigator and Internet Explorer (left). If they choose something exotic or in a very large size, your design can break apart. You can control this by using the FONT tag or Cascading Style Sheets.

OPTIMIZING THE WORKFLOW BETWEEN GOLIVE AND PHOTOSHOP

Adobe introduced (in GoLive 5.0) a set of new functions and commands that improve the workflow between GoLive and Photoshop, Illustrator, and Live-Motion. These functions include:

Smart Objects, which allow you to directly place into a GoLive HTML document a Photoshop, Illustrator, or LiveMotion file that is saved in the Site folder as GIF, JPEG, SVG, or even Flash. Any changes made to the original file or to the dimensions of the smart object will automatically create an updated version of the HTML document, making it much easier to work in GoLive.

Tracing Image, which allows you to load a Photoshop file and display it in the background, making it easier to re-create a design in GoLive. You can even use the Crop tool to slice the image, automatically importing the cropped areas.

Photoshop layers to floating boxes, which will import every layer of a Photoshop document and place it in a CSS layer.

These features make it much more convenient to work with Photoshop files and other page elements in GoLive and beg you to find new, more efficient ways to work. Let's look at how you can put these features to best use.

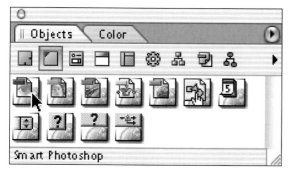

The smart objects are listed on the Smart tab of the Objects palette. They will appear only if the software is also installed on the computer.

Working with Smart Objects

To access a smart object, click on the Smart tab in the Objects palette. The first three icons are Smart Photoshop, Smart Illustrator, and Smart LiveMotion, which let you position files created in those applications in your GoLive HTML page. (Only icons for installed applications will appear.) Drag, for example, a Smart Photoshop placeholder onto a page and select your Source image from the Basics tab of the Inspector. GoLive

presents you with the Save For Web dialog so that you can optimize the image's GIF or JPEG settings; do that and then click OK. GoLive prompts you for the name of the destination file; specify the Images folder of your mirror site. Now if you edit the original file (double-click on it to launch Photoshop), the smart object is automatically updated in GoLive. If you scale the smart object in GoLive, the application creates a new file with those new dimensions under the destination's filename. The original file is left untouched.

Smart objects allow you to work in GoLive much as you would in a layout program such as InDesign. Theoretically, you could design your entire interface this way, but that is not advisable. It is still more efficient to design the interface in Photoshop and to use smart objects when designing the content of the pages.

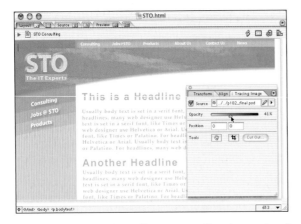

The Tracing Image palette allows you to adjust the opacity of the image in the background. Positioning the image is easy with the Move tool, and the Cut Out tool lets you import parts of the image into a layer.

Using Tracing Image

The Tracing Image command makes it easy to load a Photoshop file as a backdrop and trace it so that you can easily re-create a design. As with smart objects, this command is best for "converting" a mock-up of a content page; it is not necessarily the best tool for importing your interface design, mostly because it doesn't support rollover effects.

To use this feature, choose Tracing Image from the Window menu to access the palette. Check the Source box and browse to select the Photoshop file that you want to use. The image will be dimmed when loaded; adjust it using the Opacity slider. To reposition the image, you can either type in Position values to offset it from the upper-left corner of the page or drag it with the Move Image tool. You can then eliminate parts of the image by dragging with the Cut Out tool to select an area and then clicking the Cut Out button. GoLive will display the Save For Web dialog box; after choosing an image format and the optimization settings, you can save the file in your Site folder.

Importing Photoshop layers to floating boxes

If you plan to use layer-based animation, GoLive's ability to import Photoshop files as HTML (**File > Import > Photoshop layers to floating boxes**) is particularly handy. This command does exactly what it says: After you select the Photoshop file and choose a destination folder, GoLive displays the **Save For Web** dialog box for every layer in the image, letting you choose to optimize each one individually. One limitation of this feature is that it does not render any layer effects, and it includes hidden layers. So if you have a Photoshop file with 20 layers but you want to import only some of them, it is not enough to hide those layers by toggling off their visibility in the Layers palette. Another tip: The layer names in Photoshop will become the names of the layer's corresponding floating boxes in GoLive. Some browsers have difficulty handling floating boxes if their name begins with a number, so it's important to name the layers properly in Photoshop, including not beginning a name with a number or using numbers exclusively.

Converting Layers into layout grid

The "Photoshop layers to floating boxes" command and Tracing Image feature both place image layers in GoLive documents as floating boxes. But unless you have to use HTML layers (for animations, for example), it is better to use HTML tables instead. Luckily, converting HTML layers to HTML tables is a snap: In the GoLive Floating Boxes palette (**Window > Floating Boxes**), choose Convert to Layout Grid from the palette's pop-up menu. If the command is grayed out, then the selected layers are overlapping. Fix this by selecting the layers individually and repositioning them so that they don't overlap. After you choose the Convert to Layout Grid command, GoLive re-creates the layout in a new HTML document. Either overwrite the original document (after closing it) or copy and paste the layout grid into the original file.

After selecting a file and a destination folder, the Import as HTML command goes through each and every layer, displaying the Save For Web dialog box.

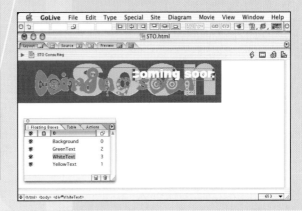

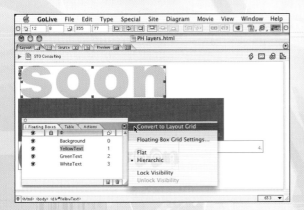

The Convert to Layout Grid command works only if the layers in GoLive don't overlap.

TUTORIAL: HTML AUTHORING

At first, creating a Web site may seem difficult and complex. Indeed, you have at your disposal two of the most complex and powerful tools that are available for designers—Photoshop and GoLive—but reading through the manuals is an almost impossible task. But when you know what to do and which buttons to press, you can create a Web site—from the design phase to the actual HTML authoring in GoLive—in just a few hours. Efficiency is essential: A simple mistake like creating the stationery, templates, and the site architecture before setting up the Cascading Style Sheet can be time-consuming to fix. But it will all come together when you work through this tutorial, which is designed to show you the most efficient workflow. It's a good outline for all your projects.

1 **Setting up a new site:** In GoLive, choose **File > New Site** to create a new site. The **Site Wizard** will lead you through the whole process, giving you several options for creating your site: **Copy from Server, Import from Server, Import from Folder**, and **Blank**. In this tutorial we are using **Blank**. On the next screen you are asked to enter a name for your site. I recommend using the domain name. On the next screen you can choose the location of your project folder.

After you finish the whole setup, you will see the **Site** window, and in the project folder on your hard drive, you will see three subfolders. The folder with the extension ".data" holds folders for the **Components, Diagrams, Library, Site Trash, Smart Objects, Stationery**, and **Templates**. The other folder in the project folder,

with the extension ".settings" holds all the settings for fonts or for color. The folder with no extension represents your actual site. It is the local copy of the site (also called mirror site), which will later be uploaded to the server. You can create folders inside it to organize your files; you should get into the habit of using the GoLive Site window to do this. GoLive uses its internal database to keep track of all the files and folders in the local site folder; if you place any documents or folders in your mirror site via the desktop, GoLive won't have a record of them. This can be confusing for new GoLive users since a folder or document (one that was created using the operating system commands) will not appear in GoLive's Site window. If this happens to you, simply fix it using the **Site > Refresh View** command.

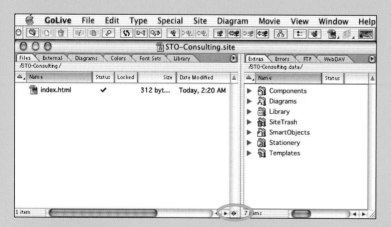

Select the folder in which to save the Web site. Use the Create Folder option to have GoLive place the information inside a subfolder. The Site window appears with the first page (index.html). Click the icon in the lower-right corner to split the window and reveal the Extras tab.

This is the Site folder with all the subfolders: one for the mirror site and one for the site data, which contains the components.

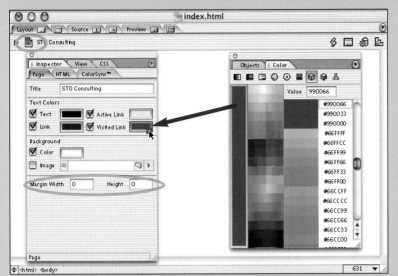

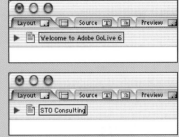

Click the Page icon to bring you to the Page Inspector, where you can set the colors and the browser offset.

Make sure you change the default "Welcome to Adobe GoLive" title.

2 **Creating the first stationery/template:** In the **Site** window, double-click the index.html page to open it. An empty page will appear. Change the page title from "Welcome to Adobe GoLive" to a title that sums up the content of the page. Because most search engines put a lot of weight on the title when indexing a document, be sure to use descriptive keywords. If your site is about music, for instance, you may want to include keywords like "music," "CDs," "MP3," or "songs" in the title.

Next, set the colors and background for your page. Click the **Page** icon next to the document title to view the **Page Inspector**. Open the **Color** palette via **Window > Color Palette** (**View > Color Palette** on Windows); choose colors for **Text, Link, Active Link,** and **Visited Link**; and drag to the color fields in the **Page Inspector**. GoLive automatically activates them (the checkboxes will be checked). Also very important: Set the **Margin Width** and **Height** to 0.

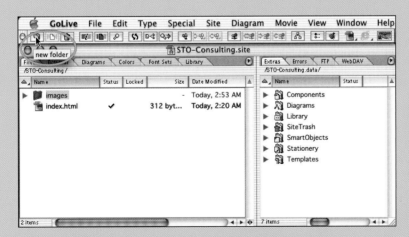

As your very first step, create an image folder for your site.

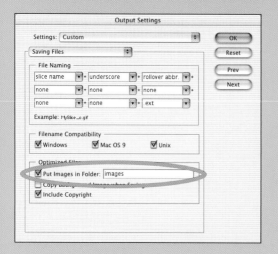

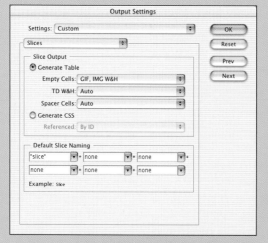

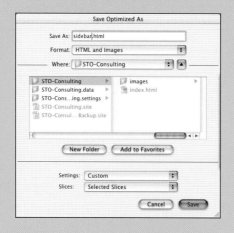

First set the Output Settings, then use the Save Optimized As command and choose HTML and Images.

3 **Exporting images and rollover buttons:** At this point we need to export all the images and rollover buttons for our design (I covered how to create the slices and rollover buttons in the tutorial of the ImageReady chapter). First, click the **New Folder** button in the **Options** palette of GoLive to create an image folder in the **Site** window, and name it **Images**.

Switch to **ImageReady** and open the tutorial design. Select all the slices for the sidebar navigation (slices 12 and 13–17) by pressing the Shift key and using the **Slices Select** tool. To set the output settings, you have to choose **File > Output Settings > Saving Files**. Here you can determine how the rollover images are named. I suggest you use "slice name + underscore + rollover abbr." to keep the filenames as short as possible (I also recommend to change the way slices are automatically named). In the **Saving Files** view you can also name the image folder and have ImageReady save the image there automatically (this is the default setting). After closing the dialog box and confirming with OK, the images are saved into the **Images** folder and the HTML is saved inside the root folder.

Choose the **Save Optimized As** command and look for the root folder of the mirror site (that is, the one that contains the index.html file). Name the file (preferably something like sidebar.html) and choose **HTML and Images** from the **Format** pop-up menu and **Slices: Selected Slices**. The images won't appear in GoLive's Site window, however, until you rescan the Site folder (**Site > Refresh View**). Drag the HTML file (sidebar.html)

over to the **Components** folder and confirm in the **Move Files** dialog box. Usually components are created by saving the HTML file directly to the Components folder, but since we are exporting so many images (all the buttons consist of two images), it is much easier to save to the root folder and just drag the HTML file to the Components folder.

It would be logical to use the same procedure for the horizontal rollover buttons, but because all the buttons use one shape layer as background (instead of individual ones), this causes some problems. Whenever we create a rollover state for one of the buttons, the areas in the other button slices change, too, and ImageReady notes this. When they're exported and viewed in Internet Explorer or Netscape Navigator, all the buttons change simultaneously. This is not a bug: ImageReady can trigger several image changes with one rollover, and that is exactly what is happening. Because we are using the inner shadow effect, we can't split the shape layer into several smaller pieces. Luckily, what seems to

be a major problem has a very simple solution: Just export the slices without the HTML and create the component with the rollover buttons in GoLive. So in the next step, we select all the remaining slices—1–9, 18, 20, and 22— and export them. Since the images are saved without an HTML file, use **Format: Images Only** and save them to the **Images** folder. Now that all the images are exported, use the **Refresh View** command again and create the component for the vertical navigation in GoLive.

After you move the HTML file to the Components folder, GoLive displays the Move Files dialog box.

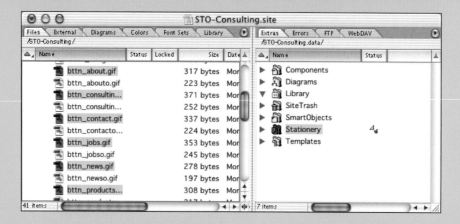

4 **Creating a component in GoLive:** For the vertical navigation, we create a new document in which we place a table with one row and six cells. In the **Files** view of the **Site window**, select all the buttons and drag them into your document (this is easier than using the **Image Object** and then linking to the image). Place each button in its own cell and adjust the width and height of the table so that the buttons fit tightly in the cells. (This is important; you don't want to have gaps. We could leave out the table completely, but that would create some problems later with the display in GoLive. The HTML code would still work correctly in the browsers, though.) Drag a **Rollover** icon from the

Smart tab of the **Objects** palette onto each button image to convert it to a rollover object. Select a rollover button: click the Over State in the **Inspector**, then use the **Point-and-Shoot** feature to locate and link to the file in the **Site** window. Repeat for each button. After all the rollover buttons are done, save the file using the **Save As** command. In the lower-right corner of the dialog box is a pop-up menu with a shortcut to the **Components** folder. The component will appear on the Extras tab of the **Objects** palette as soon as you have saved the file. Make sure that Components is selected in the pop-up menu in the lower-right corner.

Drag the button images from the Files window into the document. Then place them in a table and drag the Rollover icon onto them. Click the Over State and then use the Point-and-Shoot tool to link to the image file for the Over state.

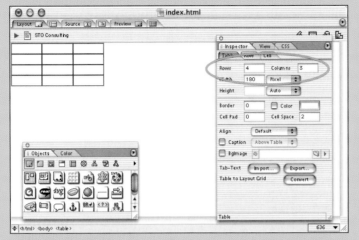

After a table object has been placed, the number of rows needs to be increased by one, and two cells need to be merged in order to create a table that can function as the container for all other elements.

All table cells should be aligned vertically to Top. This is done row by row on the Row tab of the Table Inspector.

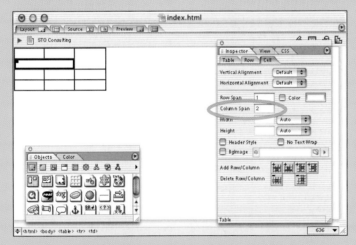

5 **Creating the master table:** As I mentioned in the ImageReady tutorial, this design can be re-created in GoLive with frames as well as with tables. Frames are somewhat unpopular nowadays because of the problems with search engines, so we will do the entire layout with tables.

Place a table in the document with four rows and three columns, and make the border invisible by using 0 for the **Border** (also set **Cell Pad** and **Cell Space** to 0). The reason we are using a table and not a layout grid is that we need some areas to adjust dynamically to the

size of the browser window. You can only do this with a table because the nature of the layout grid means that it is rather static.

Merge the first and second cells of row 2 by choosing 2 for **Column Span** in the **Table Inspector**. Merge the third cell of row 1 with the third cell of row 2 by choosing 2 for **Row Span**. (If I've lost you here, look at the screen shots or the ImageReady tutorial.) Then go through each row and choose **Vertical Alignment: Top**.

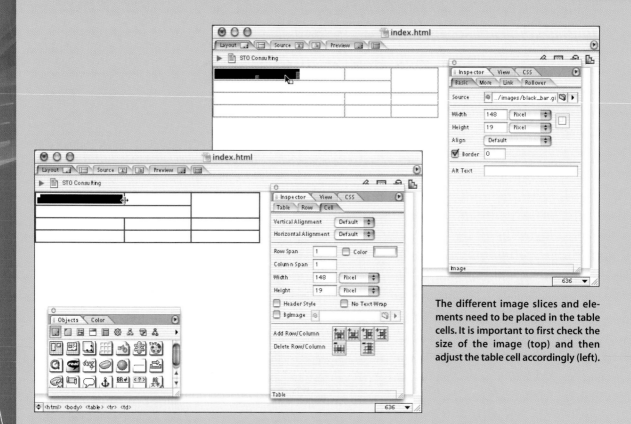

The different image slices and elements need to be placed in the table cells. It is important to first check the size of the image (top) and then adjust the table cell accordingly (left).

6 **Placing the images and other elements:** Now comes the fun part. Drag the black image of the upper left corner from the **File** window into the document and place it in the upper-left table cell. Click first on the image (and remember its dimensions), then click on the border of that particular cell. Switch the dimensions from **Auto** to **Pixel**, and enter the values for the image. Selecting might be a little tricky since the border is so close to the border of the image—you know you have selected the table when the **Inspector** changes. Place the vertical navigation bar (ver_navigation.html) into the second cell and adjust the size of that cell (its width is 461 pixels). In the first cell of the second row, place the logo (with the arch), but don't change any dimensions of the table cell. You don't have to do this because we set the dimensions of the table cells above, but most importantly, the value in this merged table cell will always reflect the value of the first cell, not the sum of both cells. Now place the component for the sidebar in the first cell of the third row.

The page is starting to come together, but the most crucial part is still ahead. On the right side, we want the design to continue to the edge of the browser window. Since the size of the browser window always changes, we can't just place an image and give it a fixed size. We have to use a trick that's not that well known, but has been around for quite some time: Use a table with cells that adjust to the width of the browser and define an image background for those cells. How do you do that? The first step is to set the width of the table to 100 percent. Since two of the table cells in a row have a fixed size in pixels, the third cell is set to 99 percent width. Are you surprised? Did you expect that **Auto** would be

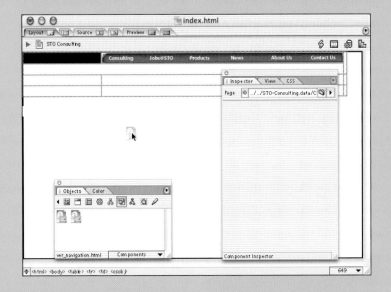

the right setting? It isn't, because **Auto** always adjusts to the content of the cells, which won't work here, but 99 percent does (welcome to the world of HTML). This makes sense in a way: Since this cell is set to almost the maximum, it will always try to fill the entire space. If it can't, it will adjust. However, we are still not done. If you preview the page in a browser after you have selected the cells and used the BgImage option to load an image background, you won't see a background in Navigator (in Explorer, you do). Navigator simply doesn't display a cell background if the cell is empty. To fix this, place a transparent GIF in the cells and that's that.

The only thing left to do is to select the sidebar cell and load an image background for that, too. One more thing: If you are using a background image, pick a background color that comes close to the overall color of the image. That way, if the background image can't be loaded (due to a network error, for example), the page will at least look as close as possible to the way it is supposed to look.

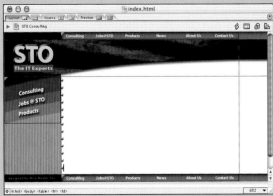

After the background for the table cells has been selected, the layout looks like this.

7 **Placing the layout grid:** The next step is to place a layout grid in the main table cell (the one that will later be used for the content). The layout grid is the first element in the palette (**Window > Palette**). When you place the grid in your document, the **Inspector** changes to the **Layout Grid Inspector**, which allows you to set the dimensions of the grid. The default setting of 16 pixels for the horizontal and vertical spacing can be changed to a more useful value of 5 pixels. To place text on a layout grid, you have to place a layout text box, which is the second object in the **Objects** palette. You should also insert some text for the next steps.

8 **Setting up the FONT setups:** As you know by now, fonts are a problem when it comes to designing for the Web. In the early versions of HTML, you had no choice whatsoever in defining fonts. Later, the FONT tag was introduced, which at least allowed you to designate a font, but with the major restriction that this font had to be installed on the user's system. So it's almost impossible to use anything exotic; it literally comes down to using Arial, Helvetica (sans serif) or Palatino, Times (serif) combinations, since these are the only fonts that come standard on both Windows and Mac systems.

Even though we are going to use Cascading Style Sheets later, it is a good idea to create font sets. They can be accessed later in the CSS Inspector, thus making the setup process much more convenient. Specify the FONT tag by choosing **Type > Font > Edit Font Sets**, which brings up the **Font Set Editor**. Make sure that you have **Default** selected, then click the **Create a New Fontset** button to insert an empty font set. Choose the font from the pop-up menu or just enter the name of the font in the text field. It's customary to pick a couple of sans serif fonts, so choose Arial, then click the button and select Helvetica. You can pick additional sans serif fonts, but it is a good idea to keep it down to just two or three fonts, since this information is embedded every time you assign the FONT tag to text. By the way, the order in which you put fonts into your font set does make a difference: If Arial is your first font, then the browser will use Helvetica only if Arial is not installed. To assign your newly created font set to text, select the text and choose the set in **Type > Font**.

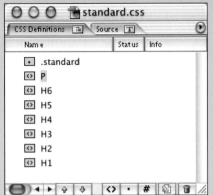

This a suggested list of elements and classes that you should create and save as an external CSS file.

Use the Font Setup menu to quickly apply a Font Family to the formatting.

An external CSS document is linked to this HTML page (below). You can see the effect right away in GoLive because GoLive is capable of displaying Cascading Style Sheets.

9 **Setting up the Cascading Style Sheet:** To create an external CSS document, choose **File > New Special > Cascading Style Sheet**. The untitled.ccs window that appears contains Classes, Tags, IDs, Imports, and Font Faces. We will create one class (that will allow us to format text that has no HTML tag) and the main HTML text marker (P and H1–H6).

Click the **New Class Style** button on the toolbar to insert a class in the CSS document. Enter a name, but keep the dot as the first character. Then switch to the second tab in the CSS Style Inspector and select the **Arial Font Setup** from the **Font Setup** menu. GoLive will now automatically list all the fonts of that setup in the Font Family; leave everything else unchanged. Later on, you can use this class to apply these fonts to selected text without changing any of the other formatting of the text.

Now define the HTML paragraph and header tags in the **CSS Style Inspector**, and then use the various tabs to set the values that you want to assign to each HTML tag. The possibilities range from text color to having a border and a background color for text—but we will keep it simple since support for some of the features varies between the browsers. All we will do for now is set the font family and a font size and then save the document in the root folder of the Web site.

Since the style sheet is an external document, it needs to be linked to the HTML page. Bring the index.html page to the front and click the stair-shaped icon in the upper-right corner of the document. The CSS window for this page will open. Click the **New Link to External CSS** button on the toolbar and an Empty Reference will appear in the window. This reference must be linked to the saved CSS document with the Point-and-Shoot tool or the Browse button. GoLive will display the CSS settings even in Layout mode, but again, to avoid surprises, check your document in all browsers that your audience uses.

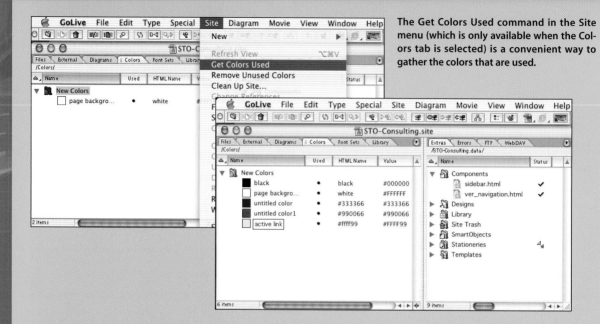

The Get Colors Used command in the Site menu (which is only available when the Colors tab is selected) is a convenient way to gather the colors that are used.

10 **Setting up the colors:** Before creating the site structure with a stationery/template page, it's a good idea to set up the colors you want to use throughout your site. Select the **Color tab** in the **Site** window and choose **Site > Get Colors Used** to import all the colors used so far. Since we haven't yet defined many colors, you'll probably get just the colors that you used for the text, links, and background. Name them appropriately so you know if you are using a link color for something else; use the link colors sparingly. It certainly is not a good idea to color regular text with the link colors, since this will confuse the visitor.

The colors that you drag into the Colors tab will appear on the right-most tab of the **Color palette**, making it easy for you to work consistently. When you're finished with the colors, save your document and use the **Save As** command to save a copy of the index.html page in your **Stationeries** or **Templates** folder (use the shortcut in the **Save As** dialog box). If you save the document as stationery, every copy of the page that you later put into the site structure will not be linked to the original. With a template this is different; every element that is marked as an uneditable region can't be modified and is linked to the original, meaning that if you

later change any of the regions marked as uneditable, they will be updated in every page that was created from the template. Since this is the smarter way of working, I will explain how to do this. Before you save the page as a template, you have to mark the areas in your page that you want to allow to be editable. Mark the table cell that will later hold the content choose **Special > Template > Editable Region**, then save the page as a template in the **Templates** folder.

Colors that you create on the Color tab of the Site window will appear as custom colors in the Color palette.

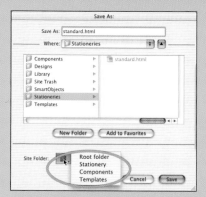

Before creating the site structure, save a copy of the home page in the Templates folder. The shortcut on the bottom makes it easy to locate that folder.

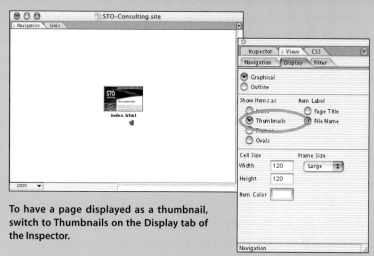

To have a page displayed as a thumbnail, switch to Thumbnails on the Display tab of the Inspector.

11 Creating the site structure: The last step before filling your site with content is to create the site structure. Open the **Site** window and select **Diagram > Navigation View** from the menu bar or click the **Navigation View** button on the toolbar and a window will appear. At this point in time, this window shows only the home page (index.html). Activate the **Site Extras** tab in the **Objects** palette and drag the template document over from the palette. As the page icon comes beneath the index.html page icon, a bold line indicates that GoLive is ready to insert the page beneath the home page. To insert pages on the same hierarchical level, just bring the template page icon along one side of an already-placed page and drop it there.

You can even move pages around by dragging them to the new location, or you can delete them by pressing Delete. But working in **Navigation View** will be much easier because you can actually see the content of the page. GoLive can display little thumbnails of the pages: In the **View** tab, click on **Display** and select **Thumbnails**. Since all these new pages are just named "New_from ...", it is time to rename the documents. You can do this by clicking on them in **Navigation View** and then changing their names in the Inspector (in the **File** tab), or you can rename them on the **Files** tab of the Site window by clicking on the name once. All the pages that you created are in one folder named "newfiles";

since this probably doesn't reflect your desired folder structure, choose the **Site > New > Folder** command to create an empty folder. Rename this folder and drag into it all the HTML files from the "newfiles" folder that you want here. A **Move Files** dialog box prompts you to confirm which files and links need to be updated.

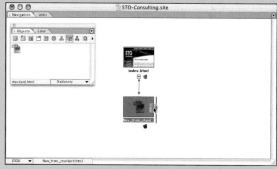

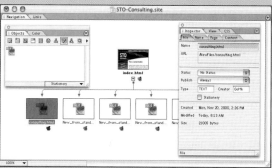

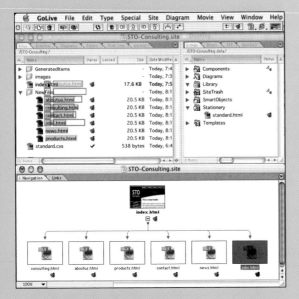

12 Updating components: The navigational elements need to be updated now to make the site navigable. To edit a component, locate it in the **Site** window. Locating the component requires you to activate the split view by clicking on the tab in the upper-right corner and then selecting **Extras**. You can also double-click on a component that is placed on a page. After the component is open, select each of the rollover buttons and create a link to the appropriate page. Use the **Point-and-Shoot** tool to point to the page in the **Files** view, make the necessary changes, and save the document again. GoLive will display an **Updating Component** dialog box, which you need to confirm.

After you've set up the entire navigational structure and the hyperlinks, the pages displayed on the **Site** tab will be connected by solid lines. Now you can fill the site with content using smart objects, for example. To preview your Web site in the browser, click the **Show in Browser** button on the toolbar.

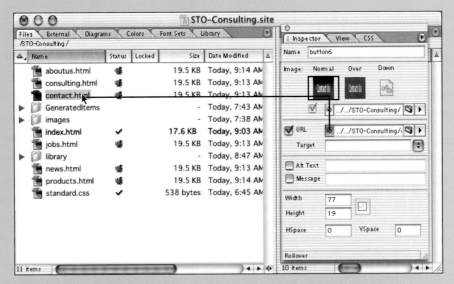

After you've renamed all files, move them out of the New Files folder to a new location in the site. Then open the components and link the buttons to the files. When saving, GoLive will ask you if you want to update the placed components.

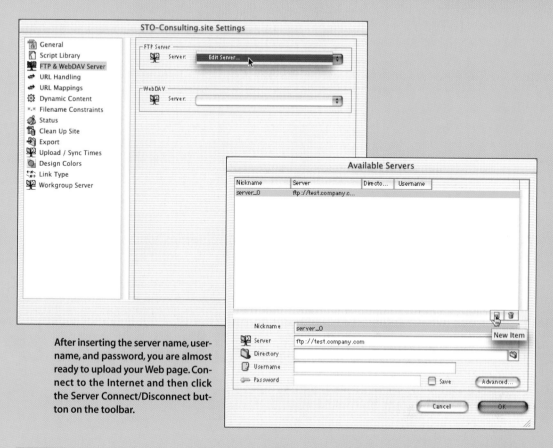

After inserting the server name, user-name, and password, you are almost ready to upload your Web page. Connect to the Internet and then click the Server Connect/Disconnect button on the toolbar.

13 **Uploading the site:** The almost-last step in the Web design process is uploading the site. First you must set up the FTP connection. Choose **Site > Settings**, then select **FTP & WebDAV Server** and enter server, username, and password for the FTP server. After closing the Settings, open an Internet connection and choose **Site > Connect to Server**. The server directory is visible only if you click the tab on the upper right, which splits the window in two (select the FTP tab). To upload, you can manually drag the folder and files from the left to the right window, but GoLive automatically synchronizes the directory of the server with your mirror site when you click on the **Upload to Server** button on the toolbar.

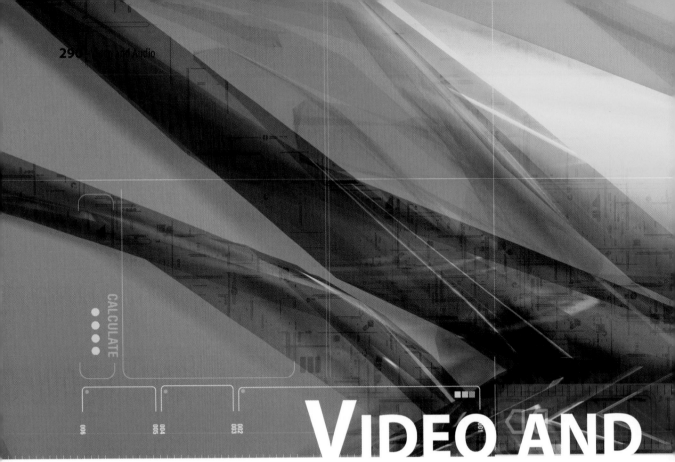

CALCULATE

VIDEO AND

Illustration: **Jens Karlsson/Vinh Kha** from the CD **Outjection**

AUDIO

High-speed Internet access has surpassed dial-up modems in the United States, according to a survey that I recently read. If true, this is good news for Web designers. As more and more people get cable modems and DSL connections, Web designers can more energetically develop sites with richer content, including video and audio. Luckily, GoLive's extensive QuickTime features make it easy to create multimedia-rich Web sites. If you are really interested in using video or audio, this chapter will give you all the information you need.

CAPTURING FORMATS

Although the Web doesn't yet allow for high-bandwidth real-time video, it's a good idea to capture high-quality content anyway. There are several reasons for this:

● Highly precompressed video cannot be compressed again—at least not with acceptable results. You can use compression algorithms, like Sorenson, that produce stunning quality even for Web use. But these algorithms won't work well on already-compressed images, and the image quality will deteriorate significantly.

● Aside from Web publishing, you might want to use your videos for CD-ROMs, high-resolution screen shots, or even your own movie edits that go back to video.

● You can always scale down a movie file, but you can't scale it back up without a loss in quality. This is especially important if you want to create several smaller clips designed for different connection speeds (a feature that comes with QuickTime and RealMedia). Scaling means that a visitor to your Web site with a 28 Kbps connection will see a movie with 160 by 120 resolution, while a visitor with a 56 Kbps modem will see a movie with 240 by 180 resolution.

● Not all compression algorithms work equally well for all purposes. Even with some experience, you might need to test the different output options (algorithms) for your particular project.

CREATING A TWO-FRAME POSTER MOVIE IN QUICKTIME PLAYER PRO

One of the problems with embedding QuickTime movies in HTML pages is that they will start downloading immediately, even if a visitor doesn't want to watch them. To avoid this, you either have to get your ISP to install QuickTime Streaming Server software or use a **poster movie**. Technically, a poster movie can be anything that acts as a placeholder, from a single image to a movie trailer. Of course, it makes sense to keep the poster movie as small as possible. I'll show you how to create a poster movie with two frames (two frames ensure that there is some animation in the movie itself).

First, create two images that have the same resolution as the movie file for which the poster movie will be used (in this example, 160 by 120 pixels). If you want to hide the movie controllers that QuickTime always displays at the bottom of the screen, add an additional 16 pixels to compensate. This is important—when you position the poster movie in GoLive, if it doesn't have the exact measurements of the movie itself, you'll end up with a squeezed movie. You can display the controllers for the poster movie, but visitors may be confused about where to click. For a poster movie to load the real movie, users have to click inside the poster movie. I recommend including a message such as "click here to start the movie" in your poster movie. In the example at right, I created the effect of flashing text. To do that, I created the first text frame in Photoshop and saved it as "poster1.tif," and then I applied an Outer Glow layer effect and saved that image as "poster2.tif." It's important to keep the files in a separate folder and to name them sequentially, because when you choose **File > Open Image Sequence**, QuickTime Player Pro loads all of the images in the folder in the order that they're listed. Choose 1 frame per second as your display rate, and preview the movie in QuickTime by choosing **Movie > Loop** and clicking **Play**.

To use this as a poster movie, choose **File > Export**. In the dialog box that appears, click **Options** to select a compression method. Cinepak yields the smallest file size but shows visible degradation. The Animation

QuickTime or RealAudio movies can be embedded into the HTML page. To avoid having movies download immediately after the page is loaded, you can use poster movies that act as placeholders.

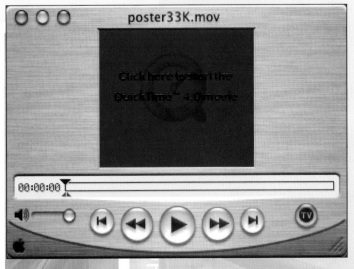

These are the two images that are looped for the poster movie.

In QuickTime Player Pro, the images can be imported as PICT sequences and saved as a movie.

codec yields good results but generates bigger files. Since file size is an issue in Web design, I suggest you stick with Cinepak. This example ended up using 20K, which is quite a lot, but it's still better than having an entire movie embedded.

Given GoLive's capability to create "sprite" tracks in QuickTime movies, you can divide poster movies into different sections, like image maps, to provide links or trigger other actions. For example, you could click one section of the poster movie to open the movie in a new window, and click another to open it in the original window. A third area could open the movie in Quick-Time Player, and a fourth section could open a universally compatible version of the movie that runs on all systems. You can make all these options accessible from one poster movie.

Save the movie and click on Options to set the codec. In the Movie Settings dialog box, click on Settings to access compression settings. For a poster movie, use Cinepak as your Compressor and select a motion frame rate. In this example the two frames will flash in intervals of 0.66 seconds because the frame rate is set to 3 frames per second.

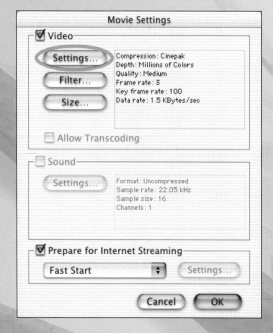

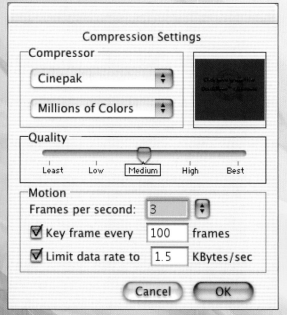

COMPRESSING AND EMBEDDING MOVIES

Compressing your movie for publishing on the Web is the last significant step of media preparation. Although there are a couple of formats, the three most popular compression codecs for Web video are Apple Quick-Time, Windows Media and RealNetworks' RealVideo. Although RealVideo offered streaming technology before QuickTime did, Apple has caught up on that technological front.

If you plan to use video frequently on your Web sites, consider buying Discreet's Cleaner. Cleaner is a dream when it comes to encoding video and audio. It supports the highest-quality compression codecs, such as Sorenson Pro, QDesign Music Codec 2 Professional Edition, Real G2, Windows Media, and original source MP3. All these formats are popular and important on the Web; if you've ever seen the amazing results that you can get with Sorenson 3, you'll understand why. And since Cleaner also does batch processing, you can

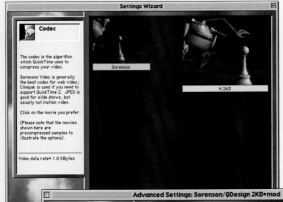

Cleaner offers an incredible variety of options, such as the audio settings of a Sorenson QuickTime video, shown here. Cleaner's robust feature set and batch processing capability make it the best choice for professional Web video producers.

In the left column, Cleaner lists all the available codecs and settings.

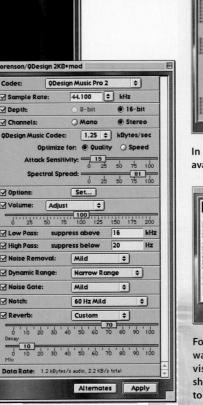

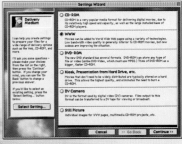

For novices, Cleaner offers a wizard that walks users though settings and gives visual examples. Here, for example, it shows how the Sorenson video compares to a regular video (left).

This is RealPlayer, which launches automatically when a RealAudio or RealVideo file is linked to a Web page. It can be downloaded from www.real.com.

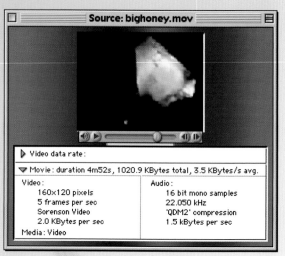

Cleaner shows a preview of the movie it's converting, as it is performing the conversion. You can even split the screen and simultaneously view the before and after movie.

Sorenson 2 offers the best video and audio quality available to date for QuickTime. It is amazing how much Sorenson is able to compress a video/audio file. It's a must-have for anyone who wants to deliver high-quality video on the Web.

set up a computer to do the time-consuming encoding task at night. This alone could justify the investment, but there is so much more.

The visual control and support throughout the program are excellent. Many of Cleaner's settings allow you to edit source material without having to leave the program: audio and video fades, several audio filters, and several video filters such as brightness, hue, and saturation, adaptive noise, and removal. You can access some special codec features only from Cleaner; for example, the "Disable saving from WWW" option prevents visitors from storing published QuickTime movies to their hard drives, thus providing copyright protection for your media. This method works more reliably than the HTML QuickTime attribute, which is supposed to do the same thing.

Working with Cleaner is very simple. A settings wizard guides you through a multiple-choice sequence to pick the right compression setting for your situation, and chances are if you're looking for a feature, Cleaner has it. At this point, it's certainly the unchallenged powerhouse of media preparation.

RealProducer Plus and Pro allow you to encode videos in the RealVideo format. RealProducer is available at realnetworks.com.

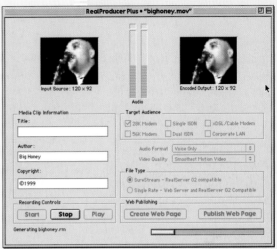

RealProducer displays the before and after when converting a movie.

Which Video Codec Should You Use?

Once you've decided to use video on your Web site, you have to choose a compression standard. Since RealVideo entered the streaming media market before Apple, it's likely that more users will have RealPlayer installed (most new content is delivered in the G2 standard, however, which requires a new player that some users may not have). If you're trying to decide among RealVideo, Windows Media and QuickTime, here are some other factors to consider:

● Generally, QuickTime requires less CPU overhead, is very responsive, and therefore works without breakups even on slow systems. With the QDesign Music 2 codec, it also sports great audio quality at low bandwidth (16-bit, 44.1 kHz stereo at 3 Kbps), and the data rate can be adjusted in finer increments. Video playback also works smoothly on slow systems.

● RealVideo creates an impressive image quality that is sharp and crisp but yields sluggish response on slow systems due to high demands on the CPU

when decompressing images. This may result in low frame rates (one image or less per second) and net congestion errors even during local playback from the hard disk.

● Windows Media creates high-quality video and audio and has reached a high level of popularity recently. Unfortunately, Microsoft offers no encoder for Macs. The only way to encode Windows Media files on a Mac is through Discreet Cleaner.

If you have Cleaner and the Sorenson Pro codec (which is about half the price of Cleaner itself), you get the best of all worlds. QuickTime's Sorenson Pro codec offers a variable bit rate (VBR) for encoding, and the video image quality will be equal to (or even better than) that of RealVideo. If you can't decide, you probably will end up using both.

How to Embed Video in HTML

Finally, it's time to embed your prepared media into your Web pages. GoLive is the best tool to use, since it supports QuickTime and RealMedia attributes. Make sure you install the appropriate plug-ins that come with the GoLive installation CD; otherwise, it will be much harder to preview the media (also, GoLive will not provide all the HTML features for the media type.)

The simplest way to integrate video in your Web page is to create a link to the file. When the user clicks on the link, the file will be opened externally in either QuickTime or RealPlayer. Although this technique does the job, I prefer actually embedding the movie in the page. But in order to have movies play directly in Web browsers, you must know at least a few attributes of the different plug-in standards. Keep in mind that since plug-ins are updated continually, authoring software may not supply all current attributes. Below you will find several QuickTime and RealMedia attributes and descriptions of their practical use.

QuickTime Attributes

Before you embed QuickTime movies into your Web page, make sure that their filenames end in ".mov." QuickTime movies also need to be flattened (their headers need to be removed) before they are put on the Web. QuickTime Player Pro and Discreet's Cleaner do this automatically.

To place the QuickTime movie, just drag it into the document window or choose the **Plug-in object** from the **palette** and click the **Browse** button in the **Plug-in Inspector**. Then set the following parameters:

AUTOPLAY=true to have the movie start automatically after the page has loaded.

LOOP=true to loop the movie after it has ended.

CACHE=true to cache or temporarily store the movie on the visitor's hard drive.

Double-click on an embedded movie in GoLive to open the movie in its own window. Click on the Track Editor button in the toolbar (circled) to edit tracks.

HREF=true.mov can be used to load another movie when the visitor clicks on the movie. HREF defines a URL that can be absolute or relative. Use the Target attribute to define where the HREF movie should play. Setting it to "self" or "myself" will open it in the original place of the SRC movie.

CONTROLLER=false to hide the controllers for the SRC movie. This attribute does not apply to the HREF movie. To avoid placement anomalies of the two movies, the SRC movie in the example should have a height of 136 pixels without the controllers, and the HREF movie should measure 136 pixels with the controllers (or 120 without).

You can set all of the above attributes in the Quick-Time tab of the **Plug-in Inspector** by checking the appropriate options. The QuickTime plug-in needs to

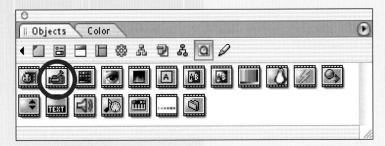

GoLive's QuickTime palette contains icons for all of the objects and modules that can be used by the Track Editor. To insert a video track, just drag the icon (circled) into the Track Editor.

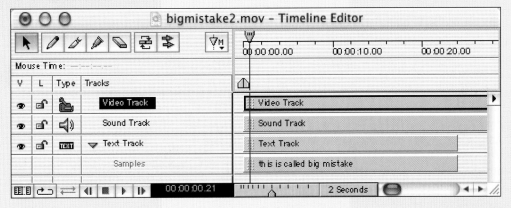

The interface for the QuickTime Timeline was updated extensively in GoLive. Here, for example, I've added a text track that will appear as a closed caption in the movie.

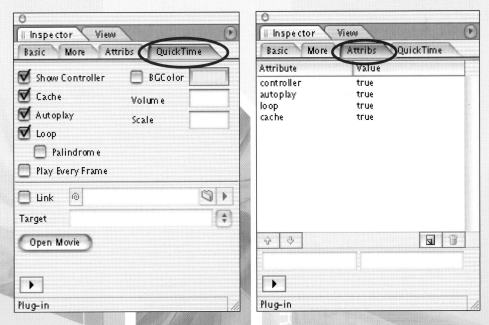

Many QuickTime attributes, such as Loop and Autoplay, can be set in the QuickTime tab of the Plug-In Inspector. For a complete list, switch to the Attribs tab. This is where more attributes can be entered manually.

be placed in GoLive's Plug-in folder for the QuickTime tab to appear. There are many more QuickTime attributes than are currently available in GoLive; to enter these attributes, click on the **Attribs** tab of the **Plug-in Inspector** and click **New**. Enter the attribute name in the left field and the attribute value (without quotation marks) in the right field. Press **Enter** to finish.

The following example will display the flashing poster movie from the earlier example in a loop and without controllers until the visitor clicks on it to load the target movie. The poster movie is 136 pixels high without controllers, and the target movie is 120 pixels high. Note that the order of the attributes isn't important:

```
<EMBED SRC="poster.mov" WIDTH="160" HEIGHT="136" AUTOPLAY="true" LOOP="true" CONTROLLER="false" HREF="target.mov" TARGET="myself" TARGETCACHE="false">
```

These are just a few examples of the many attributes available in QuickTime. If you would like to find out more, point your browser to http://www.apple.com/quicktime/.

Embedding RealMedia

Embedding RealMedia content into Web pages is a little more complicated but still is not very difficult. First of all, you need to create a metafile if you want to use Web-based streaming without a server. A metafile is a simple text file that contains the URL of the media file to be streamed. You can use a simple text editor to create such a file, or in GoLive, choose **File > New Special > Text Document**.

The information inside the metafile consists basically of a single text line with the absolute URL of the audio or video file. It could look like this: http://www.mysite.com/media/movie.rm.

Again, the URL must be absolute to work, which makes it a bit more tedious to preview your work locally before uploading to the server. If you'd like to preview the result in your browser locally, the path needs to start with "file://" and must include the complete path to the destination: file://harddisk/documents/Web sites/mysite/media/movie.rm

If you create a local path, don't forget to change it to a URL before uploading, or your link will not work.

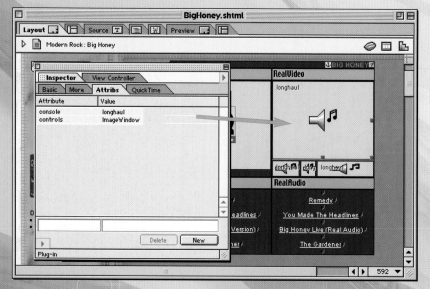

To embed a RealVideo in a Web page along with its controls, you must create several instances of the video and use the Controls attribute to specify the function. For example, Controls=ImageWindow will display the movie.

Actually, it will still work on your computer but not on anybody else's, and you might not even realize it.

Another very important thing is that the name of this metafile must have the extension ".ram" or ".rpm." A ".rpm" file is commonly used to play movie or audio content inside a Web page, while a ".ram" file will play a movie or audio in RealPlayer. To play the ".ram" file, all you need to do is create a hyperlink to it in the Web page. If the RealPlayer plug-in is installed on the visitor's browser, the associated MIME type will automatically direct the file to RealPlayer.

To display the video (or play audio) in the Web page, you need a few attributes; just like QuickTime media, RealMedia is embedded in the page using the **Plug-In** object from the palette. One major difference between RealMedia and QuickTime is that QuickTime displays its controllers as part of the video window, while RealMedia doesn't. The way RealMedia works is that you place instances of the movie in the Web page and use the CONTROLS attribute to define what the SRC window should contain. It could be the video itself or just the controllers for it. This gives you the flexibility to display, for example, just a Start and Stop button, or you can also show a progress bar. Among the values available for this attribute are ImageWindow, which will display the movie content, PlayButton, StopButton, PositionSlider, and VolumeSlider.

You might decide to use the CONSOLE attribute to have the PositionSlider control the movie. Here is an example of a movie file measuring 160 by 120 pixels with associated play, stop, and position controls. The HTML code on your page should look like this:

```
<EMBED   SRC="movie.rpm"   WIDTH="160"
HEIGHT="120" _CONTROLS="ImageWindow"
CONSOLE="movie">
<EMBED   SRC="movie.rpm"   WIDTH="44"
HEIGHT="26" CONTROLS="PlayButton" CON-
SOLE="movie">
<EMBED   SRC="movie.rpm"   WIDTH="26"
HEIGHT="26" CONTROLS="StopButton" CON-
SOLE="movie">
<EMBED   SRC="movie.rpm"   WIDTH="90"
HEIGHT="26" CONTROLS="PositionSlider" CON-
SOLE="movie">
```

Note that the width and height values for the Play and Stop buttons can't vary much from the ones given in this example. This limits your placement and design choices.

To stream RealVideo, make sure that the HTML link in the browser addresses a text (meta) file with the URL of the video.

To insert a Play button, I placed an instance of the movie in GoLive and used the attribute Controller=PlayButton. Console=Name is required so that this Play button only starts the movie with this name (in this example the name is "longhaul".)

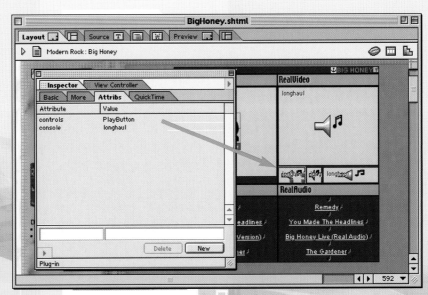

EMBEDDING MUSIC AND AUDIO

With MP3 becoming so popular and bandwidth increasing, we will probably see more Web sites using sound to enhance the online experience. There are basically two methods for delivering audio over the Web: files that have to be downloaded before playback, and audio that plays during download, which is called streaming audio.

In general, the first scenario gives you better control over the sound quality and doesn't require any plug-in. Both Internet Explorer and Netscape Navigator can play these files directly. The problem is that the download of a long audio file takes awhile. Streaming audio has the advantage that the sound starts playing even before the file has completely loaded.

Implementing a Sound File

There are several ways of integrating sound into your Web page, but the most commonly used is the <EMBED> tag, which both browsers understand and which can play WAV, AIFF, AU, and MIDI files. The EMBED tag is automatically placed when you drag the **Plug-In** object from the palette in GoLive and link it to a sound file. Here's an example of a sound file placed with an EMBED tag:

```
<EMBED SRC="music_file.mid"
AUTOSTART="true" WIDTH="144"
HEIGHT="60" LOOP="1">
```

Depending on the file type, you need to use the right attributes. In this example a MIDI file is loaded and the attribute Autostart="true" automatically plays the sound after it is completely downloaded. If this attribute is set to "false," the sound will only play when the user hits the play button in the control panel.

The Loop attribute tells the browser how many times you want the sound to be played, and it can be an integer or true/false. "True" means that the browser will continue playing the sound until the stop button on the console is clicked. "False" will play the sound file only once from beginning to end.

MP3 Audio Format

MP3, or MPEG Audio Layer-3, is an advanced audio format that provides almost CD-quality sound with reasonable file sizes. The compression ratio is up to 12:1. The resulting files are bigger than RealAudio files in best quality mode (17:1), but also superior in sound. MP3 compresses sounds by removing parts that are inaudible, while retaining the full frequency and dynamic spectrum. Streaming of MP3 files is incorporated in the file format, but requires high-bandwidth connections, such as ISDN.

If you are looking for a great MP3 player software, I strongly recommend iTunes from Apple. This software has great features, is a free download and has established itself as the standard among Mac users.

RealAudio

Thanks to streaming technology, this popular file format allows almost instant access to very long sound files, such as songs, interviews or even live transmissions. The RealAudio algorithm uses high compression rates ranging from about 17:1 to 170:1, which are based on CD-quality audio. A three-minute song can be reduced to as little as 180KB, compared to about 30 MB in CD quality. There is a definite deterioration in sound quality when using these high compression ratios with slower modems. However, the resulting low data rate necessary for those files provides real-time audio access for modems as slow as 14.4kbps.

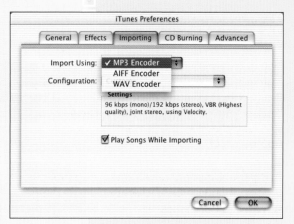

iTunes is the acclaimed MP3 player/encoder from Apple that can be downloaded for free and comes preinstalled with Mac OS 9 and OS X. It features an easy to use playlist with search function, encodes MP3s from audio CDs on the fly and offers extendable visual plug-ins for an all-around multimedia experience.

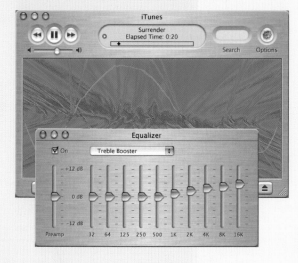

WAV (.wav): This format is the standard audio format on IBM-compatible computers running Microsoft Windows.

AIFF (.aiff): This is the standard audio format on Mac OS computers and is good for music and high-quality sound.

AU (.au): Developed by Sun Microsystems, this has a poor sound quality, but a small file size.

MIDI (.mid): If you are a musician, you are probably familiar with this format, because it is used to record music with a sequencer or to hook up two keyboards. Because MIDI is not an audio format, it requires that at least one of the following be installed on the user's computer: a sound card that supports MIDI playback, an external MIDI device, or QuickTime (which provides MIDI playback in software).

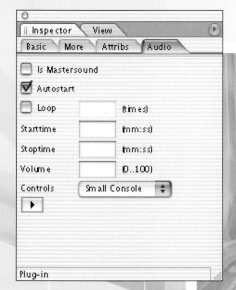

Most attributes for sound can be set in the Audio tab of the Plug-In Inspector. Only the more exotic attributes need to be set manually by switching to the Attribs tab.

APPENDIX

Normally I create my own illustrations for my books, but after coming across Digital Vision's stock photo library (www.digitalvisiononline.com), I decided to use their artwork. You can see it throughout this book. Here are some stock photo CDs that I highly recommend.

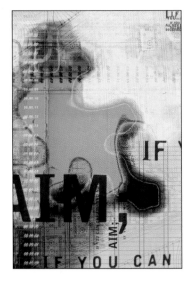

Data Funk

Alternate States

Fuse

Undercurrent

In the black

OnyFrax

Critical Mass

Business Groove

Alternate States

Wired for Business

Idioblastic

Outjection

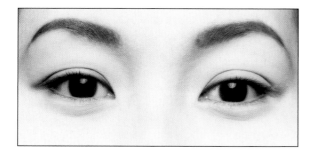

Eye of the Beholder

The Body

INDEX